GOSPEL TRACKS THROUGH TEXAS

NUMBER NINE:
Sam Rayburn Series on Rural Life
Sponsored by Texas A&M University–Commerce
James A. Grimshaw, Jr., General Editor

GOSPEL TRACKS
THROUGH TEXAS

THE MISSION OF CHAPEL CAR

Good Will

WILMA RUGH TAYLOR

NORMAN THOMAS TAYLOR, RESEARCH EDITOR

Texas A&M University Press
College Station

The paper used in this book meets the minimum requirements
of the American National Standard for Permanence
of Paper for Printed Library Materials, z39.48-1984.
Binding materials have been chosen for durability.

Library of Congress Cataloging-in-Publication Data

Taylor, Wilma Rugh.
Gospel tracks through Texas : the mission of chapel car Good Will / Wilma
Rugh Taylor ; Norman Thomas Taylor, research editor.
p. cm. — (Sam Rayburn series on rural life ; no. 9)
Includes bibliographical references and index.
ISBN 1-58544-434-0 (cloth : alk. paper)
1. Railroads—United States—Passenger-cars.   2. Chapels—United States.
I. Taylor, Norman Thomas.   II. Title.   III. Series.
TF455.T35   2005
277.64'081—dc22
2005000610

For Norman, the love of my life

CONTENTS

SERIES EDITOR'S FOREWORD

The Sam Rayburn Series on Rural Life welcomes to its collection Wilma Rugh Taylor's *Gospel Tracks through Texas: The Mission of Chapel Car* Good Will. This book focuses on several missionaries and their work on the American Baptist Publication Society's chapel car *Good Will* in Texas between 1895 and 1903. In addition, Taylor provides a compelling look at small railroad towns throughout Texas, including East Texas towns, such as Carthage, Longview, Lufkin, Marshall, and Tenaha.

Many readers may wonder at first what "chapel cars," now historic artifacts, are and what their purpose was. An article in the June 28, 1895, issue of the Kansas newspaper *Fort Scott Daily Monitor* answers the question simply and well: A chapel car is "nothing more nor less than a church on wheels."

From Taylor we learn that an Episcopal bishop introduced the concept in this country after observing the use of Russian Orthodox chapel cars on the Siberian railway in the latter part of the nineteenth century. Between 1890 and the 1940s, thirteen chapel cars—seven Baptist, three Catholic, and three Episcopal—operated in thirty-six U.S. sates, mostly west of the Appalachian Mountains. Only two, however, operated in Texas: the Baptist chapel car *Good Will* and the Catholic chapel car *St. Paul*.

Taylor is well qualified to provide this history, and her previous book, *This Train Is Bound for Glory: The Story of America's Chapel Cars,* was well received. She now tells the stories of the Baptist missionaries who caught her attention, those who served on chapel car *Good Will:* Edwin and Nettie Stucker, E. G. and Hollie Townsend, G. B. Rogers, and Alberto J. Diaz, a missionary from Cuba who served only a brief time. Her descriptions bring these personalities to life.

During the period from 1895 to 1903, Texas, like much of the West, was still unsettled. Indian raids had lessened but had not yet ended; "boom" towns had sprung up, populated by professional ruffians, gamblers, prostitutes, saloon owners, bootleggers; family feuds were at times violent; cattle barons exercised great power; and Judge Roy Bean's reign was legendary. The missionaries faced not only risks generated by people but also the natural perils of Texas heat, diseases such as malaria and yellow fever, and storms, two of which receive specific coverage in this book: the 1900 Great Storm of Galveston and the 1901 cyclone that hit Buckner Orphans' Home in Dallas. Taylor does an excellent job detailing the environmental setting in which the missionaries were called to work.

Readers will appreciate the lively style in which the stories of the missionaries' service are told; the articulate descriptions of the physical and psychological life tied to the 107 "stops" (towns and a few cities) visited by chapel car *Good Will;* and the discussions of political, legal, religious, and gender issues faced by citizens on the local level. For example, though not a surprise, prohibitionists found the chapel car a welcome sight; saloon owners and their patrons were less enthusiastic about the church-on-rails. The book is also well documented, with interviews of surviving witnesses and their descendants, local newspapers, church files, railroad histories, journals, and letters among the sources consulted.

The purpose of the chapel cars is clearly magnified in this account. They brought growth to organized religion in the towns they visited and made a positive contribution overall to the development of this unsettled land.

Within the series, *Gospel Tracks through Texas* complements Lois E. Myers, Rebecca Sharpless, and Clark G. Baker's *Rock beneath the Sand: Country Churches in Texas* by providing insight into a little-known aspect of religion in rural Texas communities. Taylor also adds a new image to the series, that of the railroad, with an intriguing look at a blend of railroad history and church history at the end of the nineteenth century. In the past few years, a quietly growing interest has resulted in the restoration of a few of the chapel cars that have survived, and the Wisconsin Great Northern Railroad now offers a "new" chapel car, *Everlasting,* for groups to charter. Taylor's book has surely helped rekindle this interest.

The Sam Rayburn Series on Rural Life, started in 1997, is sponsored by Texas A&M University–Commerce under the auspices of the Texas A&M University Press in College Station. As originally envisioned, one of the goals of this series is the creation of a historical record of rural life in East Texas and the surrounding regions. A companion to the oral-history concept, the series strives to collect factual accounts of diverse aspects of rural life. Agricultural, economic, educational, environmental, literary, political, and religious topics are among the variety sought. Each book, in turn, provides an image that together with the other collected images constitutes a montage that becomes significant in the composition of our heritage, both locally and nationally.

—James A. Grimshaw Jr.

PREFACE

One of the best kept secrets in the annals of American history may be the story of the railroad chapel cars—thirteen churches-on-rails that traveled over thirty-six states, mainly west of the Appalachians, from 1890 to the 1940s. Although mainly unfamiliar to church, as well as rail and American Studies historians, these chapel cars made a significant impact on the spreading of the gospel, the growth of organized religion, and the moral climate of railroad towns.

Like six other American Baptist Publication Society chapel cars, chapel car *Good Will* had a three-point mission and a targeted population when it came to Texas in 1895. It was to be placed on sidings at towns where there were no churches, no Baptist church, or where the Baptist church in town was struggling. At the heart of the chapel car work was a passion to witness to the growing number of railroad workers accompanying the boom of railroad lines beginning to criss-cross Texas.

The railroad was perhaps the largest industry in America at the time of the chapel car program. It supported more than 873,000 workers, who seldom would darken the door of a church, and whose jobs and lifestyles led them away from the teachings of the church, and in many cases, endangered the safety of the trains they worked on and the passengers who rode those trains. They felt the chapel cars were made just for them, and by the thousands they came. In the correspondence and journals of the missionaries who traveled on the cars are numerous accounts where the chapel cars were praised by town leaders, railroad unions, and rail officials who welcomed the positive influence on the lives of their workers.

Good Will, a Northern Baptist chapel car, came to Texas at the invitation of the Texas General Baptist Convention, associated with the Southern Baptist Convention, in turmoil over power struggles in-

volving issues of missions, education, women's role, scriptural inter-
pretation, and church autonomy. A greater issue facing them was the
influx of immigrants coming into the state in overwhelming numbers;
most of the newcomers had ethnic, religious, and cultural lifestyles
opposed to what the Texas Baptists considered to be acceptable and
were, in their opinion, in danger of losing their mortal souls.

There were other reasons to fear this rush of Germans, Italians,
Bohemians, Swedes, and Mexicans, plus the blacks who were growing in number. Their social and religious values could threaten the
morality and safety of towns and eventually the "Christian" future
of Texas. As most of these growing populations were situated in railroad towns, the Texas Baptists, sorely limited in the ability to send
missionaries to these needy areas, called to the American Baptist
Publication Society for the loan of this brand new chapel car.

At the heart of the writing of this book was my attachment to the
missionaries who traveled on *Good Will.* Not unlike the missionaries
who traveled on the other chapel cars, they were endearing, devoted
individuals who were willing to sacrifice family, health, and fortune
to preach Christ in Texas. When I first read their accounts in journals
and letters, I could not leave them behind. They tugged at my heart.
After the publication of our book on the chapel cars of America, *This
Train Is Bound for Glory,* I promised myself that I would seek out all I
could find about Edwin and Nettie Stucker, E. G. and Hollie
Townsend, and G. B. Rogers. My husband and I determined to follow their routes and find how they affected the towns they visited and
how the towns they visited affected them. We did that, visiting more
than a hundred Texas towns over a period of two years; searching
through archives, church and town histories, and uncountable rolls
of newspaper microfilm; and talking to historians and townspeople.

What we discovered is that the story of *Good Will* in Texas is a tale
of towns—yes, big towns like San Antonio, but mostly smaller established rail communities like Marshall and Denison and small
towns where the railroad had just come, like Tenaha and Timpson.
It is the amazing journey north of the Canadian River during the era
of the XIT Ranch, adventures into border towns along the Rio
Grande, and an agonizing record of the Great Storm of Galveston.
It is a microcosm of life in Texas from 1895 to 1903—the story of a
unique railroad car traveling through a unique state during a unique
time, all for the purpose of spreading the gospel.

ACKNOWLEDGMENTS

The inspiration for the Texas story began in the treasure trove of the American Baptist Historical Society in Valley Forge, Pennsylvania, where Norman and I spent many weeks researching material for our earlier book *This Train Is Bound for Glory: The Story of America's Chapel Cars* published in 1999. That book would never have taken form if it had not been for the passion and persuasion of Beverly Carlson, retired director of the society. Deborah Bingham Van Broekhoven, present director of the society, and Betty Layton, archivist, provided encouragement and support for this second chapel car book.

Much of the writing of the book was done in the lovely setting of the Green Lake Conference Center at Green Lake, Wisconsin, where my husband is restoring chapel car *Grace*. Our friends and benefactors former President Paul LaDue and President Ken Giacoletto provided safe haven and support.

We experienced so many unforgettable moments during the writing of the book; just a few must be mentioned. When Norman and I discovered the location of chapel car *Good Will* in Sonoma County, California, in 1998, after years of searching, we were welcomed to view the chapel car by Mr. and Mrs. John Diani, present owners. They have been so gracious in sharing what is left of this beloved chapel car with us, and we are so grateful for their care and appreciation of the history of the car.

While attending a forty-fifth class reunion at Ottawa University, Kansas, in May, 2001, we were introduced to Beverly Stucker Bennett, granddaughter of *Good Will* missionaries E. S. and Nettie Stucker, who were the first to serve on the Texas chapel car. Because

of the precious moments spent with the Bennetts, we were privi-
leged to view family records and pictures of this engaging couple.

When we first visited the campus of Mary Hardin-Baylor University at Belton, we were surprised to see a library dedicated to the
Townsends, the second couple on *Good Will*. We knew that E. G.
Townsend had been on the faculty after leaving chapel car service,
but we did not realize the important role he played in the life of the
university. When MHBU President Jerry Bawcom discovered that
we were writing about the Townsends, he, along with the library
staff, graciously invited us back to speak to members of the faculty
and friends. We were on campus again to speak to the Baptist History and Heritage Conference in May, 2003. Now the institution
where Townsend spent most of his career is aware of his early chapel
car years.

On our research venture to Texas in December of 1999, to speak
to the "Railroads and the West" conference of the Center for
Greater Southwestern Studies at UT Arlington, we stopped at Marshall, where we knew *Good Will* had visited many times. We decided
to visit the offices of the *Marshall News Messenger* where we were introduced to Gail Beil, an honored Texas historian. She was so kind
to show a real interest in our project and obtain microfilm of earlier
papers.

Knowing that Edwin and Nettie Stucker had spent a month visiting the little settlements north of the Canadian River, we headed
with anticipation to the Panhandle in October of 2002, our special
destination—Channing. At Channing, we found nothing but empty
storefronts and the closed headquarters of the XIT Ranch. Peeking
in dusty windows, I was shocked to see in one a magnificent painting of cowboys in progress. A truck drove up, and a man got out and
asked if he could help. He introduced himself as Don Ray, and invited us into his studio with more glimpses of his extraordinary
work, which have been exhibited all over Texas and beyond. We
asked if he knew anything about the early days of Channing, and he
brought out a scrapbook with pictures that he gave us permission to
use. He had grown up in Channing and his father has been one of
the leaders of the First Baptist Church. His pictures added so much
to our research.

Not a Texas Baptist myself, if it had not been for the work of honored Texas Baptist historian and educator H. Leon McBeth, Southwestern Seminary, Ft. Worth, I would not have been able to under-

stand the impact of Texas Baptists on Texas and the issues that challenged them during the nineteenth century. His work was a foundation for the writing of the book, along with the aid of Ellen Kuniyuke Brown, archivist, Texas Collection, Baylor University; Al La Fever, the Texas Baptist Historical Collection; Bill Sumners, Southern Baptist Historical Collection, Nashville, Tennessee; and Sean M. Lucas, Archives and Special Collections librarian, Southern Baptist Seminary.

The Center for American Studies, University of Texas, Austin, was an endless venture into Texas history, especially life in the Panhandle and the journals of Laura V. Hamner. At Panhandle-Plains Museum, Canyon, Texas, we found fascinating records of the XIT Ranch and owner John Farwell.

Professor Bill O'Neal, Panola Community College, Carthage, Texas, who has authored many books on Texas cowboy lore, was such a help, particularly on the origin of the First Baptist Church of Carthage.

Our thanks go to the Marshall Historical Society; Galveston Historical Society; W. M. Von Maszewski, manager, genealogy, and local history department, Fort Bend County libraries; the George Memorial Library, Richmond, Texas; the Kansas and Texas Railroad Museum, Marshall, Texas; Donna Green, archivist, curator, Fayette Heritage Museum and Archives; the Fayette Public Library, La Grange, Texas; the Museum of East Texas at Lufkin; the Denison Public Library, Denison, Texas; the Virgil and Josephine Gordon Memorial Library, Sealy, Texas; Bill Stein, archivist; and to many other libraries in little towns across Texas.

No children could be more loving and faithful than ours, and 2003 proved that in so many ways. In June my husband suffered a stroke while working on chapel car *Grace* in Wisconsin, and then in December, while recovering from that stroke, he had a heart attack. There were few times that we were not surrounded and lifted up by our children—Norma Faye Taylor, Timothy Mark and Catherine Elaine Taylor, Catheen Marie and Stephen Scott Hardwick, and Bethany Ann and Ronald Lloyd Warren—and delighted in our beautiful grandchildren—Chelsea Rugh Taylor, Natalie Caroline Taylor, Jonathan Troy Warren, Grace Lillian Hardwick, Grant Thomas Hardwick, and Jordan Taylor Warren. Born in Texas during our research, Jordan is mentioned here for the first time in a Grandma book.

And last, but perhaps first in the list, thanks go to editor Mary Lenn Dixon for her faith in the Texas chapel car story and her warm encouragement and wise advice; to Jennifer Ann Hobson, for her patience and support; and to the other Texas A&M University Press staff members who helped in the production of this book.

GOSPEL TRACKS
THROUGH TEXAS

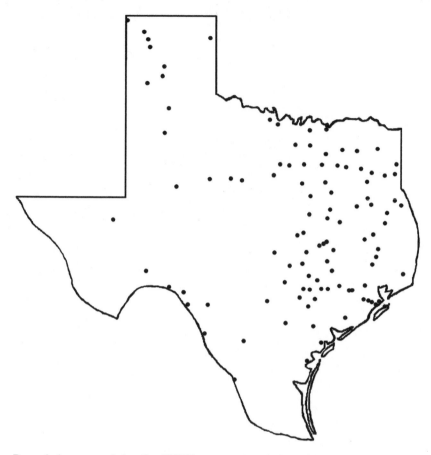

Recorded stops made by *Good Will* between 1895 and 1903 during its Texas mission. Cities and towns visited by the chapel car included

Abilene	Cotulla	Hallettsville	Milano	Sulpher
Alvin	Dalhart	Hartley	Mineola	Springs
Amarillo	Dallas	Hearne	Mineral Wells	Sweetwater
Austin	Decatur	Henrietta	Mt. Pleasant	Temple
Baird	Del Rio	Hereford	Nacogdoches	Terrell
Bay City	Denison	Hillsboro	Palestine	Texas City
Beaumont	Denton	Hitchcock	Pecos	Texline
Belton	Eagle Pass	Houston	Plainview	Thorndale
Big Sandy	Elgin	Jacksonville	Plano	Thurber
Big Spring	Ennis	Jefferson	Richmond	Timpson
Brackettville	Flatonia	Jewett	Rockport	Trinity
Brenham	Ft. Worth	Juliff	Rosenberg	Tyler
Bryan	Gainesville	Karnes City	Rusk	Victoria
Canadian	Galveston	La Grange	San Antonio	Waco
Canyon	Gause	Langtry	San Marcos	Waelder
Center	Gonzales	Laredo	Sanderson	Weatherford
Channing	Granite	Livingston	Santa Fe	Weimar
Cleburne	Mountain	Longview	Sealy	Wichita Falls
Cleveland	Greenville	Lubbock	Shepherd	Wills Point
Columbus	Gregory	Lufkin	Sherman	Yoakum
Comstock	Groesbeck	Marshall	Smithville	
Corsicana	Groveton	Mexia	Somerville	

STUCKERS HEAR
CHAPEL CAR CALL

When sweet-faced Nettie Voila Packer Stucker first heard that she and her husband Edwin Stanton Stucker were going to Texas in a brand new railroad chapel car, she was apprehensive as well as excited. She would be quite reluctant to leave Aurora, Illinois, where her husband was pastor of the Claim Street Baptist Church. They had just been married a year, and in a quiet, tree-lined cemetery nearby was the fresh grave of their first child who died February 15, 1895—a little girl born prematurely, who lived only forty hours.[1]

The Claim Street Baptist Church was special to Nettie, even if it was a cold, old building with not much space to expand, certainly not like the spacious First Baptist Church downtown. Nettie's father, a prosperous inventor of farm equipment, had retired from his manufacturing career in the Sterling, Illinois, area and moved to Aurora. The family had started attending the Claim Street church, and it was there Nettie met the tall, handsome minister. Edwin looking out from his vantage point at the pulpit could not have missed Nettie—petite, demure, with soft brown hair. It would not be a long engagement.[2]

Aurora was not Edwin's home. His family resided in Ottawa, an eastern Kansas town on the banks of the Marais des Cygnes River. Baptists had been a part of Ottawa history from 1862 when the U.S. Congress set aside twenty thousand acres of Ottawa Indian land in an agreement that missionaries would start a college to help train Indian children. By 1867 the Ottawa tribe by treaty had moved to Indian Territory, leaving the town and a college with its name.[3]

In 1880 fourteen-year-old Edwin was baptized at the local First Baptist Church. After graduation from Ottawa public schools, he set off for post–high school studies, but he did not choose to attend the local college. Instead, he boarded a northbound Santa Fe coach at the Ottawa depot and traveled to Chicago and the respected, if somewhat controversial, institution created by millionaire John D. Rockefeller. Many Baptists of that day disapproved of the so-called liberal, non-scriptural teachings at the University of Chicago, under the presidency of the Reverend W. H. Harper, D.D.[4]

After college, Edwin did not return to Ottawa; instead, he worked as an engineer/surveyor for one of the new lines of the Chicago & NorthWestern (C&NW) Railway. In the building of a railroad, the first step is to make the surveys and locate the position of the intended road and to make maps and sections of it so that the land may be bought and the estimates of cost be ascertained. Edwin's college degree, although his major is not known, would have helped in preparing him for the mental accuracy required in a job that would also include hard physical labor, all of it spent in the out-of-doors. Most of his experience would be working with a surveying team not directly working with the railroad workers, but he would have many opportunities to observe railroad life and the conditions of the men who worked the trains.

During his time surveying along the C&NW lines in Minnesota and the Dakotas, he determined to follow what he felt was a call to preach, especially to witness to railroad men. He was ordained August 26, 1891, and in 1893 that "call" led him to the little Claim Street Baptist Church in Aurora, an important rail center.

Edwin and Nettie were married June 6, 1894, in a lovely ceremony in her parents' comfortable home. Both were almost thirty when they wed. The bride carried a small white Bible trimmed with embossed lilies. In it Edwin wrote, "To my Nettie, whom I receive as a direct expression of the love of the Author of this precious Word. May our God, whom we love and whose we are, receive, develop, and use us as we offer Him our lives, saying together, *Anywhere, Anything, at Anytime for Jesus.*"[5]

Edwin excitedly planned their month-long rail honeymoon to take them along the same C&NW lines that Edwin had surveyed. He wanted his bride to see the sights of the vast wheat fields and prairies of Minnesota and Nebraska and the mysterious Black Hills of the Dakotas. Before returning to their home in Aurora, the newlyweds visited Edwin's family in Ottawa, where they took time to attend the famed Ottawa Chautauqua at Forest Park, a block from the

The Reverend Edwin Stanton Stucker of Ottawa, Kansas, was the first missionary to be assigned to chapel car *Good Will* for its Texas mission.
Courtesy the Beverly Stucker Bennett family

Santa Fe station. From 1883 to 1914, the immense tabernacle held as many as ten thousand people and drew speakers like William Jennings Bryan, Gen. John A. Logan, and Jane Adams of Hull House.[6]

After their extended honeymoon, Edwin and Nettie returned to Aurora and the responsibilities of the Claim Street Baptist Church. Aurora was a bustling town, with as many as twenty churches, a free library, several daily and weekly newspapers, shops, pleasant parks, and a good share of genteel people. The Panic of 1893, with the run on banks, the closing of industrial plants which threw millions out of employment, and the destruction of credit and loss of homes had not affected Aurora as much as many American towns.

Aurora was more fortunate because the main division of the Chicago, Burlington & Quincy (CB&Q) Railroad was located there, and several hundred train and shop men made it their home. Numerous manufacturing companies employed the working-class citizens in town; in fact, just across the street from the Claim Street church one of three corset factories employed hundreds of workers, mainly women. Certainly some of those young women were a part of Edwin's congregation.

Not isolated from big city influences, Aurora had twenty-five trains a day coming and going to Chicago, and along with the traffic was a fair share of crime. The town produced just enough immorality from thievery and assault to gambling, drunkenness, and prostitution to provide Nettie's scholarly husband with sermon fodder, although it must not have provided him with enough of a challenge. After two years in the ministry there, he was ready for a change.

Nettie loved her husband, although the thought that she would be a minister's wife with that difficult role to play had probably never occurred to her. A quiet young woman, rather sheltered by her family, she was one of the youngest of six, one of two girls. Family records indicate that she had no advanced education beyond that of a high school or female academy. She loved domestic things, like cooking and sewing, and she must have had some training in the musical arts, as she would play the organ and sing at services during their chapel car year.[7]

The death of their first child had scarred their first year of marriage. Nettie's heart was broken and her body had not yet recovered from the difficult birth, but she knew that Edwin had felt the call to the chapel car ministry. He had proved that he had a gift for soul saving. In less than a year at Claim Street Baptist Church, he had

Just one year after her wedding to Edwin S. Stucker, and just a few months after the death of their first child, Nettie Packer Stucker left for Texas with her husband on chapel car *Good Will. Courtesy the Beverly Stucker Bennett family*

baptized thirty-seven, adding to his congregation of 136 more new converts than the other three Baptist churches in Aurora put together. Even if she were reluctant to leave their home and the comforting nearness of her parents and wanted time to grieve and recover from her recent loss, she knew this opportunity was important to him.[8]

Besides the religious implications and the fact that he had worked for the railroad, a railroad gospel car would have held a real attraction to Edwin. Like other town boys, he had watched the trains going through Ottawa and knew some of the men who worked at the Santa Fe yards there. His bachelor home in Aurora, at 254 Claim Street, several blocks from the church at 742 Claim, was adjacent to the yards of the CB&Q Railroad, and his and Nettie's first home at 83 North 4th Street was not far from the shops. The Aurora yard, with a forty-stall round house, machine shop, and paint and carpenter shops, was completed in 1856, and in 1883, the NorthWestern Railroad opened six miles from Batavia south to Aurora. The Stuckers seldom would have had a moment when they were not aware of the sights, sounds, and smells of the railroad and the men who worked there.[9]

So when the American Baptist Publication Society offered the opportunity to serve on brand new chapel car *Good Will*, Edwin heard the call to follow his heart to bring the gospel to railroad men. Nettie's heart reached out to home and family. The decision was made to follow Edwin's call.

CHAPEL CAR UNIQUE
GOSPEL MINISTRY

The chapel car ministry was an exciting, innovative approach to evangelism. Beginning in 1890 and ending in the late 1940s, thirteen rail chapel cars ministered to thousands of towns mainly west of the Mississippi: The Episcopal Diocese of North Dakota cathedral car, seven American Baptist Publication Society cars, two Episcopal Diocese of Northern Michigan cars, and three Catholic Church Extension Society cars.

It was Episcopal Bishop William David Walker of North Dakota who first took the chapel car concept, produced a chapel car, and put it into service. On a trip to Russia in the late 1880s, Walker saw the elaborate Russian Orthodox chapel cars on the Siberian Railway. The construction had been announced by the *Spirit of Missions,* an Episcopal publication.

> A traveling church will be put upon the Trans–Caspian railway shortly to provide occasional services for the Russian officials of the line and the settlers scattered about. Externally the church resembles an ordinary railway carriage except for a cross over the roof and a little belfry at the entrance. Inside, however, it is beautifully fitted up for the service of the Orthodox Church, with a carved wooden altar and accommodation for seventy worshipers. The priest and his assistants travel in a tiny coupe attached to the church-carriage.[1]

The people who lived in eastern Siberia existed in an environment that could be described as bleak, and their situation was parallel in many ways to the plight of those living along American western routes. As with the American transcontinental railways in the

1860s and 1870s, the Siberian Railway, the longest continuous rail line in the world, was to fulfill Russia's version of Manifest Destiny —to develop the resources of Siberia and to constitute a new commercial route for rapid travel and exchange of products between the East and West.[2]

The sight of the Russian cars caused wheels to whirl in the bishop's head. He conceived of how he could reach the thousands of faithful scattered across the vast territory of North Dakota who were without religious services. In April, 1890, while the American Baptist Publication Society, which had initiated plans for its own chapel car, was out gathering support, Walker contracted for such a car to be built by the Pullman Palace Car Company in Pullman, Illinois, and took possession of it in November, 1890. Called the *Church of the Advent, the Cathedral Car of North Dakota,* Walker's car was the first American chapel car put in service. The Baptist car, *Evangel,* contracted in August at the Barney & Smith Car Company shops in Dayton, Ohio, would not be completed until the spring of 1891.

Harper's Weekly described the *Cathedral Car of North Dakota.*

This car is sixty feet long, and arranged with what has been known to the manufacturers as a "state-room" at one end. In the center of the exterior on either side is an elevation with sunken panels to give in some degree the cathedral appearance. . . . The finish is in oak, and the car is equipped with double windows on account of the cold country in which it will be used. A Baker heater is selected for warming this moving house of worship. Toward the rear of the car is the chancel with its altar, lectern, and font. A cabinet organ provides the music. The seating space is filled with portable chairs to the number of about eighty. The room partitioned off in the rear is ten feet long by about nine feet four inches wide.

Its twofold use as vestry and bedroom is best signified in the bishop's words: "In it I can put on my robes. It will also be a dormitory for me when the people of the hamlet will not have room to shelter me. It will be simple in decoration and in its equipment."[3]

Despite clearance problems with the elevated transept rose window and the protruding steps on the car, the Episcopal chapel car was well received. Its compactness, dignity, and simple churchly beauty, along with the bishop's Spartan way of living, probably ac-

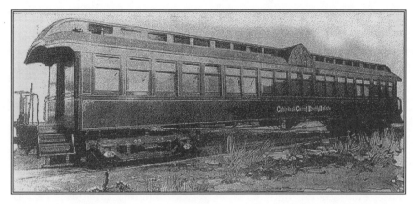

Built by the Pullman Palace Company in 1890, the *Cathedral Car of North Dakota, Church of the Advent,* was the first American chapel car. *From* Illustrated American, 1890

counted for much of his success with rough pioneer men. He cooked his own meals, made his own bed, swept the floor, distributed leaflets, made the fires, and kept the car in order; he usually had to play the organ as well. Bishop Walker acknowledged that many people were prompted to come to the church car by curiosity alone. One farmer told him, "I've been to a good many circuses, and I've seen all the grandest exhibitions that have come west; but this is the biggest show yet."[4]

The bishop and his chapel car were a familiar sight from the rolling woodlands of the Red River Valley to the Montana border as Walker officiated at church services, conducted marriages and funerals, and tended his scattered sheep. Bishop Walker with the cathedral car visited Drayton, a town of seven hundred inhabitants, in 1895. It touched his heart to hear a farmhand singing beautifully at one of the meetings and to learn that this man used to sing in the choir of Lincoln Cathedral, England. "Your car," said the man, "seems like a bit of home to me."[5]

Two Episcopal chapel cars of Northern Michigan were believed to be in operation from 1891 to 1902. In the Michigan case, the cars were not built new. The first chapel car, a loaned railroad car most likely from the Chicago & NorthWestern Railroad, was outfitted with an altar, organ, pews, and a tiny living compartment. By late 1893 it appears the first Upper Michigan chapel car had been retired. Bishop G. Mott Williams told the delegates to the 1894 convention at St. Paul's Church in Marquette, "I want also to report on the chapel car. It was operated long enough to prove serviceable, but was an old affair, borrowed at that, and inconvenient. I am having a new one built, it will be rigidly plain, but very strong, and I hope, convenient. It can be used to much greater advantage here, I think, than in any other part of the church."

This second Upper Peninsula car, put in service about the same time as chapel car *Good Will,* was earlier reported as being used on the Union Pacific, but it may also have been a NorthWestern car. For church purposes, there were three separate compartments: chapel, sleeping quarters, and a place to prepare and eat meals. The usual business car bedrooms, observation room, and dining room could have been removed, leaving the small kitchen and the attendant's room for the person traveling in the car. Then the rest of the car could be fitted with an altar and other church furnishings.[6]

In the year of his election, 1896, Bishop Williams visited many towns along the shores of Lake Superior, such as Thomaston, Ballentine, Marchwood, Three Lakes, Humboldt, and Champion, in view of multi-colored sandstone cliffs and lush forests. In the heyday of the railroads, seventy-seven different lines operated across the Upper Peninsula. The chapel car was given free use of their tracks, traversing the peninsula, east to west and north to south. Williams himself was a frequent traveler on the rails, baptizing and confirming new members.[7]

Starting in 1891 with *Evangel,* six more American Baptist Publication Society cars were put into service—*Emmanuel, #2* in 1893; *Glad Tidings, #3* in 1894; *Good Will, #4* in 1895; *Messenger of Peace, #5* in 1897; and *Herald of Hope, #6* in 1900. All the cars were built in the Barney & Smith Car Shops in Dayton, Ohio. The last American chapel car to be built would be Baptist chapel car *Grace* in 1915. The Baptist chapel cars' main mission was to minister to railroad workers and help to establish churches in areas where there were no churches.

Evangel was a beautifully appointed oak chapel complete with pews, platform, and stained glass trim, and separate living quarters for missionaries with berths, office, galley kitchen, and washroom. Its area of service was Minnesota, North Dakota, Montana, Oregon, Washington, California, Arizona, New Mexico, Arkansas, Kansas, Missouri, Louisiana, Oklahoma, Indian Territory, Colorado, Nebraska, and Wyoming. In November of 1925, *Evangel,* which had been condemned for travel, was presented to the Rawlins, Wyoming, First Baptist Church by the American Baptist Publication Society, and sections of the car body were incorporated into the Church.

Emmanuel, 1893, featured a 76-foot, 8-inch by 10-foot (over side sill) Catalpa wood exterior and was divided into two sections: chapel and living quarters. On the car's roof was mounted a brass church bell. The car served in Arizona, California, Oregon, Washington, Nevada, Idaho, Montana, Missouri, Colorado, and South Dakota. Retired from active service in 1942, it was rescued by preservationists at Prairie Village, a pioneer museum near Madison, South Dakota. In 1975 the car qualified for the South Dakota Register of Historic Places and is also on the National Register of Historic Places.

Glad Tidings, 1894, was similar to *Emmanuel.* This third car served in Minnesota, North Dakota, South Dakota, Iowa, Wisconsin, Nebraska, Missouri, Colorado, Wyoming, and Arizona. In 1926 *Glad Tidings* was moved to Flagstaff, Arizona, its final resting place, where the car was dismantled and some parts were incorporated into the Glad Tidings and Mountain View Baptist Churches.

Good Will, 1895, with the same basic plan as *Glad Tidings,* served in Texas, Missouri, Colorado, Idaho, Utah, Oregon, Washington, and California. In 1938 *Good Will* was placed on a permanent foundation in Boyes Spring, Sonoma County, California. It is in the same location today, owned by a private individual, in poor condition off its trucks.

Messenger of Peace, 1898, also similar to *Glad Tidings,* served in Kansas, Missouri, Colorado, Illinois, West Virginia, Montana, Nevada, California, Oregon, and Washington. The car was exhibited at the 1904 World's Fair in St. Louis and served briefly with the Railroad YMCA. A private citizen purchased the car in 1949, and it is assumed to be on private property near Ocean Shores, Washington, in poor condition off its trucks.

Herald of Hope, 1900, the last wooden car, worked in Michigan, Illinois, Ohio, Iowa, and West Virginia. Spending much of its time amid the coal mines during the coal wars of the 1920s, the car was retired in 1935 and later was dismantled near a coal tipple in Quinwood, West Virginia.

Chapel car *Grace,* 1915, was the first steel Baptist chapel car. Not only longer than the other cars, with a separate bedroom, 85 feet, 3 inches by 10 feet (over side sill), *Grace* was designed in a more "churchy" style with many Gothic arch features borrowed from the design of Catholic *St. Paul,* in the Barney & Smith shops at the same time. *Grace* served in Nevada, California, Colorado, Wyoming, and Utah. After supporting a mission for government workers at Orem, Utah, during World War II, *Grace* was retired to the grounds of the American Baptist Assembly at Green Lake, Wisconsin, where it is being preserved. Thousands visit the chapel car where it is still used for worship.

It was not until 1907 that the Catholic chapel car *St. Anthony* was put into service, followed by *St. Peter* in 1912 and *St. Paul* in 1915. The Right Reverend Francis C. Kelley had not forgotten the concept of the Baptist chapel car *Messenger of Peace* he had seen in 1904 at the St. Louis World's Fair. In a 1906 issue of *Extension* magazine, he described the appeal of the unique gospel car, how its very novelty would draw non-Catholics to hear a missionary, and that literature could be carried in quantities in the car, which would also be the home of the missionary. He wrote that the railroads pulled chapel cars free of charge and they cost little to maintain, opinions that he would have cause to take back in the years to come. He concluded by asking, "If the Baptists can do it, why not the Catholics? Who will give us a chapel car to place in the service of the scattered ones of the flock?"

Ambrose Petry, president of the Ambrose Petry Company of New York and Detroit, and Richmond Dean, a vice president of Pullman and also a board member of the Extension Society, saw the potential for such a car. Pullman was disposing of the old Wagner cars, and Pullman records show that on July 7, 1907, Petry bought Wagner Palace Car Mentone #187, Plan 3049, Lot 1205, built in September of 1886, and it was renovated as a chapel car. Seventy feet long, *St. Anthony* was capable of holding sixty-five persons. The altar was constructed so that at the center of the altar was a painting of St. Anthony. The candlesticks and a beautiful ivory crucifix, carved in the eleventh century, were donated by Count Santa Eulalia, the Portuguese consul in Chicago. The movable communion railing could be converted into a confessional. Two small rooms for the chaplain and attendants—a kitchen and dining room—completed the arrangement. *St. Anthony* was especially adapted to the Western and Southern sections of the country where Catholics were few and where small congregations could be housed during services.

The *New World* newspaper reported, "The car left the LaSalle

The first chapel car put in service in 1907 by the Catholic Church Extension Society was *St. Anthony,* a Wagner Car renovated by the Pullman Company. *From the author's collection*

Street Station at 6:30 Sunday evening [June 16, 1907,] for Wichita, Kansas, where it will be at the service of Bishop John J. Hennessey until next December. During this time the Bishop or a missionary priest will tour the branch lines of the railroads running through Kansas, stopping at towns where there are no Catholic Churches to administer the sacraments and bring the consolation of religion to the isolated members of the Faith." On board and in charge was lay-man George Hennessey, a Canadian Irishman who was a first cousin of Father Kelley. In Northwestern, South Dakota, Father O'Neill, the priest on board, wrote, ". . . In Mobridge down the line . . . forty confessioners, mostly railroad men, had the opportunity to go to the Sacraments for the first time since they came to this country eigh-teen months ago."

As was true with the Episcopal and Baptist chapel cars, there were those in the Catholic church who did not agree that the chapel cars were a great idea. In the fall of 1907, opponents of the chapel car were heard and quickly rebutted by Bishop Hennessey in *Extension*.

> Our critics might say that all this could be done and is done by ordinary missionaries everywhere without a chapel car. Per-haps it could if conditions were favorable, if a suitable hall could be rented, and an organ provided, and an organ player imported, and a convenient dry goods box could be borrowed for an altar, and a codfish box for a credence table, and a couple of empty beer or catsup bottles for candlesticks, but we believe those who are listening to us will still be persuaded that the chapel car is way ahead in every respect, and that it is worth all the money that was paid for it.[8]

St. Peter, the second Catholic Extension Society chapel car—this one built by the Barney & Smith Car Company in Dayton, Ohio, home of the Baptist chapel cars—was said to be one of the longest cars in the world at that time, just as Baptist car *Emmanuel* had been in 1893. The overall length was eighty-four feet with the part set aside for the chapel measuring forty-three feet. Finished in a rich St. Jago mahogany, with dark green ceilings touched with graceful de-signs, the sanctuary platform, elevated six inches above the car floor, had a storage area underneath. A handsome communion railing in the English fashion—a rood screen of scroll nature on which is mounted the "rood" or the cross, separated a neat altar and a per-manent confessional from the nave. Stations of the cross were built in to form a part of the car's interior decoration, and an organ, built by the Hinners Organ Company of Pekin, Illinois, was installed near the entrance. The compartments used as living quarters by the chaplains, managers, and porters included a study that could also be used as a dining room, a library or office, a sleeping compartment, a washroom, and a kitchen.

St. Peter would serve in Illinois, Ohio, Kansas, Minnesota, Montana, Oregon, North Carolina, Idaho, and Utah. After a mix-up at the Pullman shops in Chicago when *St. Peter* and *St. Paul* were in storage in the 1920s, both cars were sent to the wrong destination. *St. Peter* ended up serving as a chapel in North Carolina until it was dismantled in 1953.

Peter Kuntz paid $35,000 for *St. Paul,* his second chapel car gift to the Extension Society. *St. Paul,* 1915–54, was constructed in the Barney & Smith Dayton shops at the same time as Baptist Chapel car *Grace. St. Paul*'s floor plan was an improvement over *St. Peter*'s. The kitchen ran the full end of the car, and in both the toilet room as well as in the kitchen there were provisions made for filling the tanks for water supply both by hand and by force. Attending priests had requested that the confessional be made in the folding style so the prie dieu could be attached and folded. *St. Paul* would serve mainly in Louisiana, North Carolina, Oklahoma, Montana, Idaho, Iowa, Indiana, and Texas. After being sent to Gardiner and East Glacier, Montana, *St. Paul* was sold for a token price to Senator Charles Bovey in 1967 for his rail museum in Nevada City, Montana. The car is presently being restored at the Lake Superior & Escanaba Railroad shops in Michigan's Upper Peninsula.[9]

The only chapel cars in service when chapel car *Good Will* was commissioned to go to Texas in May of 1895 were the second Episcopal chapel car of Northern Michigan and sister Baptist cars— *Evangel, Emmanuel,* and *Glad Tidings.*

HEARING THE TRAMP
OF TEXAS MILLIONS

In comparison to their comfortable life in the railroad community of Aurora, for Nettie, going to Texas on a rail chapel car would be a different story. Even those who lived in Texas acknowledged the state's daunting uniqueness. The members of the Home Mission Board of the Baptist General Convention of Texas declared that Texas was a world, and not a very small world, in itself, and that no state in the Union could possibly be compared with it. Although its territory does not "stretch from pole to pole," it does stretch 800 miles east, west, north, and south. "Some of the people of nearly all the nations of the earth have found a home within her borders. The children of Europe, Asia, Africa, and Mexico have come to our doors, and are begging for bread, shall we give them a stone?"[1]

Besides native Texans—mainly ranchers, cowboys, merchants, and professionals—there were thousands of Bohemians, Swedes, and as many as three hundred thousand Germans who had migrated to the state, plus a large Norwegian settlement in the Texas Basque country. Around San Antonio, San Marcos, along the Rio Grande, at El Paso, along the border, and up into New Mexico Territory, there were many needy Mexican settlements. A growing population of African Americans posed unique problems for mission outreach.[2]

Good Will, #4, was not the first American Baptist Publication Society chapel car to work in Texas. *Emmanuel, #2,* built in 1893, came to El Paso to conduct a mission for the Chinese with the Reverend and Mrs. E. G. Wheeler on board. This second Baptist chapel car, considered to be the longest railroad car operating at the time at almost 77 feet long, had been serving in California. Brother Lum Chow had been laboring to explain Christianity to the hundreds of

Chinese in El Paso and had distributed tracts and Bibles in Chinese sent by the Publication Society.[3]

In the spring of 1895, the Wheelers established a West End mission on Main Street, a night school to teach English under the direction of the First Baptist Church, and an American Sunday school. They worked extensively among the railroad workers, and the Chinese were a large segment of the work force. The El Paso *Daily Herald* reported, "Mr. Wheeler is a forcible and interesting speaker, and his wife is a lovely and entertaining woman. The public are taking very kindly to them both and the car may be expected to be crowded at all of the services."[4]

Leaving El Paso, *Emmanuel* headed northeast to Roswell in New Mexico Territory. In February, 1895, a small band of Baptists started a two-room church under the leadership of Missionary O. P. Miles. Miles was looking for ways to encourage the growth of the fledgling fellowship, and he heard through Publication Society chapel car superintendent Boston W. Smith that the chapel car was in El Paso. On April Fool's day, *Emmanuel* rolled into the Roswell depot on the brand new Pecos Valley Railroad in the midst of a terrible sandstorm. Methodists in town were stirring up a storm of their own, revival-style, when *Emmanuel* arrived. According to the *Roswell Register*, evangelist Abe Mulkey was "turning Roswell upside down, as it were, and giving it a cleaning out, . . . with strong men with tears streaming down their faces." It is likely that Baptist Miles needed the spark of the novel chapel car to offset the excitement created by Mulkey's presence.[5]

Wheeler had already proven that he too had a gift for stirring up souls. Twenty-three came forward after the first meeting in *Emmanuel,* and sometime the next day he baptized a number in the artesian springs that helped make the area famous. Since the chapel car could not hold the crowd, including the employees of the Atchison, Topeka, and Santa Fe railroad shops and roundhouse, meetings were moved to the New Mexico Military Institute. With his knack for public relations and perhaps a sense of one–upmanship over Mulkey, Wheeler took pictures of the baptism and had them displayed in the lobby of the prominent El Capitan Hotel.[6]

A week later after considerable success in spite of the Mulkey competition, the Wheelers and *Emmanuel* left for Eddy, later changed to Carlsbad. The Home Mission Board of the Southern

Brand new chapel car *Good Will* on a siding at the MK&T shops, Sedalia, Missouri, on its way to Texas shortly after its dedication at Saratoga Springs, New York, in the spring of 1895. *From the author's collection*

Baptist Convention had reported that along the Roswell & Pecos Railway, the Pecos and Penasco Rivers and Valleys, the White Oaks and the Sacramento Mountains, there were growing populations "absolutely destitute of missionary labor, except for some work at Eddy." But who reached Eddy before *Emmanuel* did? Abe Mulkey, drawing huge crowds and turning Eddy "upside down." The Wheelers must have felt it was not worth another revival battle for they left Eddy after only a few meetings. They worked their way back west to Arizona's southern frontier, after a brief stop at Pecos, Texas, about the same time chapel car *Good Will* began its Texas mission. It would not be the last that the chapel car missionaries would hear of Abe Mulkey.[7]

Texas Baptist leaders were aware of the good work done by *Emmanuel* and were eager for *Good Will* to minister to snowballing colonies, many without churches. German immigrants had made their homes in the state around New Braunfels, Fredericksburg, and Brenham, and spread south peopling as many as forty counties. As early as 1869, the State Convention had missionaries working with the Germans, and in 1884, a German Baptist Conference was organized. The proportion of the foreign population was greater in southern and southwestern Texas, but there were colonies or settle-

ments scattered over different parts of the state. Specifically of concern were "the souls" of Mexicans, principally Catholics, and of Swedes and Norwegians—almost all Lutherans. Texas Baptists had a narrow view of those who could enter the kingdom of God, and Catholics and Lutherans, in their opinion, did not make the cut.[8]

Blacks who came to Texas as slaves before the Civil War or after as freedmen were also a targeted group for missionary effort. Even after reconstruction, it was the majority opinion that blacks be retained in the white churches segregated in the balcony. In some instances, they were allowed to form separate churches, but they were required to be supervised by whites. In spite of the restrictions, across Texas there were a growing number of black churches.[9]

The Stuckers had heard of the concern of the Texas Baptist General Convention, which reported at its 1894 Atlanta meeting, "Hard as the times are, these vast regions are being settled. There is nowhere else for the people to go, and he who has an ear to hear can already hear the tramp of the oncoming millions. Our missionaries should not wait to ride on the cowcatcher of the first engine of the new railroad, but should be on the ground ready to welcome the engineer and his passengers, preaching the gospel to them, and baptizing them as fast as they believe."[10]

Its sides resplendent in varnished Pullman green, *Good Will* was constructed to ride not on the cowcatcher of the figurative "first engine of the new railroad," but coupled behind a real steam engine, announcing its message to all who could read the gilded letters "American Baptist Publication Society" and "Chapel Car *Good Will.*" Near the vestibule end, where people would enter the chapel, was hand painted the scripture from Mark 16:15, "Go ye into all the world and preach the gospel to every creature."

The dedication of this chapel car at the depot in Saratoga Springs, New York, its cost of $7,500 paid for by donations of Baptists nationwide, was a highlight of the annual meeting of the Publication Society. The Reverend Wayland Hoyt, pastor of the First Baptist Church of Minneapolis, Minnesota, gave the dedication address. His brother, Colgate Hoyt, vice president of the Northern Pacific Railroad, trustee of the Wisconsin Central Railroad, and soon to be vice president of the Missouri, Kansas & Texas Railroad, was a Baptist layman.

The Hoyts; William Hills of the Hills Bros. Coffee Co.; New York businessman Charles L. Colby, whose father was president of the Wisconsin Central Railroad; James B. Colgate of the Colgate–Palmolive Co.; John R. Trevor, a stocks exchange dealer; and John D. Rockefeller, millionaire financier and oil mogul, were the members of the syndicate who financed the first chapel car, *Evangel.* E. G. Barney, a Baptist layman and owner of the Barney & Smith Car Shops of Dayton, Ohio, agreed to build the Baptist chapel cars at cost. His company was known for the quality of its wooden passenger cars, the work done by German and Hungarian artisans who were brought over by Barney and who lived in Kossuth, a company town surrounded by walls of wood.[11]

The Barney & Smith Car Company, then E. Thresher & Company, started production twenty–four years after American railroads began operation, and they built their shops on the banks of a canal because there were no railroads to serve them. By the time the first Baptist chapel car was being constructed in the Barney & Smith shops in 1890, business was expanding. Although oak, ash, and hardwoods were generally used for passenger cars, it is likely that the exterior wood of *Good Will* was catalpa. Eliam Barney promoted catalpa wood as a material of choice in the construction of railroad rolling stock. He had run tests that proved catalpa wood was of remarkable strength and power of resisting decay, even in the most exposed situations. Barney promoted among the citizens of Dayton the planting of catalpa trees for possible use for car construction and also for shade.[12]

Barney & Smith competed for orders with other respected car companies, including The Pullman Palace Car Company, and received such prestigious accounts as Northern Pacific President Villard's private car in 1883 and seventy–five sleepers for Pullman from 1860 to 1875. When *Good Will* was in the shops in the fall of 1894, the company had survived the Depression of 1893 but was suffering as a result of its delay in switching to steel cars. Less than eighty cars shared space with *Good Will,* significantly less than normal. E. G. Barney would have been in the crowd gathered around the Saratoga Springs depot on the day of *Good Will'*s dedication. He must have appreciated the crowd's admiration of the fourth of his magnificent chapel cars.[13]

The Reverend Hoyt braved the noise of the crowd of excited delegates as he proclaimed that the purpose of the chapel cars was to travel to "struggling, too often sadly irreligious" western towns. "It advocates your Lord's gospel. It summons the crowds. It is a distributing center for your literature. It is a great and thoroughly appointed evangelizing instrument thrust among the people." He told the delegates, "You have hitched your gospel to the nineteenth century. You have said, and in a splendid way, nothing is too good, or swift or modern or convenient, for the use of the Lord and Savior Jesus Christ."[14]

At the dedication, the delegates sang a hymn written especially for *Good Will.*

> With trailing light, the gospel car
> Moves over all the land
> Till sin and death bow down before
> The bounties of thy hand;
> For thou hast ever present been
> A guide in all our ways,
> A heavenly leader, thou shalt win
> All joyous notes of praise.

Nettie Stucker, sitting in the audience, must have wondered where this "gospel train" would take her. Perhaps of prophetic en-

The glass panel with "God is Love" stenciled on it was in all the Baptist cars.
Through the door can be seen the upper bunk in the living area. *Courtesy
Norman T. Taylor Collection*

couragement was the thought that Saratoga County, where she was
now sitting, was where her parents, Harvey S. Packer and Charlotte
Prudence Bass, had married before coming to Illinois.

After the June 1, 1895, dedication, Edwin and Nettie headed toward Texas and settled into their new life on *Good Will.* The 76-foot
car featured an oak-paneled 9 feet, 4 inches by 52-feet, 2-inch sanctuary, trimmed with moss-white glass clerestory windows. It was
equipped with seats, fixed three on the right and two on the left
along a center aisle; an ornate brass podium; and an Estey reed organ, donated personally by Col. J. J. Estey of Brattleboro, Vermont.
Since the distribution of religious literature published by the society
was one of the main purposes of the ministry, tracts, Sunday school
literature, scripture cards, and Bibles translated in as many as seventeen languages were stored under the seats. These items were not
to be sold, but given away.

Stucker was delighted with the row of Bible commentaries con-
veniently placed near the roll-top desk with etched glass doors. On
a shelf under the desk was a typewriter that he could use to prepare
his reports and sermons. He would not be so delighted with the
complexity of having to feed coal to the perverse Baker Heater in
those occasions when Texas weather would turn cold. He was more
fortunate than many of the other chapel car missionaries in that he

had spent several years working around trains and had a working knowledge of the mechanical aspects of the car.

Nettie may have had second thoughts about their Texas assignment, but the diminutive parsonage to the rear of the chapel must have charmed her. It was newer than their little Aurora home near the railroad yards, although much smaller, with a total living area of nine by eighteen feet. The compact space consisted of a tiny galley-style kitchen with a copper-lined sink, an icebox, cabinet space, and an oil burning stove. Upper and lower sleeping berths, chairs, storage space, and a table that folded out from the wall crowded the living area. She even had a homey rug, given by a Ladies' Missionary Society in Dayton, Ohio, under her padded rocking chair, and in the pass-through cupboard nested a set of delicate rose-patterned china. On the fold-down table, Nettie would have placed a favorite bowl or other items she had brought from home, perhaps family pictures. An Aurora newspaper glowingly reported, "It [the chapel car] contains everything calculated to serve the needs of its occupants and conduce to the comfort of those who attend services within it." [15]

Not all was perfect. Nettie would discover that the wash room with its hopper-style toilet had health and aesthetic limitations, although the mirror over the marble-topped sink, with water pumped from a tank beneath, was a nice addition. Missionary societies from across the country had donated kitchenware and linens, but keeping those household and personal items clean in the 10-inch square by 12-inch deep sink required heating a teakettle of water and emptying the water into the sink and drying them on a narrow counter. The teakettle would also serve as the source of sponge baths as there was no room for a tub. It would prove to be difficult at many stops in arid Texas to get water. Usually the stations and shops were good places to fill the tanks under the washroom and kitchen sinks, so with every stop, one of the priorities would be to load up on water. At times, the source and quality of the water would be questionable.

In spite of inconveniences, when Nettie would look up at the living area ceiling, she would see panels glowing with a decorative stencil of rococo turquoise waves set in a pale gold background. This graceful touch seemed almost decadent along side the more modest interior of the chapel with its recessed square panel design on the walls and the restrained ceiling trim—a leaf-like motif tucked away in the corners. [16]

Good Will arrived in Texas after completing a well-attended, week-long mission in the Stuckers' home base of Aurora. An Aurora newspaper article printed, "The railroads thus far have esteemed it a privilege to haul the car and its missionary free, and keep it supplied with ice water, oil, etc., without being asked. It came over the New York Central and Michigan Central roads to Chicago and over the 'Q' to Aurora from Saratoga Springs, New York. The latter company has expressed its readiness to transport the car wherever desired upon its lines." The reporter concluded, "It is a beauty and no surprise exists that Mr. Stucker and his wife should be proud of their portable home." From Aurora, they stopped at Sedalia, Missouri, for services, and at Fort Scott, Kansas, the car was sided on the Wall Street spur at the Gulf Depot in meetings with the YMCA. The newspaper at Fort Scott said of the chapel car that it is "something new in the world. It is nothing more nor less than a church on wheels." [17]

Although the Stuckers were delighted with *Good Will*, not everyone in the Texas Baptist General Convention, beset with internal strife and at odds with the concept of the role of missions in the local church, shared their pleasure with the presence of the American Baptist Publication Society car. The relationship of the Publication Society and the American Baptist Home Mission Society to the Southern Baptist Convention traced back to the beginnings of Texas Baptist work. James Huckins, a graduate of Brown University and Andover Theological Seminary and an appointee of the Home Mission Society, landed in Galveston in 1840 to help establish a Baptist presence in Texas. [18]

But before Huckins came, a Baptist presence was already in Texas, although carefully hidden. In 1833 Elder Daniel Parker, founder of the "Two–Seed" sect of Baptists that would become the arch enemy of missions on the frontier, found a way to circumvent the Texas law that forbade the introduction of non–Catholic faiths into the state. From Illinois, Parker and a group of Pre–destinarian Regular Baptists set out for Texas, and in violation of the law, secretly met in homes until after the War of Independence. In the years between 1840 and 1895, several schisms, theological skirmishes, and a devastating Civil War had loosened the ties that had bound the Northern Baptists and their southern brethren. Other movements such as that of the Primitives, who were "stubbornly anti-missionary, anti-intellectual, and extremely class-conscious," as well as "strongly predestinarian," widened the gap.

Texas Baptist leader J. M. Carroll defined the state of affairs in 1895 as "times to try the patience of the saints." Martinism, with its belief of absolute assurance coming simultaneously with conversion and lasting forever, bordered on heresy. The Anti–Education remnant band permeated pockets of Texas life and impacted not just Baptists but Methodists as well. The financial situation at Baylor University was tenuous, with attempts to consolidate smaller Baptist colleges failing. Criticism of Carroll and other Baptist leaders by opposing factors verged on libel, much of it instigated by Samuel A. Hayden and his "Landmark" reforms. In frustration, the General Board pleaded, "Shall we wait until the mission cause, now bleeding, is stamped out of existence?"[19]

It was not a time to wait. The coming of the chapel car, although sponsored by what many considered to be the more liberal Northern Baptists, was a testament to that commitment. As praise for the chapel car's work in churchless towns and with needy churches began appearing in the *Texas Baptist Standard*, there were more requests for the services of the Stuckers and chapel car *Good Will*.

RAILROADERS LOVE
A RAIL CHURCH

Good Will was placed on a siding in the busy, sweltering Denison
yards on July 8, 1895. Hundreds of freight shipments and passengers rode the "Katy" from the union depots of St. Louis,
Hannibal, Kansas City, Moberly, and Sedalia, on their way through
Indian Territory to Denison and beyond. The Missouri, Kansas &
Texas (MK&T) Railway, also known as "The Emigrants Route,"
reached Denison in 1875, and the town became an important cattle
shipping point as well as a bustling rail center. The railroad advertised Denison as the "Gate City of Texas" hoping that the colorful
promotion posters, promising every married man along the route
160 acres and every single man eighty acres of land, would entice
settlers to stay.[1]

In Denison's early tent city days, professional ruffians, gamblers,
and "off-scourings" of society made up half of the town; in fact, the
first formal business when the town was established in November,
1872, was a one-foot by twelve-foot plank nailed to two trees from
which liquor was served. With every third building a saloon or gambling house, the town was so wild that town fathers called in the
Texas Rangers. Along with some law and order, in 1873 the Houston & Texas Central Railroad came to town. In the mid-1870s, the
MK&T created at Denison its Texas Terminal to serve the southwest's greatest cotton compress and vast cattle yard.[2]

An early newspaperman around 1873 delighted in saying that
people went to Sherman for religion and to Denison for fun. As Jack
Maguire writes in his book on the Katy, that was not entirely true,
as the First Presbyterian Church was organized on December 23,
1872, two days before the first Katy train arrived. By the mid-1870s,
the Episcopalians, Methodists, Baptists, and Catholics all had con-

gregations organized and one had built a sanctuary. Town life quieted with the coming of families, businesses, and the churches, although in the 1890s the saloon trade was still the controlling influence in almost all railroad towns, including Denison. A census taken by the *Daily News* March 13, 1873, was evidence that houses of amusement outranked religious institutions in numbers if not popularity. It listed twenty saloons, ten brothels (dance halls included), and only one church actually standing.[3]

In 1886 the Prohibition Party in Texas pushed for a constitutional amendment to prevent the production, sale, or exchange of alcoholic beverages in Texas. Randolph B. Campbell in *Gone to Texas* reports that in the spring of 1887 the legislature let the wets and drys have it out in a nonpartisan contest. Prohibition foes did not risk a pro-alcohol position, but argued against state interference with personal freedom and called for temperance through private and religious efforts. Prohibitionists presented themselves as the champions of "virtue, thrift and prosperity . . . right, justice and humanity." During the campaign, B. H. Carroll, Baptist minister, called Congressman Roger W. Mills "Roger the Dodger . . . [who] finally would not dodge the devil," and Mills replied that hell was "full of better preachers" than Carroll. The wets won, and voters later would remember the bitter 1887 vote as a time "when friendships were severed and family ties subjected to the keenest trial."[4]

For Baptists, as well as for the Methodists, Presbyterians, Congregationalists, and later Disciples of Christ, temperance had been an issue since colonial days. The stress then was not on total abstinence but on the "intemperate use of alcohol." Later the focus shifted to condemning hard liquor but permitting the use of wine and beer. Some Baptists even argued that wine and beer, which they proclaimed never or seldom led to drunkenness, could be deterrents to the use of "strong" drink. Farm columns in some Baptist journals encouraged farmers to grow grapes and berries for the purpose of stimulating wine manufacturing in the South, but by the end of the Civil War, temperance leaders began an all out assault against all alcoholic drinks. By the 1880s Southern Baptists had committed to a battle against "demon rum" in all forms but avoided a national crusade because they viewed drinking as a personal sin to be dealt with by personal regeneration, not legislation. Most Methodists agreed with this view of prohibition until the 1890s when Methodists declared at their General Conference, "We are a prohibition church. . . . We stand for the complete suppression of the liquor traffic [and] are opposed to all forms of license of this iniquity."[5]

Denison was the seat of Grayson County. The Grayson County Baptist Association made clear its view of the consumption of alcohol in its minutes: "We consider the whisky traffic the greatest and most aggressive evil that ever invaded our fair land. We believe it to be an inveterate opponent of our greatest and most sacred institution, and that it is using all its combined power to retard the progress of Christianity and destroy the great principles that underlie the temples of American civilization." The members believed that every church should refuse to fellowship any member who drank intoxicating liquors as a beverage or visited saloons for such indulgence. Even if the men who worked at the shops did not have to work seven days a week, and even if they had Sunday off, it would have been difficult for them to adhere to the standards set by the town Baptists. Most of them probably would not have darkened the door of the Denison church.[6]

Railroad life tended to be rough. Even Edward Henry Harriman, who would take over the management of the Southern Pacific and Union Pacific System in 1901, was concerned about the amoral atmosphere of railroad life. He considered the number of accidents as well as loss of life and property as a consequence of what he called "ubiquitous saloon" influence. He hoped that "clubs established by the company would counter the influence of the saloons and at the same time increase morale, efficiency and safe working habits." Railroad Men's Clubs and Railroad YMCA buildings began to appear in many rail centers, and were warmly embraced by both management and labor. The time when there would be conflict with the Railroad Ys occurred during strike time when the Y leadership faced having to take sides between the men who permitted them to witness in the rail yards and the men to whom they wanted to witness.[7]

Among the early supporters of the Railroad YMCA was Cornelius Vanderbilt, who in 1897 contributed $215,000 for the erection of an association building in New York City. Along with his financial support, he stressed the necessity for a maximum of autonomy for railroad associations. He saw that the policy of corporate gifts from the railroads could create problems, especially during times of labor disputes when the issue became whether striking workers could still be served by the railroad associations that were supported by the management. Related to that same concern was the criticism that since the Railroad Y was primarily a Christian movement, and that since railroad employees were of all creeds and of no creed, railroads should not contribute to its existence.[8] In response to that charge, L. H. Turner, superintendent of motive power of the Pittsburgh & Lake Erie Railroad, said that railroads will realize that when facilities for the comfort of their men and libraries and opportunities for instruction are provided, and religious events are voluntary, that they are not contributing to a charity but simply taking a common sense view of a business proposition—that "a railroad that has the greatest number of sober and intelligent men is bound to set a high mark in economical and efficient operation."[9]

Whereas the Grayson Baptists disdained anyone using alcohol, most of the railroaders frequented the saloons and gambling places in town, and there were an abundance of them. Bootlegging and prostitution continued to thrive in Denison for more than half a century, including the infamous Skiddy Street. Some of the men would have been under the influence of alcohol when they stepped up on the platform of *Good Will* and entered the chapel. That did not deter them from coming to the services; for railroad men, to be able to hear the gospel preached in a railroad car was a different matter. The men who crowded into the seats in *Good Will* were amazed at the beauty of the chapel area. The scripture "God Is Love" etched on the transom glass above the podium was not amended by a list of church rules for behavior or reasons for exclusion.

The Texas General Convention had not yet officially approved the Stuckers, although they were in Texas at the request of convention leaders. They had stopped in Dallas to arrange for permission to travel on the MK&T lines at free passage as had been agreed upon by most all the railroad companies.

Free passage began with the maiden journey of the first Baptist chapel car, *Evangel.* After a visit by chapel car superintendent Boston W. Smith with William S. Mellen, the general manager of the Northern Pacific system at Minneapolis, Smith was provided with a letter to superintendents and conductors that issued free movement of the chapel car along railroad lines. "You will pass Mr. Boston W. Smith and one attendant, with chapel car *Evangel* over our lines. You will arrange to take the car on any train he desires; you will sidetrack it wherever he wishes. Make it as pleasant for Mr. Smith as you can. Signed: Wm. S. Mellen, General Manager." Perhaps one of the reasons Mellen was so accommodating was that Chapel Car Syndicate member Colgate Hoyt was a vice president of the NP.

Regardless of the motivation, the chapel cars' free and unlimited

Railroad workers would flock to services in the chapel cars during stops at rail shops. The diversity of the group includes black and white, young and old, and management and laborer. *Courtesy the American Baptist Historical Society, American Baptist Archives Center*

passage was a generous gift. In the late 1890s the rate for hauling cars was around 54 cents per mile—a considerable amount. Without free passage, chapel car *Evangel*'s initial trip could have cost $1,080. The railroads continued to grant free passage to the chapel cars during the early years of their existence, greatly reducing the cost of their operation. Without the free, and later reduced, transportation fees, the chapel car program could not have succeeded. Many times not only did the railroads provide free passage but also free repairs and service, like coal and water.[10]

Because of the welcoming attitude of the officials of the railroads, the chapel cars were able to witness in the train yards and loco- motive and car shops. After the race to complete the Trans- Continental Railroad and the explosion of "hell-on-wheels" towns along the routes, railroad management came to acknowledge that the riotous lifestyles of their employees were a threat to safety as well as detrimental to the wellbeing of the men themselves. In order to improve the moral climate of the railroad towns, managers encour- aged religious groups to move to their towns, gave lots for churches, and provided free transportation to the chapel cars until the beginning of World War I.

Texas railroads were eager to support the chapel cars but Texas Baptists were slow to seal their commitment. The *Baptist Standard* of Thursday, July 4, 1895, ran a letter from El Paso pastor L. R. Millican in support of the chapel car ministry. After describing the work of *Emmanuel* at El Paso and Pecos, he stressed, "I cannot be too lavish in praise of the car work. Let us get one for Texas." Millican was not aware that there was a chapel car in Texas, not yet approved by the Texas General Baptist Convention, as there was still concern about the influence of a Northern Baptist chapel car on their churches.[11]

Witnessing to railroaders was the major focus for the ministry, and the American Baptist Publication Society reported that there were hundreds and thousands of railroad men who never had or seldom chose to avail themselves of the opportunity to hear the gospel of Christ. "Most of you will be surprised to know how many men are in the railroad service." The society credited the Facts and Figures Company of Chicago with the following figures for 1895. There were employed in the United States 873,602 men. Of these, 38,781 were engineers; 40,359 firemen; 27,537 conductors; 72,969 trainmen; 40,048 switchmen, flagmen, and watchmen. The balance was employed at stations, offices, shops, and yards.[12]

At the Denison shops of the MK&T, it was a wet welcome, as Stucker would recall. "Mud and rain were not lacking for a single twenty–four hours while we were there," and the torrents, considered to be the heaviest in several years, were well documented by the Denison paper. Nettie soon discovered that life on the chapel car could be quite unpleasant—sided in the busy railroad yard with its discharge of soot and cinders and the constant bumping of cars and movement of engines. Even with screens on the windows to keep out insects, sleeping was difficult; the combination of heat, noise, and smoke prevented them from staying in the car, so the couple found a room in town.[13]

Company officials placed *Good Will* between the roundhouse and the machine shops, which must have reminded the Stuckers of the Aurora yards. Services were held noon, evening, and midnight for ten days. The midnight audience averaged forty men whom Stucker reported would hurriedly eat their lunches and come "just as they were."[14]

The boilermaker came, his face streaked with oil and dirt, as did the brakeman, who wrestled with the wheel that slowed and stopped the train. The trackman came, weary with the grueling labor; the fireman with his backbreaking grind; the switchman with his risky coupling tasks; the conductor watching his watch; and the office helper with his starched collar. The man most closely connected to the chapel cars in the yards would be the shop carman, as he would have "hands on" experiences with *Good Will,* repairing panels, windows, and steps; retouching paint; and checking the airbrakes. Even the engineers who "had come from the ranks and were hard as nails" would find themselves shaking the hand of the missionary, thanking him for the opportunity to attend a chapel car service.[15]

The Stuckers would follow the traditional services for railroad men. There would be much singing—congregational, duets, solos —all to the delight of the men. A favorite song would be "Beautiful River," written by Robert Lowry.

> Shall we gather at the river,
> Where bright angel feet have trod;
> With its crystal tide forever
> Flowing by the throne of God?
>
> Yes, we'll gather at the river,
> The beautiful, the beautiful river,
> Gather with the saints at the river
> That flows by the throne of God.

Edwin would preach simple sermons geared to railroad life, like "Down Grade" and "On Time." One sermon titled "The Way" began, "In the construction of a railroad, a line, or a route is first decided upon, the grading and bridging follows, and last of all, that which is most important, the ties and rails are placed in position. In our little conversation today, let us see if we may learn a practical lesson from the study of the track, without which there could be no movement of trains." In closing, he said, "There are valleys through which we may pass in this part of the way, but we know that here as elsewhere, he [God] will keep us with his eyes of love."[16]

At Denison, men who had not been in a church service for years were seen in *Good Will* with tears rolling down their begrimed faces. No doubt many of them were remembering the wreck that had occurred just a few days earlier. An eastbound T&P train consisting of a mail car, baggage express, two passenger coaches, and two Pull-man sleepers, left the depot in charge of Conductor Mahoney, with Engineer Al Hamer, and Fireman John Devine in the engine. When they approached Hadley switch, about four miles east of Dallas, the engine left the track, carrying with it the mail and express cars. En-gineer Hamer and Fireman Devine were buried beneath the demol-ished cars, their bodies mangled beyond recognition.[17]

Stucker reported his experience at the shops with a pun. "The men seemed to realize that we were there with 'good will,' when we left our lodging in Denison and traveled back to the yards in mud and rain to hold the services in the car, in the midst of the activity of the rail yards." The result was more than fifty public professions among the men, many who had not been in a religious service in five to fifteen years. Although the Reverend Stucker mentioned only "men" in his account, women worked in the shops, too, gener-ally as clerks and office help, and they would come to chapel car meetings.[18]

Although a matter of concern for the Stuckers, the spiritual con-dition of the hundreds of men employed by the MK&T did not seem to be a pressing issue for Denison and Grayson County Bap-tists. Their immediate focus was that "we have a large foreign pop-ulation that [is] calling for the gospel and if they are not converted to the Christian religion they will corrupt and mislead our chil-dren."[19] It was not that Texas Baptists did not care about the souls of railroad men, for they sponsored two railroad evangelists whose duty it was to visit the rail centers and to distribute Bibles and hold services. With the explosion of rail towns and shops and yards in Texas, it would have been impossible for just a few men to cover this need.

The Reverend Charles H. Rust, missionary on chapel car *Glad Tidings, #3* traveling in Minnesota during this same time, would re-call his experiences at a rail shop. "Look at this man who is rushing up now in such haste. He is the engineer of a stationary engine in the shop. He has been coming to the car each noon, but cannot stay to the entire service, as he is obliged to run to his engine to blow the whistle at 12:45. He hardly can part with the missionary, and says in parting, 'God alone knows what the chapel car has meant to me. I have not been in church for years, but you have brought the church to me.'"[20]

Stucker had passionately dedicated his life to the personal regeneration of railroad men. This first stop witnessing in a rail shop touched his heart. Of his Denison experience, he would say, "It was not easy to leave these 'babes in Christ' who, because of having to work seven days each week, have little or no religious privileges." [21]

From Denison, the Stuckers took *Good Will* and headed to Dallas where they arrived July 17 and remained for a few days. The *Dallas Morning News* welcomed them with an article describing *Good Will* and the Stuckers. "The car is used to spread the gospel light among railroad men and the car is filled with pews sufficient to seat 120 people. The car is on the north side of the Missouri, Kansas & Texas Railroad and will be open to visitors any hour after 10 a.m. A special meeting of the Baptists and their friends will be held this evening at 7 o'clock. At Denison there were 40 converts and 9 railroad men. There are four of these cars built by the American Baptist Publication Society for mission work on wheels." [22]

On the day after their arrival in Dallas, the *News* announced a meeting in the chapel car at five o'clock to which all children were invited. For the parents, it was stressed that the car was in a safe place, not far out in a yard where it would have been dangerous to walk. The men's meeting at six o'clock included the local YMCA, and visitors, perhaps intrigued by the newspaper coverage, came to the car daily to see what a chapel car looked like.[23]

The reporter, on the last day of services before the car left for Ft. Worth and Waco, mentioned a matter of domestic interest. "It [the chapel car] contains everything to serve the needs of the occupants. Whenever it rains, there is a cistern to receive the soft water." He added more details about the chapel. "Just back of the organ, which is also used for a pulpit, is a blackboard and above it a transom bearing the motto 'God Is Love' in recognition of the fact that the work for which these cars are designed is purely a labor of love, the society bearing the expense." [24]

SCATTERING CANADIAN
GOSPEL SEEDS

The Denison and Dallas meetings had provided Nettie and Edwin with insight into what life would be like on the chapel car. They may have been feeling somewhat confident about the success of their experiences. But their next journey would take them into another world—the world of the Staked Plains, sometimes called the Llano Estacado, especially the land north of the Canadian River, which flows for 190 miles across north Texas.

Along the lines of the Fort Worth & Denver City (FW&DC) Railroad, settlement did not begin until after Native American tribes were subdued by General Miles at the Battle of the Tule and by General McKenzie at the Battle of Palo Duro in 1885. In 1888, in response to immigration associations, settlers began pouring into the Panhandle from Missouri, Georgia, Arkansas, Virginia, New Jersey, Illinois, Indiana, and other states. Many of those newcomers would seek their fortunes in little settlements on the fabled XIT ranch.

The XIT came into existence through a fascinating chain of events. In 1876 the Texas state government began to feel cramped in the old capitol building at Austin and decided to set aside 3 million acres of what they thought was worthless land in the Panhandle for funding the building of a new capitol. Governor Oran M. Roberts called a special session of the legislature that let a contract to Charles B. and John V. Farwell, Chicago brothers, to build a $3 million capitol and take the Panhandle land in payment.

Texline was the northernmost post of the immense XIT, on the state line between Texas and New Mexico. When *Good Will* arrived in 1895, the FW&DC junction was changing from a tent city into a permanent town. Texline was mainly made up of men employed by the FW&DC Railroad, although immigrant cars, known as Zulus, arrived daily carrying prospective settlers and all their earthly goods—from quilts to cows. Settlers even received free transportation from the railroad if they purchased up to a maximum of forty acres, provided they requested this within sixty days of the date on the ticket.[1]

The editor of the *Pioneer,* Tascosa's newspaper, wrote June 2, 1888, that "a half dozen immigrant wagons, loaded with women, tow-headed progeny and other plunder, passed through yesterday morning." Another week brought another account: "Wagons and wagons with white tops, rope-bottomed chairs, tow-heads, brindle cows, yellow dogs, and a pervading air of restlessness have poured through this week in the direction suggested by Horace Greeley." On September 8, the *Pioneer* wrote that Texline would be "the biggest and best and the fastest and the hardest and the busiest and the wildest and the roughest and the toughest town of this section." If this was not enough to establish this hell-on-wheels character, the editor informed his readers that the Texas Rangers had already established a base in Texline. "When that is said, enough said," he concluded.[2]

There was an attempt to civilize the town. The XIT Ranch owned Texline's first school building and helped the railroad build a hotel to receive prospective settlers. The FW&DC planted produce along the right-of-way so sightseers would be impressed with the richness of the soil and be convinced to buy farming land. They also brought in advisers from Texas A&M University and the Department of Agriculture (DOA) to assist farmers in making the most of the arid soil. In the early nineties, the financial crisis of 1893 and an extreme drought caused many of those same settlers to turn their wagons back east, "cursing the West and the men who painted it 'golden.'"[3]

On Tuesday evening, July 29, 1896, the chapel car left on its mission to the Panhandle, accompanied by Missionary Superintendent M. D. Early and his wife. Early was to assist Stucker in selecting the most available points along the FW&DC line at which the chapel car work would be done. For two months, *Good Will* held two to three services daily in the frontier towns above the Canadian where the gospel was seldom preached.[4]

A woman who loved the profusion of trees in Aurora, Nettie would have scanned the range and seen few here, except for stands of black locust, which the DOA decided was the best tree for Panhandle planting, and copses of cottonwood and hackberries along the banks of the Canadian. Laura V. Hamner would write in her memories of the area that in this new land were "no softly rounded hills or kindly meadows, no streams babbling a spring song, no forests or little fields or clover patches. Instead, bare prairies stretching into the horizon."[5]

What Nettie could have seen from the chapel car's windows was mile after mile of windmills supplying the power for water to thousands of acres of ranch land. She could not have ignored the Russian thistle tumbling before the wind, leaping ditches and crowding under fences. Russian settlers that poured into the Texas frontier carried on their clothing and goods the thorny bramble's seeds, shaking them out like pepper from a box at every jounce—not unlike the immigrant cars, shaking out families and belongings at little settlements along the lines.

Edwin described the town in his monthly report: "Texline is a town of one hundred, near the line between Texas and New Mexico, and in the Llano Estacado or Staked Plains, junction of two railroads which connect Texas and Colorado. It is largely made up of men employed by those roads in the shops; no religious organization or preacher being in all this section." For two weeks, the Stuckers held meetings twice a day and four times on Sundays in the chapel car. Practically everyone in town was in attendance.[6]

This was Nettie Stucker's first glance at a young, raw Texas—with its few frame businesses, tents, sod houses, and dugouts. It certainly did not look like Aurora, Illinois, or even the neat dwellings she had seen in Denison. For a young lady raised in a sheltered environment, it was a view that could prove unsettling.

The job of caring for the domestic needs of chapel car life was daunting enough. Nettie could not keep perishables in the little ice box loaded from the platform for more than two or three days, depending on the climate. As ice was not easily accessible, at almost every town she needed to replenish supplies. Shopping in Texline would have been quite an experience, providing Nettie with the opportunity to make contact with town women and shopkeepers who would have been very curious about *Good Will*, sided near the depot.

Women's meetings in the morning included the settler wives in their mother hubbards and sunbonnets. A collection of immigrant wives—their dresses, shawls, and head scarves testifying to their places of origin—had come with their husbands from Great Britain and Europe, fleeing oppression and starvation and following the promise of working for the railroad. A mixture of Mexican women from the ranches, although probably Catholic, would have ventured to the car out of curiosity.

Women whose husbands were in positions of responsibility on the XIT Ranch, or who owned the town businesses, or who were in the management of the railroad would have welcomed Edwin and Nettie and offered the hospitality of their tidy homes, many carpeted and outfitted with fine furniture. They fully recognized the importance of organized religion to the growth of the town, and their names would appear on the charters of Texline churches.

From the doors of the saloons and brothels, the town prostitutes and rail camp followers could watch the services, see the lights shining through *Good Will's* windows, and hear the singing and the hymns played by Nettie on the Estey organ. Some of the tunes may have been familiar, and tears may have tracked down the painted facades of these "soiled doves." The Reverend Stucker would notice them, though. Unlike the practices of many churches to condemn "fallen women," his custom was to enter the saloons and make contact with those inside, if only to give them religious tracts or Bibles and offer to talk with them in the privacy of the chapel car before or after the services. Stories of distressed "ladies of the night" coming to the chapel cars appear in several reports.[7]

There was a frontier saying, "This country is fine for men and cows, but hell on women and horses." Lillie Mae Hunter wrote in her history of Dallum and Hartley counties, " . . . the cowboys who came to work on the big ranches were assured of a living. The chuck wagon food might be monotonous, but they were never in danger of starving. Not so the settlers who came a few years later. Filing on land and building a dugout—just a room dug into the ground and then built up to allow a small window to supply some light; or an adobe hut with a dirt floor, they struggled to make a bare living for their families."[8]

Nettie would discover that most of the women had not been to a church for years, some not at all. Some could not speak or understand English. Imagine their surprise when Nettie offered them Bibles and tracts in Swedish, German, Bohemian, Spanish, and Italian. Some would have been lonely for the sight of other female faces or a change from their dingy existence in their shanties and tents; but for many, their main interest in coming to the chapel car was concern for their children. Most longed for a better life for their boys and girls and felt that religion might provide a semblance of morality and culture to their scanty existence.

The children would crowd into the car in the afternoon, their little faces bright with promise and wonder at the beauty of the chapel car's polished pews, brass lectern, carpeted platform, and library of books. Many of the children had never heard a Bible story and could not recite scripture verses or sing a hymn. Perhaps they spoke little English, but they were eager to see what the pretty lady in her modest gown would do with the colorful charts and the large blackboard behind the platform. They loved the scripture cards, even if they could not read them. Generations later, some of those cards, decorated with vines, flowers, and delicate birds, would appear in family collections.

In the evenings, the men would come, railroaders whose faces and manner were similar to those the Stuckers met at Denison. Cowboys from the ranch came, as did some of the ranch management. For many of the cowboys on the XIT, attending worship was not a new experience. Edwin and Nettie had been told that the men who ran the XIT were men of faith, for *Good Will* would not have been invited into XIT towns without their knowledge.

Owner John V. Farwell, who regularly led services at the Spring Lake camp, insisted on the observance of Sunday as a day of rest, although many times in theory alone was that practiced.

During the years he resided in Chicago, Farwell had been greatly influenced by evangelist Dwight L. Moody. Some even said "he made Moody," and he was also a friend of evangelist Billy Sunday. Farwell had come to Chicago in 1845 to earn a living with only $3.25 in his pocket, a gift of his father, and a Bible from his mother with the words, "You will be known by the company you keep." Long years afterward he used to give away to his ranch hands the Gospel of John and in the flyleaf he would write, "This is a pocket book that never runs dry." [9]

It is not surprising that Farwell was against any saloons, brothels, gambling, shooting, wasting time, swearing, drinking, and not going to church, but he was not alone in his strict rules of conduct. Another moral influence in the XIT was A. G. Boyce, general manager of the XIT for eighteen years, who was a "stern but just man who earned respect from all his hands." He was said to have been the greatest civilizing influence in the early days of the High Plains country. A devoted churchman, he served as Sunday school superintendent of the Channing Methodist Church for many years. Soon after coming to the XIT, he issued an order forbidding the carrying of six–shooters or the playing of cards.[10]

According to reports submitted by Stucker to his superior at the Publication Society, a little church was formed—the first in Texline. "At the end of the first two weeks a congregation of fourteen members was organized. . . . Many accepted Christ but did not at once join the newly organized church."[11]

No other record has been found of that church organized by the Stuckers. The dozen or more faithful who decided to organize a church may not have been able to carry out their intent, for in 1900, the Reverend W. B. McKeown, responsible for the Methodist work north of the Canadian River, preached to three families and a few railroad employees. He reluctantly concluded that Texline was not ready for any church organization. According to church records, it was not until 1905 that the charter group started by the Stuckers reorganized and built a church on land donated by Boyce.[12]

Dalhart, the present seat of Hartley County, was just a station called Twist Junction when the Stuckers were working along the line. A designated station may have had a spur track, a corral for unloading livestock, a freight-loading platform, maybe a shelter of some sort, or often a tiny, unattended freight house. Many stations had no depot at which to buy a ticket and wait for a train or a place where passengers were allowed to board. Some were elaborate facilities with many different structures, including shops, engine houses, water tanks, freight houses, and passenger depots, but Twist Junction was just a marker post with a small settlement of tents, shacks, and holding pens.[13]

Texline, the most northern of the XIT ranch towns, was not the headquarters for the ranch. Wild and wide–open Tascosa was the first base for the XIT, but when the FW&DC Railroad came through, crossing the Canadian River at the mouth of Cheyenne Creek, Channing sprung up and headquarters were moved there in 1890. Tascosa struggled on for a number of years.

Channing, once called Rivers, straight down the line, would have been the town *Good Will* visited after leaving Texline. At first, Channing, recognized as a post office on January 30, 1891, was merely an unloading station on the old XIT ranch. Newspaper editor C. F. Rudolph of the Hartley *County Citizen* (later known as the

Amarillo Northwestern) tried to promote the town, but local ranchers said that the newspapers favored the farmers. The cattlemen were reluctant to see settlers take up land because it meant the loss of much–needed grass land. As whole trainloads of people—or "home–suckers" as ranchers sometimes called them—flooded into the area, their influx reduced the value of the XIT lands as ranges, so the company began to sell.[14]

Many settlers traveled to the Panhandle from cotton-producing territory and moved to get away from the malaria–infested lowlands of the south and the unprofitable raising of cotton. They longed to scrape together a small claim to raise any crop other than cotton. They faced the daily dangers of wolves, bobcats, rattlesnakes, coyotes, and even panthers, and the search for water and adequate housing increased the hardships of Panhandle living.[15]

Nothing caused as much dire alarm on the ranchlands as a widespread prairie fire. Loss of grass meant loss of the reserve essential to existence and posed immediate bankruptcy for the owner. One of the worst prairie fires of the western Panhandle broke out in November, 1894, just a year before the Stuckers arrived. Syndicate land almost twenty by sixty miles, from the Canadian breaks to the sand hills, had been burned clean of grass, causing ranch employees to quickly move 4,500 head "above calves" on the trail to grasslands. Adding to the fuel that fed the spreading fires were the cow chips that stoked many settlers' stoves and the Russian thistle that Nettie would have come to know well, tumbling along with every wind that blows, carrying with each prickly mass sparklers of disaster.[16]

Life was arduous, but Channing was not without social graces. Nettie could see the two-story gables of the Rivers Hotel, one of the finest buildings in the Panhandle, from the chapel car siding near the depot. Many famous people were housed in the Rivers Hotel, known for its "fancy" meals. She and Edwin may even have walked through the lobby or had dinner in the dining room, a pleasant change from the more Spartan chapel car menu.

Although there were no churches in Channing when *Good Will* came to town, occasionally preachers would hold services. Hunter recalls in her *Book of Years* that the itinerant ministers spent most of their time on horseback or in a light buggy, preaching wherever a small group of people gathered. These circuit riders would be welcomed by couples waiting to be married or families hoping for a proper service at the burying of a loved one. His equipment was simple: a slicker and two saddlebags that contained a few articles of clothing, a Bible, and a hymn book. One of the first regularly or-dained ministers assigned to the Panhandle territory was the Rev-erend R. F. Dunn, a Methodist circuit rider who began his duties in 1881, preaching in one-room schoolhouses, courthouses, dugouts, or outdoors to roundup crews. Often he held service in saloons, where the bartender draped his apron over the bar in token that it was closed for the duration.[17]

Many women refused to live in a town without a church and Bessie Powell was an example. William Powell was the first breeder of purebred Hereford cattle in the Panhandle, having established a ranch in the Channing area in the late eighties or early nineties. In 1896 he persuaded his brother James to return from England to help care for his herd and become a partner in the ranch. James's wife, Bessie, was reluctant. She said, "I don't see any reason for us to go clear across that ocean again, and live on a ranch with a lot of rough cowboys, when we can live here in comfort." But James pleaded that Texas would offer him an opportunity to get ahead.

Bessie brought up another objection. "But we would have to give up too much, James. It would be hard enough for me to leave my brothers and sisters, but it would be harder still for me to leave my church." James told her that his brother said that "there was a church right across the street," and so with this promise, Bessie came to Channing. When she arrived at her new home and looked across the street, the "Episcopalian Church" was the adobe school-house used for services when an occasional preacher, almost never Episcopalian, came through town. This usually was about twice a month.[18]

According to church records, the First Southern Baptist Church of Channing was organized in 1899–1900. It is likely, because of the visit of *Good Will* in the late summer of 1895, that a small band be-gan meeting, but early church records that would verify that are missing.

Stucker while at Channing would have visited now fading Tas-cosa, noted for such legends as Charles Goodnight, John Chisum, and Billy the Kid. When heavy rains flooded the Canadian after a drought in 1893, Tascosa fell into decline, and most of the busi-nesses moved to Channing. Tascosa was not on a rail line but within a few miles of where the car was sided. Stucker would have traveled the distance by horse or buggy, and some folks from Tascosa would have traveled to Channing to see the gospel car-on-wheels. The Palo Duro Canyon Baptist Association recorded at its 1893 meeting: "We cover nineteen counties, and only the portion near the railroad ever sees a Baptist minister." [19]

When a priest or minister could be obtained, women arrayed in braid-trimmed capes and feathered hats and men in shiny-from-wear black suits and string ties, probably brought forth from trunks not opened for months, would come from far and near to hear the gospel preached. Stucker would have found a warm welcome at Tascosa if notice had been sent ahead of his visit.

Heading south from Channing, *Good Will* would have stopped at Hartley, platted in 1890 two years after the right-of-way was sold to the Ft. Worth & Denver City Railroad. The railroad agent did not even have an office in the new town. He simply set up a desk on the prairie, and accounts tell that he never locked that desk, which sometimes contained as much as $500.

A school district was created in 1890 with a population of sixty-eight, but still there was no church. Uncle Tommy Dunn, who ran a general store and who kept "all the necessities of life and some of the luxuries," permitted his adobe building to be used for a Sunday school and preaching services whenever a minister of any faith happened along. During that time, a "sketchy Baptist organization" met, but lapsed. It would not be until 1903 when the Reverend G. B. Rogers came on the chapel car that a church would be established in Hartley. [20]

Soon after beginning their mission in the settlements above the Canadian River, Edwin and Nettie heard heartbreaking news. After placing chapel car *Emmanuel, #2,* in the shops of the Southern Pacific Railroad at Sacramento, California, the Reverend and Mrs. Wheeler, who had visited in El Paso and Pecos in the spring, were on their way home to Minnesota for a family vacation. On route on August 7, 1895, Wheeler was thrown from the platform of a Santa Fe Railroad car and killed in a washout near Mitchell Station, New Mexico.

Mrs. Wheeler was not injured, and she would recall, "a sudden shriek of the whistle, a sudden putting on of the brakes, a crash, and all was over, and my dear one was gone." Nettie's heart must have gone out to her chapel car sister, Mrs. Wheeler, sensing what such a great loss would mean. [21]

CHAPTER
SIX

FINDING SURPRISES
IN EAST TEXAS

Five months after *Good Will* entered Texas, the Baptist General Convention finally passed a resolution relating to the operation of the chapel car. Control of the Northern Baptist car was the issue. After much discussion, they unanimously agreed that under their terms *Good Will* could stay in the state and continue its mission. "Resolved, that with our present understanding of the only conditions under which the American Baptist Publication Society proposes to employ the 'Chapel Car' in Texas, this board cannot cooperate in that service, and that without our cooperation the service will be an embarrassment to and complication of our mission work in the railroad towns."

The Texas Board demanded that the missionary on the chapel car be a man of their choosing and that the car, as long as it remained in Texas, should be under the sole direction of the Texas superintendent of missions, "to prevent any disorder, clash, or complication of the work." The chapel car missionary was to report to the Publication Society on the financial status and to the Texas Board on the evangelistic work. The agreement resulted in Texas getting the benefit of the chapel car work and the Publication Society footing the bill.[1]

After the state convention at Belton in October, the Stuckers, who by now were perhaps learning more than they desired about Texas Baptist politics, took the chapel car to central and eastern Texas for the rest of the year, much of the time evangelizing railroad men and miners. That did not mean they neglected women and children.

Along the Texas & Pacific line at Big Sandy, like in the other towns on their travels, expectant boys and girls lined the tracks as the train pulled into the station. The click of the telegraph would no-

The chapel cars were not the only special cars pulling into small towns across Texas. Circus trains, theater trains, agriculture cars, and photography cars drew crowds at stations. *From the author's collection*

tify the dispatcher at towns like Big Sandy of *Good Will*'s arrival, and the missionaries would be standing on the car's platform under the green and white–striped awning throwing scripture cards and papers to the children along the track.

Embarking at the station, Edwin would pass out tracts, and after tending to business with the station master (also called agent) about the siding of the chapel car, he would put up handbills around town announcing the services. Other flyers might have announced the coming of a circus train—the sides of the train decorated with colorful billboard advertising and its construction perhaps, as with *Good Will*, the work of the Barney & Smith Car Company. Often an agricultural demonstration train from Texas A&M, a car with actors for a Shakespearean production, or even a photography car would pull into the station. It would not be long until the word got out that a different kind of car was in town, that "a church on wheels is down on the side track." The children who had lined the tracks filled the car in the afternoon, followed by women and men in the evening services.

From Big Sandy, the car was attached to another Texas & Pacific (T&P) train and headed south to Marshall. Jay Gould plotted the T&P through Marshall in 1868, and the town tripled in size with the presence of the railroad. In 1872 the town approved giving the T&P $300,000 in thirty-year bonds bearing 7 percent interest payable in gold if the railroad would establish its Texas offices and shops in Marshall. Although the shops did come to Marshall, the taxpayers soon found the tax burden "unbearable" and negotiated a scaled-down payment plan.[2]

At the T&P shops, the chapel car was the center of a circle of eight large buildings, employing five to six hundred men. Stucker reported, "During the seven months since the dedication of *Good Will,* it has traveled five thousand miles and witnessed the preaching of over three hundred gospel sermons. It has not found a single railroad over which it may not freely journey on its mission of love." A reporter for the *Marshall News Messenger,* November 4, 1895, praised the presence of *Good Will.* "The car . . . has worked all through the Panhandle. The T&P makes no charges for handling the car—a service appreciated by the society, as it enables them to do just that much more in the good work." His praise turned to Nettie, as well as Edwin. "Mrs. Stucker accompanies her husband; plays the organ, sings, and in every way possible assists in the work, which is a grand and noble one, and the *Messenger* especially requests every railroad man in Marshall to meet Mr. Stucker, visit his car, and attend his meetings."[3]

Marshall, in the piney woods of eastern Texas, was an area entirely different from Denison or Waco or the Panhandle, as the couple would discover. With its "deep South" tradition, it was more like towns in neighboring Louisiana. The rich lands surrounding Marshall were abundant with cotton, producing fifteen thousand bales, and fruit and other crops.

The first occupants of the Marshall area were the friendly Caddo Indians, but from 1840–1900, Germans, Russians, Poles, Alsatians, and Scandinavians inhabited Harrison County, many coming through the ports of New Orleans and Galveston. Some also came via the Mississippi and the Red River and Caddo Lake. In the 1800s the Irish came in droves as a result of famines and English rule, and they sought refuge from hunger and oppression in "Amerikay." A small colony of Jewish families came to escape religious persecution and to live in a land of freedom and opportunity that they had come to accept as Marshall. Many owned stores in the community, and Nettie could have shopped for staples or items for personal or chapel car use at the Weisman & Co. stores. In 1887 the members of the Jewish community had grown to a substantial presence and formed the Moses Montefiore Congregation, although they were not able to erect a temple until 1900.[4]

Since First Baptist Church of Marshall was without a pastor, Stucker provided services for the congregation. Unlike many of the towns E. G. and Nettie had visited and would visit, Marshall was a town of churches. Shortly before Texas became a state, John Bryce, missionary and secret agent for President John Tyler during the Texas War of Independence, and the Reverend George Washington Baines Sr. (great-grandfather of President Lyndon Baines Johnson) organized the Baptist church. Baines, who lived in North Louisiana at that time and who was considered "the foremost preacher of any denomination," would soon move to Texas. He would rise in Texas Baptist ranks to be president of Baylor University.[5]

Services were held in a brush arbor or nearby log schoolhouse until 1849 when a church building was erected at 405 West Austin on a lot donated by State Legislator James McCowan. The small frame building was replaced by a Gothic structure in 1892, with a high-vaulted roof and a tall steeple that became a town landmark. The talk of the town would not have been the steeple but the baptistry filled with well-drawn water replacing the previous baptisms held in a small stream called Cold Water Creek.[6]

Since the Presbyterian Church then had no building, the Baptists invited them and other denominations to worship in their edifice until they were able to build one of their own. As Nettie and Edwin walked the streets of Marshall, visiting with families and inviting them to services, they would have seen the First United Methodist, the Presbyterian, Trinity Episcopal, St. Joseph's Catholic Church, and the black Ebenezer United Methodist. Bethesda Baptist Church, organized in 1867, was known as the "Colored Baptist Church." There were many blacks in the Marshall area; some were brought there with their masters before the Civil War, and others came after as freedmen. Bishop College, a school for the education of blacks by the American Baptist Home Mission Society, located in Marshall, was the only school of its kind west of the Mississippi. It offered courses from grammar school to college and theological studies, and it had around two hundred students who would assume positions of leadership among the five hundred thousand black Baptists of Texas, such as teachers in public schools.[7]

Marshall movers and shakers considered the number of blacks a detriment to the growth of the community. In their booklet, "A Pen Picture of Marshall," they wrote, "What is necessary to render this county one of the most prosperous in the State, is a change in the system of agriculture, which will be brought about when an intelligent white population occupies that place of the negroes that are so largely in the ascendant." [8]

Nettie would have been delighted with Marshall. She could not have ignored the beautiful homes located just across the street from the depot and the railroad yards. From *Good Will*'s platform, she could view the home of Charles Ginocchio, an Italian immigrant and Confederate veteran who followed the railroad from Little Rock via Texarkana to Marshall. He had acquired vast holdings in Arkansas, Louisiana, and Texas, and operated hotels and restaurants along the railroad lines, and he would build the Ginocchio Hotel adjoining the railroad shops in 1896, but not in time for the Stuckers to spend a night and enjoy a bath there. [9]

One particular home was just a few yards from *Good Will*'s siding—the stately two-story white frame with the wide veranda that belonged to the Reverend and Mrs. W. M. Allen. Allen was the beloved longtime pastor of the Marshall Presbyterian Church. In February of that year, the Allens had celebrated their fiftieth anniversary with an elaborate party, talked about for days in town. The tables, as well as the decorations of the parlors, halls, and dressing rooms, were decorated with flowers and fruits and pyramids of oranges. [10]

Nettie had been on *Good Will* for seven months and, by now, the novelty of living on the chapel car had been replaced by some sense of claustrophobia. The graceful home of the Allens probably stirred her heart·with a longing for a more spacious home of her own.

Leaving Marshall and traveling on the T&P seventy-five miles west of Fort Worth, the Stuckers arrived in Thurber—a town within a town. As locomotives consumed large amounts of coal, the development of mines was critical to Texas' economic expansion. The most famous coal district in Texas around the turn of the century was Thurber, owned by the Texas & Pacific Coal Company, no kin to the railroad although the Thurber mines were tied to the building of the T&P Railway.

The town began mining operations in 1886 with miners recruited from all over Great Britain and Europe. Following the inability to meet a payroll and a resulting strike by miners, the owners sold out to the founders of the Texas & Pacific Coal Company, who chose to deal with the dissident Knights of Labor miners with an iron hand. The company erected a six-foot, four-wire barbed fence in the winter of 1888–89 to enclose the nine-hundred-acre compound and to keep out labor rousers. Within the enclosure they constructed a complete town. Eventually the strike ended and the miners and families moved into the new town. The Texas & Pacific Coal Company owned not only the mines where the men worked, but the houses, schools, churches, recreational facilities, and saloons. The company furnished preachers for the churches, teachers for the schools, doctors for the sick, and in the company store—even caskets.[11]

Marilyn D. Rhinehart, in her extensive study of Thurber, wrote that in most coal camps companies designated a building for church services or constructed one especially for that purpose. The various denominations then shared the facilities. In 1899 the *Texas Mining and Trade Journal* listed three denominations holding services on alternate Sundays at the Union Church in Thurber—Methodist, Presbyterian, and Baptist. Rhinehart wrote that religious services in Thurber performed another function. Revivals, first communions, conversions, musical presentations, weddings, baptisms, funerals and burials, picnics, fundraisers, and charitable assistance helped to strengthen social ties.[12]

Edwin described Thurber as "a mining town of about two thousand people representing, so it is claimed, every nationality but the Chinese." He would have missed seeing the Chinese because in most railroad towns they were an integral part of the work force. Stucker also would have noticed that the miners lived along ethnic and racial group lines. The 1900 census showed that southern and eastern Europeans generally populated the north and south sides of Hill #3, or on Italian Hill on the West Side. Many Irish lived at the base of nearby Stump Hill, while the American–born and English, Scots, and Welsh miners and brick plant workers lived on Park Row to the north and east of town. The company's barriers enclosed all enclaves.[13]

As in every mining camp, liquor was a catalyst for controversy. Not only the Baptists but even the Good Templar Society saw the consumption of alcohol as "the town's most serious infectious ailment." Rhinehart writes that "the advocates of abstinence never succeeded in winning many converts among the residents of the hard-drinking town," as the saloons earned the company considerable profit and provided a social gathering place.[14]

Stucker reported to the *Standard,* "The place, from the 'Union' Church building to the saloon, is owned absolutely by the Texas & Pacific Coal Company. There is no local pastor, though different

Chapel car *Good Will* would stop frequently at Thurber by invitation of the management to hold services for the men in the mines and their families.
Courtesy Special Collections Division, University of Texas at Arlington Library

preachers visit here from time to time, and all are welcomed in the company's pretty little church edifice on the hill."

Edwin held three meetings daily in the car, and handed out dozens of Bibles and tracts in the languages of the miners, and, in an analogy he used frequently, reported that God richly blessed "the seed sown by both the preaching and the printed page." Company officials invited the chapel car back several times, and it would have been the custom for some of them to have attended services hoping perhaps to "have an intimidating effect, intended or not."[15]

The beginning of 1896 found the Stuckers at Temple, a key rail hub that *Good Will* would travel through frequently. W. R. Maxwell visited with a small boy who had heard the Reverend Stucker speak while at Temple, and he commended Stucker for his work with the children: "On our mission fields his services will be of incalculable value, and I most heartily commend him and his Christly wife to our brethren everywhere."[16]

It was at Temple that the Stuckers heard of their new Publication Society boss. Robert G. Seymour would be the field secretary in charge of chapel car work, although Minnesota missionary "Uncle" Boston W. Smith would continue to be the superintendent and major booster.

The Railroad YMCAs could be found in many rail towns. This Y in Smithville was built in 1899 for $7,000. *Courtesy Valerie Kite Johnson*

Smithville was the next stop. The Katy management provided a convenient siding for *Good Will* as the company had always had excellent relations with the chapel cars. In 1894 the shops and a working force of five hundred men were brought to Smithville from Taylor and Alvarado, causing the town to double in size. Many of the enterprises along Main Street catered to the needs of the railroad men. Some of the businesses thriving at the turn of the century included five groceries, four general stores, four dry goods stores, three barbers, two tailors, a restaurant, a drug store, a jewelry store, and a confectionery.

The Masons met in a room called the "Upstairs." In the early 1890s fraternal organizations grew in membership. In addition to the Masons, other names like the Knights of Pythias, Odd Fellows, Knights of Columbus, Order of Red Men, Fraternal Order of Eagles, Protective Order of Elks, and Modern Woodmen appeared on buildings in Texas cities. The presence of the lodges did not necessarily mean that they would encourage the establishment of churches in town. Frequently the lodges were active long before the establishment of churches. At Marshall, for example, before the Civil War there was no church or school building; the only gathering place in town was the Masonic Hall.[17]

It was the saloons, not the lodges, that would have been the cause of concern for Edwin and would have been the objects of pointed references in his sermons. A history of Smithville recorded, "There were many saloons in those days where the men went to drink warm beer. They would then order mugs of beer which they brought out on trays to their waiting women in the carriages." On Saturdays, farmers, ranchers, and their families would come to town to buy supplies, and excited children, many of the more than 150 bright, little faces that Nettie had seen in the chapel car, would be tugging mothers toward candy stores. During their stay, Edwin would be out in the streets inviting everyone to the services in the car that night.[18]

Although the women of the Smithville Baptist Church would have brought cakes, fried chicken, and other goodies to *Good Will*, Nettie still would have taken the opportunity to visit the stores to replenish their supplies—coffee, beans, canned peaches, corn meal and flour for biscuits, and bacon and eggs. There were always items to purchase at the dry goods stores—combs, shaving soap, powder, stockings, and other personal needs not supplied in the mission packages from Baptist missionary organizations.

In spite of or perhaps as a result of any public references Edwin might have made about the beer-drinking townspeople, the attendance at the services grew and the Stuckers had to use the Opera House instead of the chapel car. Stucker charmed even the Presbyterians. Mina F. Sayers wrote, "The Chapel Car *Good Will* has just left us. To use our Presbyterian minister's words: 'He [Stucker] is the most God–like man I ever knew!' Everything good and commendable is couched in those few words. His influence is great and will be felt for many years. We ought to feel very proud that we have had such a man among us."[19]

The Stuckers received shocking news while at Smithville. On February 2, 1896, the Baptist Publication Society building in Philadelphia was completely destroyed by fire. The printing presses, the retail store, the offices, the holdings of the American Baptist Historical Society, the chapel car records, all gone—most of the loss irreplaceable. This news would have greatly disturbed the Stuckers, although they, like the thousands of Baptists across America, were thankful that there was no loss of life.[20]

On March 28, 1896, when *Good Will* was miles away from Smithville, Austin and much of the central part of Texas was struck by a severe storm. Trains were stilled, rivers like the Brazos over-flowed, and some reported that the rain was the heaviest in ten years. On the same day as the Austin-area storm, Smithville was struck by a cyclone, and although no fatalities were reported, property damage was great. About ten houses were destroyed or seriously damaged, including the Baptist church.[21]

BORDER TOWNS,
BIG DECISIONS

The chapel car seldom stopped in the larger Texas cities as the emphasis of the work was in small towns and rural areas where there were no religious services or no Baptist church. San Antonio was an exception, not only because of the number of railroad shops but also because of the poverty of the Mexican population. *Good Will,* sided near the San Antonio International depot, began a series of meetings February 14, 1896.

Since the inauguration of the early Spanish missions, San Antonio had been a center of Roman Catholic strength. Because of the Catholic influence, for many years the city was considered a poor field for Baptist growth. J. M. Carroll, general convention leader, would say that no other place in all Texas proved to be so impervious to Baptist mission work. Corpus Christi and Laredo were difficult fields, as Carroll would testify from personal experience, and El Paso was a hard field, as George W. Baines Jr. (great uncle of Lyndon Baines Johnson) could testify. Eagle Pass and Del Rio belonged in the same category, but none of them, according to Carroll, were ever so unpromising as San Antonio. In addition to the Catholic stronghold, Methodist and Presbyterian work had preceded the Baptists by something like fourteen years. By 1878 a Baptist church was under construction that would consist of Texas limestone, forty by sixty feet in size, facing Travis Street at the corner of Jefferson.[1]

In the twenty years after the building of that first church, more than twenty-five Baptist churches—combined white, Mexican, German, and black—would be in existence in the old Spanish town. Stucker reported, "We are presently at work in the 'mission fields' of San Antonio." Nettie explained, "We have found great destitution, especially among the children, many of whom have never learned the meaning of the words 'sin,' 'Bible,' or 'Jesus.'"[2]

In response to some criticism, Stucker explained that they were not selling books, even Bibles, advertising periodicals, or "making money" but seeking to help those who would not otherwise receive help. "We have nothing but the 'old gospel' and insist on it as the solution of all life's problems. Our work is, of necessity then, far from self-supporting. We have received as little as $1.25 for thirty services and as low as $8 for an entire month."

The *San Antonio Daily Express* reported, "A church on wheels is something new in evangelistic work in this part of the State, and the chapel car 'Good Will,' now on the International & Great Northern tracks, in this city, is attracting a great deal of attention." The *Express* explained that the car had been in Texas several months, and services had been held in nearly all the railroad towns in North and West Texas, and the International & Great Northern, Southern Pacific, Missouri, Kansas & Texas railroads had helped Stucker in every way possible.

Probably because the reporter did not wish to ask such a personal question, he did not mention that the Reverend Stucker was paid $2,200 a year for his labors by the American Baptist Publication Society.[3]

After several days at the International Depot, the car was moved to the Sunset Depot, which was named for the Sunset Limited route, and placed on the Duval Street spur, near the corner of that and Austin Street. The Sunset Lines was another name for the Galveston, Harrisburg, and San Antonio Railroad that later became the Southern Pacific. When the railroad reached San Antonio in 1877, accompanied by a great celebration of torchlight parades and speeches, it was the beginning of "an immense change in the city's fortune."[4]

The afternoon services at the Sunset Depot attracted so many that all the seats were filled and some people had to stand outside, causing the Reverend Stucker to move the evening service to the Sunset Baptist Church.[5]

From a brief stop at the capitol in Austin, the Stuckers headed to Granite Mountain, one mile west of Marble Falls, where they stayed for about ten days. The Stuckers considered Granite Mountain a very pleasant stop in a lovely Hill Country setting including views of the huge pink stone quarry—at that time the largest in the United States. The stone was used in the building of the state capitol in Austin.[6]

Many who filled the chapel car, besides railroad workers, were employees of the Texas Capitol Granite Company, although the prisoners who were used as labor in the quarry would not have been present. The church closest to the location of *Good Will* in Granite Mountain was St. Frederick's Baptist Church, a black congregation, organized in 1893, with a building called the "Church in the Hollow." The members of St. Frederick's would not have been present. Although the Reverend and Mrs. Stucker would have welcomed them, they knew the whites in town would not welcome them. Because many drummers, including politicians and other notables, stayed at the Roper House near where the car was sided, they could have seen the crowds around the car and have been drawn by the lights and music. The First Baptist Church had grown from an open–air sanctuary in Johnson Park fitted with benches made from railroad ties to a wooden structure at Fifth and Main, but Stucker decided to hold the meetings in *Good Will*, hoping to attract more people.[7]

A letter in the *Baptist Standard* praised the work at Granite Mountain and said that Brother Stucker had done able and faithful preaching, and there was not a more important place in the state for such work than at Granite Mountain. Why the writer came to this conclusion is not clear, but it could have been because of the increasing flow of tourists or the presence of the many workers at the mine. "No greater blessing has come to Texas than the Chapel Car. Let our people know that they can get the best books, best in matter, best in material and best in price at the American Baptist Publication Society, which society has so generously fitted up and sent this church on wheels to Texas."[8]

From Granite Mountain to Eagle Pass would have been a journey through different worlds for Nettie and Edwin—from the pastoral Hill Country with its winding streams and stands of pecan, oak, and cedar to the mesquite-, prickly pear–, and yucca-covered landscape of the Rio Grande border. Eagle Pass, the first American settlement on the Rio Grande, at the turn of the century had an American population of around 1,200 and a Mexican population of around 2,800. There was no Anglo or Mexican Baptist church when the Stuckers arrived, and they hoped to start a mission. The Methodists, Episco-palians, and Presbyterians had buildings already, as did the Catho-lic church that served the majority of citizens.[9]

The small trading town still had rough elements of its earlier days. Just a few years before the visit of the Stuckers, the local Methodist minister decided to hold a service in the Lone Star saloon, known for its elegant fixtures and brilliant electric lights. Although those present listened politely to the sermon and contributed liberally to a collection, it was reported that after a run on the bar, the "fre-quenters settled down at their usual places around the different tables, and soon three kings were running up against four tens to their sorrow, and five on one color were pronounced no good when 'pitted' against a full hand."[10]

Good Will, parked in the yards of the Mexican International Rail-road, could be a hot house in April, and Edwin reported, "Little warm out here, thank you; 110 degrees in the shade for ten hours one day." Stucker said, "We are spending this week with the officials and employees of the Mexican International R. R. at the station called 'C. P. Diaz' opposite Eagle Pass. About 5000 men employed in shops here, half of them English speaking. Sorry we cannot preach in Spanish too. Expect to begin at Del Rio with our beloved Brother Haile not later than next Sunday." Edwin and Nettie would have passed out Spanish translations of the New Testament and have written on the blackboard behind the podium John 3:16: "Porque de tal manera Amó Dios al mundo, que ha dado a su Hijo unigénito, para que todo aquel que en él cree no se pierda, mas tenga vida eterna."[11]

Good Will had been working in Eastern Texas when Baptists in the border town of Del Rio first called for support in organizing a church. In May, 1896, the chapel car pulled into Del Rio and the Reverend Frank Marrs joined the chapel car fresh from his studies at Southern Baptist Seminary in Louisville. Catholic priests had held the first religious services in Del Rio around 1808, and a priest of the Episcopal church and a chaplain in the U.S. Army stationed at nearby Fort Clark held Protestant services in the 1850s. The Methodists did not organize until 1878, and from 1887 through 1890, the few Baptists who were in Del Rio held only occasional meetings.[12]

John Perry, a town merchant, allotted part of his building for school and religious services on "the rare occasions when a man of the cloth appeared and offered to preach." Pastor E. R. Robles from Manor, Texas, who claimed to be "American, Mexican, and Negro," had attempted to hold services and start a church the previous February, but he had found opposition from the Methodists in town. He asked them for the loan of their church for services, but they refused. In many towns, the churches of other denominations would not encourage the building of a Baptist church as that would draw members away who had been attending their services and contributing financial support. Perhaps he did not know about Perry's offer, but Robles was obliged to rent a house for the first night, and on the second, he preached on the banks of the Rio Grande. He reported to the *Standard* that he baptized thirteen members and organized a Baptist church.[13]

When Stucker and Marrs came to Del Rio, along with Robles's small band, they chartered a church in August, 1896, probably much to the dismay of the Methodists. They began meeting in the courthouse, later occupying a two-story frame building in town. Stucker said, "The little Sunday school in newly rented building, the good congregation that followed us from the court house, the first observation of the Lord's supper, the many men and women who so earnestly sought the Savior, all are objects of sweet remembrances."[14]

By the 1890s, Del Rio had grown to 1,980 people, and the Southern Pacific Railroad was the town's biggest employer, with salaries amounting to nearly twelve thousand dollars monthly. When construction on the Southern Pacific stretched across the federal territories in the late 1870s and early 1880s and reached Texas, the inveterately thirsty crews demanded that saloons move along with the building of the town tracts. They would spend much of their pay in establishments like Mr. Ware's Hell's Acre and the legendary Judge Roy Bean's Saloon.[15]

These taverns, mainly tents, still flourished during the time *Good Will* was in Del Rio. Soon it became apparent to the railroad officials that the saloons were detrimental not only to the welfare of the workers but also the safety of the railroads. One Southern Pacific official told Stucker that he welcomed the chapel car and could only wish that all his men were Christians. He said that, from a business point of view alone, a church was better than a bank in any western

community. The ever–present saloons served as focal points for
many a chapel car sermon frequently preached on sidings just a few
yards from the raucous saloon rows.[16]

Keeping to the border, the next stop after Del Rio was Laredo. In
1881 the Catholics were the only church with a building or school,
but with the coming of the Texas–Mexican Railroad and the International & Great Northern Railroad, Laredo boomed. By 1890 the
population had doubled to 11,319, many of these Anglo–Americans.
New businesses had appeared, land values skyrocketed, an international bridge replaced the ferry in 1889, and the Hamilton Hotel offered travelers first class service. Crop farming became profitable
with improved irrigation projects.[17]

By the Stuckers' visit, several other Protestant churches had been
built, but the first Baptist church established in Laredo was not an
Anglo church but the Mexican Baptist Church, and it had been ac-
complishing a fruitful ministry. During one of the meetings in
Laredo, Stucker, who was still limited by his lack of Spanish,
preached a sermon based on "God's Workmanship." As this was a
general meeting, not just for railroad men, his approach was more
general.[18]

> I once visited an organ factory and was shown first the rough
> lumber at the rear of the lower story, then I was led through
> one room after another, and from one story to another, where
> I saw the slowly growing instrument and the different steps in
> the process until by and by I found myself with the master
> workman in the front room of the highest floor looking upon a
> beautiful organ. I had seen some suggestions of beauty and
> heard an occasional strain of music of suggested sweetness but
> now I beheld it in all its beauty and drank in the sweet tones of
> harmony which in time to come shall delight many beside my-
> self, and bring much honor to him who conceived and realized
> this instrument of beauty and harmony.
>
>   Some of us visited the World's Fair and there saw on exhi-
> bition the finished work of man's brain and hand, but not un-
> til the Great Fair of the Universe shall we see what God can
> make in the way of character.[19]

It would be in April, 1896, that Nettie would become pregnant
with their second child, the first having been buried in a little plot in
Aurora a few days after birth. Del Rio, Eagle Pass, and Laredo were

the farthest points that Nettie would travel on the chapel car from her home in Aurora, Illinois. Nettie knew that Mrs. Rust on chapel car *Glad Tidings* had recently given birth to a little girl while in service and that she was staying on the chapel car with the baby. Mrs. Rust had described in correspondence how they would place the baby in a hammock between the two sleeping berths and the little one would fall asleep with the movement of the car and sound of the tracks while en route. Nettie wanted to go home for the term of her pregnancy, probably remembering the tragic times surrounding the loss of their first child. Nettie was beginning to understand how difficult chapel car life could be for a chapel car wife or mother.[20]

After Laredo, Edwin placed *Good Will* in the shops at San Antonio for cleaning and varnishing, where the wooden sides of the car would have new coats of varnish applied and then rubbed with linseed oil to a high gloss. The chapel cars were supposed to have this treatment done at least once a year when Publication Society funds would permit and a shop could be found that would do the work. After attending the Texas State Baptist Young People's Union (BYPU) meeting in San Antonio, Edwin and Nettie traveled back to Aurora. Along with the happy expectation of a child, their future on the chapel car must have been a matter of serious thought to the young couple as they traveled the tracks between the Texas border and Aurora, Illinois. Leaving Nettie in the care of her parents, Stucker returned to Texas in August to pick up the chapel car from the San Antonio shops. In the *Baptist Standard,* he explained that Nettie would not be traveling with him on the chapel car. "I fear however that another so helpful to her husband and so important to the work will not be able to return so soon if at all. How sweet to know there is one who understands and appreciates all." He did not mention to readers that Nettie was expecting a baby. That would be an indelicate subject for a church publication for those times.[21]

Stucker's plan was to work a line of fifty miles of railway where he could visit towns of populations from fifty to two hundred where a gospel sermon, a paper, a Bible to read, and a friendly visit to the home would be an invaluable blessing. He wrote that the chapel car could get its best hearing in these little towns. Practically every citizen was present at the first service held along the line, even though it was only two hours after the arrival of the train that brought the "church on wheels." What was better, they would continue to come as long as the car remained. "We are glad to remain from 10 days to two weeks in towns of 150 or more where the gospel is not preached."[22]

According to sketchy records during this time, Stucker visited towns between Denison and Henrietta on the MK&T. While the chapel car was safely attached to a southbound Katy, a promotion stunt gone wrong was occurring on the Katy a few miles north of Waco. Fifty thousand people, including lawmen, pickpockets, reporters, and photographers gathered to watch a train wreck—a planned train wreck by general passenger agent William G. Crush to promote the power and presence of the Katy in the Southwest. At ninety miles an hour, two unmanned engines plowed into each other, but in an unexpected twist, the exploding boilers tossed "thousand of chunks of metal hundreds of feet in the air, to rain down on the helpless spectators," many who died or were injured.[23]

About the same time, the Baptist church at Denton, southwest of Denison, was having its own explosion. Not quite as exciting as the Katy wreck and no publicity stunt, yet it earned its place in the Gainesville newspaper. A Mrs. Mays horsewhipped J. F. Riley, a prominent druggist in Denton, on Thursday night, August 25, during a meeting of an investigation committee of the church. Riley had been testifying against Mrs. Mays concerning a matter of church discipline. Denton was not one of the towns visited by *Good Will*, and obviously, there was not much goodwill among members.[24]

At Hillsboro Stucker preached to the men in the shops, although his mind was on the absence of his wife, their coming child, and their future on the chapel car. He was considering other avenues of service that were connected to the work he had come to love but that would permit them to have a more stable lifestyle for raising a family.

The Baptist General Convention's fall meeting was at Houston, and the mission board "encountered numerous and very serious difficulties." Besides the Hayden agitation and the opposition from some factions against Carroll and M. D. Early, missionary secretary, the fate of women at Baylor University was decided. For ten years, as a trial arrangement after the consolidation of Waco University and Baylor, women had been granted admission to Baylor University. It was recommended that the general convention continue this arrangement but also give support to the Baylor Female College

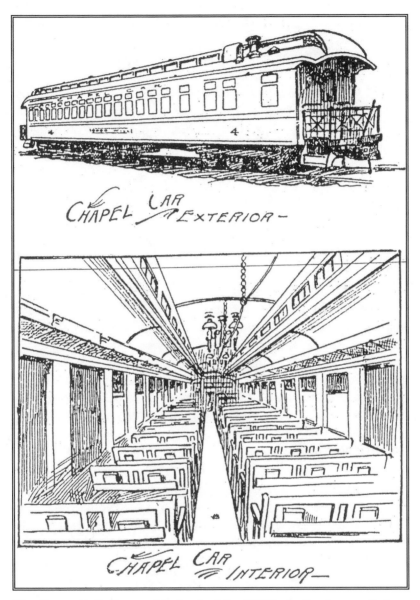

The *Houston Daily Post* ran this sketch of *Good Will* in its October 14, 1896, edition, praising the beauty of the car. *Courtesy* Houston Daily Post

at Belton. Thus those who desired a coeducational experience for their girls could continue to send them to Baylor University at Waco, and those who desired an all-female education could send them to Belton.[25]

The *Houston Daily Post* announced on October 14 that chapel car *Good Will* had been removed from its siding near the Grand Central depot where it had been holding public meetings to the shops of the Houston & Texas Central Railway. In addition to the article, the paper showed drawings of the interior and exterior of the chapel car. Now all Houston readers would know what a chapel car looked like.[26]

Edwin had made up his mind. He told Texas Baptist officials of his decision to leave the chapel car ministry and become a district secretary for the American Baptist Publication Society, working out of the Chicago office. The *Houston Daily Post* on October 21 announced that he was resigning the chapel car work.[27]

Before leaving Houston for Aurora and Nettie and his new work, he sided the car near the Grand Central depot then at Washington and Tenth Streets. It was fitting that his last sermon preached on the chapel car was to the railroad men at the Houston railroad shop. The *Daily Post* reported his visit: "He is himself a former railroad man and he will know how to talk to the congregation of railroad men. He is a firm friend of that class of people and he has always found courteous treatment from them. He has a pamphlet, 'Good Will to Railroad Men,' which he will distribute from the car." With a heavy heart, Stucker left *Good Will* in the Houston shops, where it would await the assignment of a new chapel car missionary.[28]

The scattered seed concept of the tumbleweed Nettie and Edwin saw in abundance during their travels may have left an indelible mark. Stucker would use the analogy of "seeds" many times, along with a scripture from 2 Corinthians 9:6 to describe his experiences: "But this I say; he who sows sparingly shall also reap sparingly, and he who sows bountifully will also reap bountifully." In a pamphlet for the Publication Society, Stucker wrote about how the scattered seed of an earlier witness had born fruit in the life of a little boy. Though it was yet early, Stucker was dismissing the last of his visitors when, stepping upon the platform of the car, he noticed a little boy nervously twirling his cap. The little fellow, pulling out a well–worn Bible, asked Stucker to help him study the scriptures. Stucker said, "We discovered that the Bible," which had been published by the American Baptist Publication Society, "had been given this boy by his mother several years ago."

When the mother came to the station with others to bid the chapel car good-bye, the Reverend Stucker asked her to tell about the source of the Bible. She said that some years ago she and her husband had come to Texas and settled upon a ranch, and within a radius of fifteen or twenty miles there were a few families, and they desired to do some gospel work among their neighbors. Soon they started a small church and Sunday school and needed literature, so because of their connection with a Baptist church in the east, they wrote to the Publication Society for material. In return, they received free Bibles and material for their Sunday school. The Bible in the little boy's hand proved to Stucker that the scattered seeds of the mother's witness had borne fruit.

CHAPTER EIGHT

HERO DIAZ'S FALL
FROM GRACE

W hen passionate, articulate Stucker left the chapel car in November, 1896, another passionate man, not an ordained minister, became the second missionary on *Good Will*. Blackballed from practicing medicine in Cuba because he preached Baptist doctrine, a Cuban physician had come to the attention of the Southern Baptist Mission board. The Committee on Cuban Missions described Alberto J. Diaz as an "earnest, godly man whose zeal, enthusiasm, and unfaltering faith, even through bitter persecution, were mighty factors in carrying on the work." Diaz would become both a hero and an aggravation to the convention in years to come.[1]

How did Diaz become such a hero as to be called "The Apostle of Cuba?" The Cuban fight for independence that began in 1895 was a result of many years of Spanish rule, lack of reform, and the financial crisis that prompted the United States to repeal the tariff act permitting the importation of Cuban sugar into the country. These combined factors brought personal and economic hardships to Cuban citizens, and Cuban patriots gathered support and troops to fight for independence. Eventually, Spain would send more than two hundred thousand troops to try to crush the rebellion.[2]

During the early years of the rebellion, Diaz, a young captain of the rebel army, was sent by his commander to one of the outposts to notify its occupants that they were in danger of an attack by Spanish forces. In attempting to execute this order, Diaz and several companions were surrounded by the enemy at a point on the seaside. Finding it impossible to escape by land, they plunged into the sea, hoping that the strong current that sweeps eastward along the island of Cuba would bear them beyond the reach of the soldiers and that landing at some secure place, they would be able to make their way back. But the currents carried them far out from the shore, and about midnight, a small vessel that was passing along the coast picked them up.

Having thus escaped from the island, Diaz, a graduate of the University of Havana in both its literary and medical departments, decided to go to New York to prepare himself to treat diseases of the eye. During the winter, Diaz contracted pneumonia. Among those who came to know him during his illness was a young woman, a Baptist, who tried to tell him about Christ. Diaz could speak little English, and she did not understand his Spanish, but from her he learned that he could procure a Spanish translation from the American Bible Society. One day, while reading Luke's account of the cure of blind Bartimeus, he was strongly attracted to the story and saw parallels between his own life and that of Bartimeus. Inspired by that revelation, Diaz was baptized into the fellowship of the Willoughby Avenue Baptist Church in Brooklyn. He began to think of the loved ones in his native island who were living in utter ignorance of Christianity, and he yearned to share his new faith with his brethren.

Diaz again set sail for Cuba. At his Cuban home he told his family of finding Jesus, who had cured him of his spiritual blindness, and he urged them to accept Christ. They looked upon him with pity and surprise, fearing that their son and brother had forsaken the Catholic church of his parents and embraced a foreign superstition. They refused to hear him. He began preaching to a small group of friends in the parlor of the Passaje Hotel, and the group grew to about a hundred converts and finally to more than a thousand. Through his preaching and work, he became known to the Mission Board of the Southern Baptist Convention and was commissioned by that board.

One day while passing along the shore of the bay, he saw two men fishing, and he stopped and talked to them about Jesus. Soon a great crowd gathered; then two policemen stepped up and took position on each side of him. Diaz thought they were there to protect him and preserve order, but instead they placed him under arrest. Upon appeal, the American consul was able to release him from prison.

In Cuba at the time, no religious service could be held except indoors. One day Diaz and his brother went to town to preach and distribute books. The priests had warned the people about him, and no one would allow him to hold religious services on their premises. He

Alberto J. Diaz, a celebrated Cuban hero and short-term *Good Will* missionary, experienced problems with the Southern Baptist Convention and the
American Baptist Publication Society. *Courtesy Norman T. Taylor Collection*

found an old, unoccupied frame building near the Catholic church,
and began to preach in the plaza nearby. While he was preaching, a
shot was fired from above him, and the ball that was intended to
strike Diaz instead struck a boy in front of him. The missile had
come through an opening in the weather boarding from the tower of
the Catholic church. A priest was the assassin, and he was tried for
the offense, convicted, and sent to Spain for punishment. The cries
of the fatally wounded boy had incensed the crowd though, and they
began to cry "Kill the Protestants," "Shoot the heretics!" Diaz and
his brother were barely able to escape with their lives, but later he
was thrown in prison again.[3]

J. M. Carroll printed an impassioned plea on April 23, 1896, in the *Standard*. "If Havana could know that ten thousand Baptist churches by one concerted movement swelled a fund for Diaz's protection and freedom, how that would hold back the threatened blow and change the purpose to destroy. How it would affect our authorities at home to know that a million and a half Baptists were in earnest in their efforts to save a man so honored of God—a star of the first magnitude among the missionary heroes of the world."[4]

The Washington correspondent of the *Philadelphia Press* reported of Diaz, "The Baptists in this country are greatly interested in his fate. The awakening of their sympathy with the Cuban cause through their interest in him is likely to result in material aid to the revolutionists. Should harm come to him, this sympathy would probably set at defiance the laws of neutrality. A minister of one of the leading churches of that denomination here said to me the other day that if Diaz were not set at liberty, there would be an army of Baptists ready to fight the battles of Cuba, and thousands would find means of joining the Cuban army."[5]

An announcement in the April 23, 1896, issue of the *Baptist Standard* reported, "Our missionary in Cuba, and one of the most eminent Baptist preachers of this century, has been thrust into a Spanish dungeon by General Weyler. This is but another evidence of Spain's brutality. Steps will at once be taken to rescue Diaz from his perilous position." In the April 28 issue, another article pleaded and said that the horrors of Spanish prisons were confirmed by the multitudes of diseased, vermin-infested, half-starved inmates. "We cannot shut our eyes to the fact that the life of our great brother Diaz is in great jeopardy."[6]

The following week, the *Standard* rejoiced that readers' "prayers to God and their memorials to Congress have prevailed." Diaz was freed from prison, was coming to the United States, and would appear at the Southern Baptist Convention to be held in Chattanooga the following week.[7]

Two years previous to his celebrated return to the Chattanooga convention, Diaz had been given a broad power of attorney as was the custom under Spanish law for the management of property on the island. Without the board's knowledge or consent, he put a mortgage of $12,000 on what was called the Jane Theatre property. The Jane Theatre was where his church was meeting. With nearly $8,000 of this money, Diaz purchased a Buenos Aires property in his own name. It would not be until June, 1896, Dr. Belot of Havana, agent of the board in charge of the property, would inform Southern Baptist Board treasurer Walker Dunson of the transaction.[8]

Diaz had again left Cuba, and since the early part of 1896, he had been in the employ of the Southern Baptist Board to do canvassing work in the United States. Boston W. Smith, chapel car superintendent, met Diaz at the American Baptist Publication Society gathering in Milwaukee, Wisconsin, in May, 1896. Chapel car *Glad Tidings* was on display, and Diaz took a tour of the chapel car and was excited about what he saw. Smith, who had been eager to start a chapel car mission across the border, asked Diaz, "How would you like to take charge of chapel car *Good Will* and go to Mexico to preach the gospel?" By all accounts, neither the Publication Society nor Smith was aware of the problems that Diaz was having with the Southern Baptist Board.[9]

The tide had begun to change by August, 1896, and seeing the opposition against him after the release of the misuse of funds, he voluntarily ceased to work for the Southern Baptist Board. Hoping to find some means by which he might be able to return and continue his work in Cuba, Diaz traveled to New York. While there, he learned that the Ladies' Bible Society of Philadelphia wanted a colporteur for Cuba, and Diaz offered his services and was accepted. Once more, he was among his people, and while on weekdays he scattered Bibles and testaments among the people, on Sundays he met his congregation.[10]

At the time of the discovery of the irregularities about the Cuban property, Diaz was brought before the committee of the board. He made no claim that either Tichenor or the board had authorized the transaction. He did not deny that, although there had been a period of more than two years and many convenient opportunities, he had never given information of the transaction. Diaz, on demand, executed a deed conveying the Buenos Aires property back to the board, acknowledging the right and title of the board and renouncing all claims or authority of any kind whatever on any property of the board in Cuba. His power of attorney was revoked, and another agent was appointed. The board had to pay the mortgage with its interest in the course of the next four years without any assistance whatever from Diaz or his church.[11]

So it happened by a series of events—either because of lack of pertinent information or as an act of faith—that in November, 1896, the Cuban national was the missionary on board *Good Will,* although still under a cloud of distrust by the Southern Baptist Board.

Diaz picked up chapel car *Good Will* in Houston, where Stucker had left it. During his initial tenure on *Good Will,* Diaz was reported to have been in Laredo and perhaps Eagle Pass for brief visits. His visit to Eagle Pass in November, 1896, may have been to support the new congregation that would organize on January 24. Frank Marrs would become their first pastor.

Just a few weeks after his appointment to the chapel car, Smith visited Diaz in San Antonio and was surprised by what he found.

Sidetracked in the most densely populated section of that quaint city, among the Spanish-speaking people, I found *Good Will.* As I entered the beautiful study, I found the bookcase, instead of containing a well-selected library, filled with surgical instruments of all kinds. Opposite the bookcase was an operating table. "Why, Doctor, what does this mean?" I asked. He told me in his broken but intensely interesting way, how from nine to eleven o'clock each morning he treated, free of charge, all the sick and afflicted who came to the car. This, he said, gave him entrance into the homes and hearts of the people. After lunch each day, he visited from house to house, reading the word of God, distributing Spanish tracts, and praying with the people.[12]

Within three days large congregations gathered in the car to hear the gospel preached in Spanish. Boston W. Smith would say, "I could watch the dark faces and see them filled with deep interest."

The *Texas Baptist and Herald* praised the coming of Diaz to the chapel car. "No man in America would receive a more cordial [welcome] than our own A. J. Diaz. Brother Diaz with the chapel car will cross the Rio Grande into Mexico where he will preach to the people." The *Baptist Standard* reported that Diaz planned to go to El Paso from San Antonio and then return to San Antonio. In December, Diaz took the chapel car to San Marcos for a few days of services. The Mexican community in San Marcos was in bad shape and without a pastor for their little church. During the services, the car was crowded with Mexicans who were thrilled to hear the gospel preached in their language. One of the Baptist missionaries in the area said, "This is a reflex action of missions and Cuba is now helping us. Here is a foreign mission field just at our doors and while the field is white unto the harvest and the men are at hand we should occupy it."[13]

Nobody seemed to know or claim what organization Diaz repre-

sented—the American Baptist Publication Society or the Southern
Baptist Home Mission Board. It was reported a week later, Brother
Early, Texas Baptist missionary secretary, claimed that Diaz had a
full commission from the Home Mission Board, but W. Luther of
the American Baptist Publication Society countered that Diaz was
in the employ of the society and that they paid his salary.[14]

Smith and the Publication Society hoped that Diaz would carry
Good Will into Mexico as was originally planned, but the disturbing
events that had occurred in Cuba regarding his relationship to the
Southern Baptist Convention, and his concern for the war for independence, led him to return to his native land. The confusion over
whom he worked for and his tenuous relationship with the Home
Board was also a factor. He left the chapel car sometime in late November, 1896, after just a few weeks on the chapel car. On December 10, Diaz traveled to Houston to pick up mail and to confirm
what the Southern Baptist Home Board expected of him.[15]

In 1898, Teddy Roosevelt arrived in San Antonio to recruit
Rough Riders to fight in the Spanish-American War. During the terrible and trying period of blockage and siege of Havana, when fam-
ine and pestilence was abroad in the city and violence a constant
menace, the Southern Baptist Home Board succeeded in keeping up
and continuing its work with gratifying success with other missionaries serving in the city. The American Consul in Washington placed
all the board's property in Havana under the protection of the English Consul.[16]

After the siege had ended and Havana was in the hands of the
American army, Diaz again took the pastorate of Gethsemane
church, but soon complaints reached the board about differences
between Diaz and Southern Baptist board agents. The board sent a
committee to Havana in November, 1898. On their return, they reported that all matters could be settled under arrangements recommended by them, but Diaz took offense with their decision and appealed to other agencies like the American Baptist Publication
Society for recourse.[17]

For several years, the situation was not resolved to a peaceful conclusion between the Southern Baptist Home Board and Diaz. The
Havana Post, September 5, 1902, reported the events leading to the
ouster of Diaz from his church.

The *Post* article explained that ejectment proceedings brought by
the board against Diaz took place on time. About 8 o'clock on the

fifth the judge and his assistant appeared as well as the "procurador" representing the law firm of Ernest Lee Conant. At about nine o'-clock the janitor and Diaz opened the house and a number of the members of his church gathered within. The official representing the judge entered the building, and on seeing the people gathered there, asked if they wanted to pray, because otherwise he would commence at once his ejectment proceedings. Diaz asked for a few minutes, but as there was no motion made toward the holding of the services, the judge proceeded to remove the property from the church. This was the signal for general weeping among the women present and hot words from the male representatives of the church and those representing the court, and some bad words were exchanged.

Everything that was not considered personal property of the board or Diaz was put into the street, with the exception of the church Bible and the communion service, which out of respect was left within the church. Diaz piled his goods up in the street in anything but an artistic way and then had pictures taken with those of the weeping women, "so as to make an altogether dramatic effect." Many people attracted by the unusual scene stopped and watched the proceeding and were included in the picture also.[18]

For years, the struggle between Diaz and the Southern Baptist Home Board would continue, and even the American Baptist Publication Society finally would withdraw any support for his work.

HONEYMOONING
IN PINEY ARBORS

Newlyweds E. G. and Hollie Townsend climbed aboard *Good Will* in March, 1897, prepared to spend their honeymoon mainly among the brush arbors of East Texas. Townsend had pastored at Central Baptist Church in Dallas, and Hollie Harper was a "Bible Woman" for the First Baptist Church of Dallas, working with women and children.

Eugene Gale Townsend was born in October, 1867, in Calhoun, Missouri, the son of Cornelia and Joel Townsend. Eugene's mother was from New York and his father, from Rhode Island. The family moved to Texas when Eugene was seven, and he grew up on a ranch in southwest Texas near San Antonio, where he attended school. As a young boy, he was very active in the First Baptist Church of San Antonio. The Reverend A. S. Bunting, who ordained Townsend in 1888, recalled that on that day "the rains came down in great torrents and I asked God to let great showers of blessings follow his ministry." After graduating from Baylor with honors in 1893 with B.A. and D.D. degrees, E. G. traveled to Southern Baptist Seminary in Louisville, Kentucky, for a Th.D. degree. He became a pastor in Dallas and actively participated in the life of the Baptist General Convention.[1]

Hollie's family moved to Dallas in 1880 when she was ten, and she was baptized into the membership of the First Baptist Church of Dallas—perhaps the most notable church in Texas. That church helped mold her religious experiences and encouraged her to reach out for ways to serve. "I yearned to go away to a foreign land, to China if I might, to tell the women and children about our Christ. This dream was realized in part when I was appointed by our home church and the Sunday School Board of our State to do city mission

The popular young Texas Baptist pastor E. G. Townsend and his bride would be the second missionary couple on chapel car *Good Will. Courtesy the American Baptist Historical Society, American Baptist Archives Center*

work in Dallas, my home town. I served three years in this capacity and oh, the lovely work that opened before me among the very poor, the neglected in the mission districts of our city!"[2]

When she was twenty-two, Hollie became the editor of the women's section of the *Baptist Standard* and was the first woman to edit a woman's department in any Texas Baptist paper. Well-known for her dedication to the Baylor Female College Cottage work, a program to help disadvantaged young women, Hollie was "an attractive, energetic young woman." In Hollie's column for the *Baptist Standard,* she reviewed the happening of women's work in Texas churches, and among her items she frequently mentioned the activities of Miss E. C. Moore and the "Cottage Girls." Elli Moore was Hollie's closest friend. This friendship would result in a most unforeseen occurrence in the two years to come.[3]

Hollie and E. G. were excited about chapel car work after hearing an address by Boston W. Smith at the First Baptist Church of Dallas, where George Truett, a stalwart supporter of the chapel car ministry, was pastor. Townsend, who at that time was pastor of Central Baptist Church in Dallas, had for some time been reading with interest accounts of the chapel cars. The earnest, enthusiastic words of "Uncle Boston" impressed him very deeply, and he saw the wonderful possibilities of chapel car work. He said, "'Oh, if the Lord would only open this work to me!' was the desire of my heart."

Hollie Harper was also present that night, and in the chapel car service she saw an expansion of her own chosen mission among the women and children. She too thought, "How happy I would be if I could tell the story of Jesus to the women and children of a hundred towns in Texas!" A few months later, Brother M. P. Moody of the Dallas Branch House, and Brother W. C. Luther, district Bible secretary for the Publication Society, said to her: "If you and Townsend could form a partnership we would recommend you for 'Good Will.'"

"Well," she said, "as to that, the partnership is already agreed upon. You speak to Mr. Townsend, and if he is willing, I am."[4]

The Townsend-Harper wedding took place on March 16, 1897, at the Dallas First Baptist Church. Not only was the bride's elegant silk dress white, but so were all the masses of roses, edged with garlands of green, decorating the huge sanctuary. The bridesmaids, ten girls whom Hollie had taught in Sunday school for a number of years, also were draped in white silk. Hollie's brother-in-law gave her away, and E. G.'s good friend, the Reverend C. B. Seasholes, performed the ceremony. The *Baptist Standard* reported, "Nothing more brilliant than this reception has ever taken place in Baptist churches in Texas." The editor wrote this tribute to the couple, "May they live long and usefully, grow old beautifully, lead thousands of souls to Christ, and die happy in each other's love and in the love of that God who smiled lovingly upon them on their wedding night." Townsend would say, "The result was, after much consultation and prayer, I undertook the following March what few men are willing to do, the management of two brides at once!"[5]

The Baptist women of Texas loved Hollie. She had reached many of their homes through her column in the *Texas Standard*. As a wedding gift, she received a lovely silk ribbon quilt from the Cottage Home girls at Baylor Female College (now the University of Mary Hardin-Baylor). The girls, under the direction of Hollie's friend Elli Moore, would never have had the opportunity to receive a good education if it were not for the Cottage Home project. Their note explained the gift. "As you look at these numerous pieces so united and harmoniously blended resting on the solid crimson lining, think of them as emblematic of the eternal union of our hearts and the varied expressions of God's love to us who are resting upon our faith in his crimson blood."[6]

During the period of transition between the leaving of Diaz and the coming of the Townsends, Edwin Stucker returned to hold services at the railroad shops in San Antonio. His wife did not come with him, as she was home with their baby. Then he accompanied *Good Will* to Dallas, where the car would wait for the Townsends to begin their first mission. At Dallas, an evangelist who had become a familiar face to the Wheelers on chapel car *Emmanuel* at Roswell and Eddy, New Mexico, was holding a revival. Abe Mulkey was preaching to the men of Trinity church on McKinney Avenue and Pearl Street on Sunday afternoon, "turning San Antonio upside down . . . and giving it a cleaning out."[7]

It was the plan of the Townsends to visit little towns in the piney woods of eastern Texas where there were no churches or only weak churches. Z. N. Morrell, who preached to large crowds of Americans, Mexicans, and Indians in the 1830s, struggled to bring the gospel to East Texas. Mounting the timbers of an unfinished house, Morrell would call out, "O-yes, o-yes, o-yes! Everyone that wants to buy without money and without price, come this way." While the crowds gathered, he would lead in singing, "Am I a Soldier of the Cross," and then preach on the fifth chapter of Isaiah, "The wilderness and the solitary place shall be glad for them: and the desert shall blossom as the rose."[8]

The newlyweds' initial mission was to Smithville, southeast of Austin, where the Stuckers had stopped in 1896. As a result of the storm that had destroyed the Baptist church after the Stuckers left, *Good Will* was a welcome sight, and the car was filled night after night, giving the couple a great start to their chapel car life.

Townsend reported that the country along the road they were traveling on—the Houston East & West Texas (HE&WT)—was settling rapidly. "We are now at a place [Cleveland] of 500 people. Some good homes, a Baptist organization one year old, but no house, a pastor with preaching once a month." Brother Everett, a young man, was the pastor as well as a practicing physician. Townsend noted, "The Methodists have organized an organization and a house. The interest is very great here."[9]

Like the crowds that followed Morrell, when the newlyweds held their first service at Cleveland, a sawmill town of about 150, people came from miles around, filled the seats, and stood outside listening at the windows. Hollie reported, "Our meeting continues with fine interest. . . . The people in this section are very destitute of the gospel, prosperous in a financial way but careless morally."[10]

Her husband said, "We are very much in love with the chapel car," and every day they were learning more about chapel car life and each other. It is difficult enough for newlyweds to adjust to married life in the space of a home, let alone the cramped, although cozy, space of the chapel car. It was impossible to pass each other in the living quarters without touching, even when they did not want to touch. Hollie, as even-tempered as she seemed to be, would have to have some irritation over the bumps and abrupt stops of the chapel car, not only en route, but as they would be sided and moved in the railroad yards. Whether or not she was a good cook like Nettie Stucker, Hollie's meals would sometimes be tossed on the floor as the car would lurch, and E. G.'s sermons would slide across the tiny space and land under her rocker in a moment of momentum.

Texas could be hot, and the chapel car side windows and the clerestory windows that opened with a special stick would have offered little relief on the hottest days, even with the front and back platform doors open. The delicately patterned window shades were helpful, and in the storage boxes under the car were awnings to place on the sunny side when the car was stationary. In cold weather, and thankfully in Texas that would not mean blanketed in snow, heating the car was a haphazard experience as the Baker heaters were fickle to say the least. The Baker Heater had come to be known by all the chapel car workers as "The Devil's Advocate," especially by those missionaries who traveled in the northern states.

Shepherd, also a sawmill town, was the next stop along the HE&WT line. It originated in the vicinity of Old Drew's Landing, a Trinity River port where settlers landed bringing in goods, and shipping cotton, tobacco, and other products to market. Into these pioneer settlements came HE&WT investors, including Benjamin A. Shepherd of Houston, who in 1875 platted town sites, naming the town for himself.

The women of Shepherd became disgusted with the sinful conditions the town saloons had fostered, and although they were not allowed to vote, according to town history, "they talked, urged, and paraded until the men voted out whiskey by local option." They felt that after the vote the fathers of hungry children could not so easily spend the money earned by hardworking mothers, and drunken fathers would not beat their children as often. Town historians would record that Shepherd became a more respectable place in which to live. It had been started by saloons, but saloons could not be the means of keeping it growing.[11]

Jessie Fain operated an early hotel, and the first public school session was held in the Methodist church, the first church in town. In 1896 James Ephraim Tribe, a native of Canada and a carpenter, coffin maker, millwright, and wheelwright, built a church edifice. A fervent Baptist, he was said to have been the one to hire and fire preachers of the church, but he was also known as the one to give up his bed for a visiting preacher and sleep on the floor.[12]

A preacher Tribe did not fire was W. B. Everitt, a medical doctor and a bi-vocational pastor, as were many early preachers. Everitt, a friend of the Townsends, requested that they bring the chapel car to town. Perhaps deacon Tribe was relieved to learn that the Townsends brought their own little parsonage in *Good Will*, and he would not have to give up his bed.[13]

Leaving *Good Will* at Shreveport, Louisiana, Hollie and E. G. took the train to the Southern Baptist Convention at Wilmington, North Carolina. At the convention, an incident occurred that caused the relationship between Southern Baptists and the American Baptist Publication, already frayed, to break. The Publication Society sent seventeen representatives to the sessions and one of them attacked the Southern Baptist Sunday School Board, which was just beginning operation again since disbanding in 1873 because of lack of funds. This turned the tide against the American Baptist Publication Society and created problems for the chapel car. One of the reasons *Good Will* was continued was the respect that Texas Baptists had for the young Townsends.[14]

One of the Townsends' early stops after Cleveland and Shepherd was Tenaha, in the heart of the piney wood, a shipping point on the HE&WT Railway. The first train pulled into Tenaha in 1886, much to the excitement of the townspeople. When the first ticket agent stepped down from the train and looked around at the raw settlement, it made him want to take the next train out. That was before the Hotel Tenaha was built, dominating the main street of the town and giving it more an appearance of permanence. By 1897 Tenaha had grown to a population of 680 and had become a farm and lumber center although cotton was the major crop in the area, and at least two cotton mills were in town.[15]

Many of the blacks in the community who worked in the cotton fields, gins, and brickyard may have commemorated on May 19, the date for freeing the slaves in Texas. At St. John Baptist Church in the "Quarters," this was a time when families gathered behind the church near the "swishing music of the clear creek waters" and under the sweet gums and red oaks for picnics with tubs of lemonade, watermelons, and fried chicken.[16]

While blacks in town may have been celebrating, the Baptists had just moved into a former schoolhouse but were suffering from the board-party schism that had torn apart their Shelby County Association. *Good Will* arrived with the intent to strengthen the resolve of the young congregation, but they were soon engaged in a "great revival." Townsend began to preach four times a day as wagons moved through the piney woods from every direction, and families made their way to the chapel car siding. The women and children were dressed in their finest, however plain that might be, and the men outfitted in a suit, if they had one, or a vest over a shirt, or clean work clothes. E. G., who had experienced preaching to the congregation in his small Dallas church, was thrilled. He had attended camp meetings and tent revivals, but he had never preached to crowds like this.[17]

He wrote, "The people began to come for miles and miles around. They came to see that church on wheels–that wonder car, and a woman who was 'a heap better talker than the man.'" Townsend was amazed that after the singing and the preaching, as Hollie played hymns on the Estey organ, "The most hardened sinners came—people who had never been known to attend church before. One old woman, over fifty years old, walked two miles to see the car; on this visit she became deeply convicted of sin and after that never missed a service. She enlisted the interest of her husband, an old white-haired man, the judge of the district."[18]

Twice the Townsends had to move the meetings from *Good Will*, seeking a larger building or brush arbor. On the third Saturday of May, 1897, Townsend said there were a thousand people present. "More than a score of brawny lumbermen, white-haired men, young boys and girls, came pressing forward. Many of these, I knew, had never in all their lives heard a dozen gospel sermons." Townsend baptized many in a pond not far from the chapel car, and he said that of the large crowd, many had never seen a baptism before. They worked two weeks longer, baptizing forty-six in all and receiving into the church sixty-five, and some twenty joined neighboring country churches. Hollie mentioned the weather; it was "hot, but we have three services every day."[19]

Townsend's reference to the fact that his wife Hollie was "a heap better talker than the man" could have created serious problems. An issue for Texas Baptists was when, where, and to whom women could speak. In early records, "Bible women" served as missionary teachers on the frontier and Mexican border, but by the 1890s the term encompassed those who filled a wide range of ministries, both paid and unpaid. The origin of the term lies in the fact that such women often sold and gave away Bibles, as well as read and taught from them. Hollie herself, as Women's Page editor of the *Baptist Standard,* and a "Bible Woman," explained that "the selling and giving away of Bibles is but a little part of the work the Bible women are doing."

Hollie explained that they held children's meetings, visited the children of these meetings, and looked after the poor, the sick, the afflicted, the stranger, and the neglected generally. They held mothers' meetings, conducted industrial schools, did gospel work of every description—except preaching. After making her last point, Hollie emphasized, "These women do not preach. They do not want to preach. The brethren need not be alarmed. They are only trying to fill every womanly calling." [20]

Hollie knew the traditional stand against women "speaking" in the church was based on 1 Corinthians 14:34–35, "The women should keep silence in the churches. For they are not permitted to speak, but should be subordinate, as even the law says. If there is anything they desire to know, let them ask their husbands at home. For it is shameful for a woman to speak in church." Not only was it unlawful for women to speak in church, but they were denied the right to be delegates to denominational meetings. In the 1892 minutes of the Waco Baptist Association, the committee chaired by Rufus C. Burleson stated as their objection, along with the admonition from Corinthians, "that there is nothing in our Constitution directly prohibiting female delegates. But as the fathers and founders of Waco Association thirty-two years ago had never heard of female lawyers, female preachers, female policemen, and female delegates, it is fair to conclude they never intended to receive female delegates into this association." [21]

Therefore, Hollie's husband's pride in her speaking abilities was not shared by the leaders of the Baptist General Convention, even though by 1897 the convention reversed its stand and permitted women delegates. Her eloquent talks could have hampered the witness of the chapel car ministry in Texas. Mina S. Everett, a leader in Texas Baptist Women's Work and a great missionary soul and dear friend of Hollie Harper Townsend, left Texas as a result of criticism over her speaking to mixed groups and became a missionary for the American Baptist Publication Society in Colorado. Other wives on the American Baptist Publication Society chapel cars frequently "spoke" to mixed audiences—not just women and children—and two of the chapel car women were ordained. The Townsends had just read in the report of the Publication Society meeting in Pittsburg that Mrs. E. G. Wheeler, after her husband's tragic death, traveled for the society doing missionary work, and that work involved speaking to mixed groups. [22]

The men of the general convention were not the only ones to discriminate against women in the ministry. The management of the railroads generally found women not as worthy as the men in the

The chapel car missionaries led many revivals in brush arbors like the one pictured in this sketch. Hundreds of people would drive buggies, ride horses, and walk many miles to attend brush camp meetings. *Courtesy Longview Public Library*

granting of clergy passes. Clergy passes, either full- or half-time permits, were granted annually to ministers, missionaries, evangelists, Sisters of Charity, and other persons engaged exclusively in work of a religious or charitable nature. Most of the railroads, even though they had been generous in the movement of the chapel cars, would not grant full clergy passes to the wives of the chapel car ministers, and that even included chapel car women who were ordained. Some passenger associations would grant a half-time pass good on all its lines to anyone who qualified under their definition. Others would only grant passes to those residing within the states traversed by their railroad.[23]

Hundreds of people attended the brush arbor meeting at Timpson down the HE&WT line, and such numbers were not unusual in those days. The brush arbors, usually built out of poles covered on the tops and sometimes on the sides with pine branches, were filled with rough lumber benches. The tangy smell of resin, the sweet scent of sawdust, the glow of the coal oil lanterns, and the sound of the old hymns and preaching would imprint memories for a lifetime. Around the brush arbor there would be wagons and stamping horses and chattering families gathered to visit and feast on fried chicken and biscuits before the services.

Herb Walker, in his book on camp meetings, recalled his experiences. He could remember the smells brought in by the gentle breeze that wafted through the open sides of the brush arbor on a summer night: the smell of newly mown hay in Stanley's meadow, the odor of horses tethered about the perimeter of the camp ground, and the fumes emitted by the smoky lanterns. He also recalled the more immediate scent of a bag of vile asafetida that an anxious mother had hung around her baby's neck, thinking it would ward off disease germs. Walker remembered that it was considered disrespectful to pray at the meetings standing up, so those called on to lead would always kneel on the ground. Women were not allowed to pray, but they were allowed to shout, and that they did.[24]

Things did not go so well at another stop that late summer and chapel car life was taking a toll. "We found a church but it was doing absolutely nothing," Townsend reported. "Some large brick works and coal mines near the town brought a gang of drinking, gambling men. We longed to stay for weeks here, but after one week I was forced to leave, worn out with the heat and malaria fever."[25]

Townsend's opposition to the liquor trade would increase at every stop as he and Hollie saw increasingly the desolation of lives as a result of alcohol. Before he came to the chapel car, he had voiced his strong feelings about the damaging effects of liquor. At the 1896 convention in Houston, he had been a member of the committee that proposed that resolutions be passed against liquor traffic. The motion was to urge all churches to discipline any member who in any way aided the liquor traffic, and for the Texas Baptists to cooperate with all organizations laboring to crush the liquor trade. Some members recalled a different vote when an earlier association declined to support the expulsion of five members who had gotten drunk, the moderator arguing that deacons and preachers all over the land had distilleries.[26]

Townsend told of a hired man who came to the car who had quarreled with a brother in Georgia some years ago and had fled to Texas. Another convert of the meeting was a horseracer, almost dead with consumption, whose father was a millionaire in Louisville, Kentucky. All during the day people dropped by the chapel car, and often, all day long and far into the night, the car was an inquiry room. Before the Townsends left this troubled town, some girls came to the car to see them off, weeping as if their hearts would break. One girl put her arms about Hollie's neck and sobbed, "You have brought the only sunshine and joy into my life it has ever known. If I could be with you always I could be good."[27]

Hollie would not get her wish of "telling the story of Jesus to women and children of a hundred towns in Texas," but she did reach many. It would be the children that became her passion. The car would be filled with a squirming mass of young people, and Hollie would describe their heroic attempts to sing the songs, their blank dismay when called upon for scripture verses, and their pathetic apology, "We ain't never been to no Sunday school to learn one," or "We ain't got no Bible at our house." Hollie would remember their delight when she would hand out the story papers and scripture cards and use the colored chalk for illustrated talks on the blackboard hung on the wall in back of the chapel car platform. The Reverend Townsend would say, "When we get the children, it is not a hard task to get their parents."[28]

In August, 1897, Hollie and E. G. Townsend brought *Good Will*, again at the invitation of the mining company, back to Thurber. Not only was Thurber a mining town, but it had become the location of the Green & Hunter Brick Company just a few months earlier. The new enterprise was producing dry-pressed bricks in the most modern facility west of the Mississippi. Thurber brick found ready markets in the southwest for buildings, streets, highways, and heavy construction. The Galveston Sea Wall would be built of Thurber brick, as was Congress Avenue in Austin.[29]

Hollie Townsend wrote in the *Baptist Standard* her impressions of the company town—still surrounded with barbed wire and armed guards. She said that the little folks of Thurber regarded them as their special guests. At the children's meeting they filled the car and even passing trains did not tempt the boys and girls to take their eyes off the blackboard drawings while the lesson was in progress. At the first meeting, as she had experienced at almost every town, she could not get a scripture verse out of the crowd. She gave them illustrated text cards, and the next afternoon every child present was ready with a verse, and those who could not stay to the services came by long enough to give in their verses. Hollie explained, "The population of this mining camp is decidedly mixed—almost every nationality is here. I am experiencing a long felt desire—to tell the story of Jesus in a foreign land—at least I feel that I am out of America when I look into the faces of these children."[30]

Because of sickness, Townsend wrote Boston W. Smith, chapel car superintendent, they had to leave *Good Will* at Thurber after a week of services and return to Texas. It is most likely that the "sickness" was Hollie's early pregnancy symptoms and the need to go back home to Dallas either for medical confirmation or to adjust to the normal physical discomfort of the early months of her condition. Like Edwin Stucker, Townsend would not have been so indiscreet as to publicly mention his wife's delicate situation. A month later, they returned to *Good Will* at Thurber for another round of services.[31]

Nothing but a smokestack, the old depot, a cemetery, and the mercantile store, now a restaurant, remain of Thurber. The six-foot, four-wire barbed fence that protected the company town from the rest of the world is gone, but the little white church on the hill is still standing.

WINNING SOULS
IN WEST TEXAS

Townsend loved to preach. Since his youth, it had always been his desire to reach thousands with the gospel. While in Chicago at the university, he had heard the great evangelist Dwight L. Moody preach, and that had inflamed his desire. At Abilene in October, 1897, First Baptist Church set up a tent seating two thousand by the chapel car, with all denominations participating in the meetings.

It was Townsend's hope that this would be the greatest meeting ever held in western Texas. The *Abilene Reporter* wrote, "The meeting now in progress under the tent near the Baptist church is not only drawing immense congregations, but its influence is extending in all directions, permeating all classes and ages of our population. Even strangers or visitors remaining but a day or two have been converted or reclaimed, and have returned home with hearts filled with love for their Savior. E. G.'s preaching received much praise, and it was said of Hollie, 'she is just a wonder.'" [1]

The *Abilene Reporter* reported that around fifteen hundred people were in attendance. "The house was crowded in every corner and some sat on the floor while a large number stood and while a still larger number failed to obtain entrance and returned home." People from other towns came from miles away, taking advantage of the special rates offered by the railroad. [2]

The chapel car services were not without competition. Folks in Abilene had more than just the revival in the big tent to create interest. A concert was featured at the Opera House, where the U.S. court was also in session trying cases of bank embezzlement, post office robbery, and the illegal sale of liquor. The newspaper reported that many Abilene citizens were leaving town to travel to Dallas to see the state fair. [3]

One of the more important news items on October 29 had to do with the unexpected death of George M. Pullman, founder of the Pullman Palace Car Company. Although none of the four Baptist chapel cars that were on the road in 1897 had been constructed at the Pullman shops, the first American chapel car, the Episcopal cathedral car of North Dakota, the *Church of the Advent,* was built in the Chicago Pullman shops in 1890. All the Baptist chapel cars, seven eventually, would be built in the Barney & Smith Car shops in Dayton, Ohio.[4]

Abilene was a railroad town, but the fact that it was a one-railroad town, the Texas & Pacific, caused concern. For some citizens that was not enough to secure a promising future for the town. A reader expressed in a letter to the *Reporter* that while it was true that the Abilene country needed thousands of thrifty farmers to raise cotton and cows, Abilene as a town needed something else first and must have it. Abilene needed at least three more railroads.

"Providence has given to Abilene not only a position to be a clever town, but as every intelligent visitor from abroad say[s], 'This is a place for a grand city, —a distributing point for a vast territory, where there should be and can be fifty wholesale houses, and factories of every description. But do the wide awake men of Abilene need be told, that this never can, and never will be done with only one railroad.'"[5]

From Abilene's success, the Townsends left the chapel car and headed to San Antonio for what was touted as the "Greatest [Baptist] State Convention in History," and the culmination of "The Great War" on the board. At the convention, Samuel A. Hayden's right to a seat was challenged. He was accused of being "a breeder of strife and dissention and contention," because, including other dissentions regarding anti-missionary Landmarkism, he charged that the convention was made up of churches and thus had no authority to expel a church. The Convention voted 582 to 104 to expel him, although this would not be the last vote taken on the Hayden matter. Hayden was not the only problem. Heresy charges against the Reverend E. R. Carswell, the advocate for Martinism, were upheld by a three to one vote.[6]

The San Antonio *Daily Light* described the mood of the gathering as "stormy and the clouds are yet low" and mentioned the "babble of voices, one man hardly having time to conclude his speech before another took the floor. . . . The gavel was kept constantly striking the table and shouts of 'order' and 'question' were to be

First Class Ticket Good for

ONE PASSAGE

On a
Chapel Car

through life, from
EARTH to the
NEW JERUSALEM

Subject to the following conditions

1st - Be sure you take the right road.
John 14:6
2nd - Take immediate passage.
2 Cor. 6.2
3rd - No stop-over allowed.
John 8: 31-32
4th - Implicit trust in the Conductor.
Acts 16:31
5th - This ticket is not Transferable.
Gal. 6:5
6th - No person has any authority
to alter or change any of these conditions.
Acts 4:12

REASONS FOR TAKING THIS ROAD
1st - It is the cheapest of all roads.
Isaiah 55:1
2nd - It is a delightful Road.
Prov. 3:17
3rd - You will not be Crowded.
Matt. 7:14
4th - No accidents on this road.
Ps. 91:11
5th - The end is glorious.
1 Cor. 2:9

These "First Class Tickets Good for One Passage on a Chapel Car" published by the American Baptist Publication Society were given out to the people who visited *Good Will*. *Courtesy Norman T. Taylor Collection*

The curtain in front of the chapel car would be used to provide some privacy
when the deacon's bench behind the organ was pulled out and used as an
extra bedroom. *Courtesy Norman T. Taylor Collection*

heard in all parts of the audience, and 'for a time it appeared as if
there would be a pitched battle or a bolt from the hall.' Through the
times of disorder, Rev. Jarrell stood on the stage with Meel's parlia-
mentary rules in his hand, attempting to substantiate his points." [7]

George Truett summed up the significance of the turbulent San
Antonio meeting. "We are coming to recognize the fact that a Baptist church which is not missionary is not worth its room in the
world." Chapel car *Good Will* was the embodiment of the "Go" in
the revitalization of the Great Commission of the Baptist General
Convention. It combined all the elements to strengthen the work of
the Sunday school and Colportage Boards and the work of the home
missionaries—if given the chance. [8]

Baird, another T&P town, was the first stop for the Townsends
after the excitement of the San Antonio convention. In July, 1895, a
cyclone hit the little town and destroyed the Baptist church and par-

sonage, killing the pastor's son, "a young man of great promise." All of the other churches in town, along with many residences, were also destroyed. By November, 1897, when the train steamed into the Baird station trailing *Good Will,* churches in town were still rebuilding, and the church-on-wheels was a welcome sight.[9]

Hollie had been revived by her visits with her Bible Women and Cottage Home friends at the convention, and she may have shared with them her happy news of the impending birth of their child. Although excited about the baby, she was even more determined in her evangelistic efforts with the children in Baird. The *Abilene Reporter* did not mention her specifically in the story on the Baird meetings, only stressing the abilities of her husband, "He made strong impressions and is an excellent preacher."[10]

The end of 1897 brought them to Sweetwater where town fathers, after the T&P capriciously avoided the original town site in 1882, decided to move the town to meet the rails. After two weeks of services, the Townsends headed west to Pecos, another T&P ranching community. Small settlements scattered up and down the (Pecos) river had few churches, and as the *Standard* reported, "Some of the stockmen are Christians and Baptists. Many of them are unsaved."[11]

Hollie would have been delighted at Pastor S. B. Calloway's fruit trees, grapes, and figs flourishing in the dry land of West Texas because of the rare presence of an artesian well. The lack of water kept the railroads from establishing points, or offering free land, so West Texas was thinly populated. E. G. found that the First Baptist Church of Pecos, organized in 1885 by just eight people, began within one year to build a 30-foot by 50-foot by 14-foot high house of worship. The small flock, even with a loan of $400, had difficulty in fulfilling their commitment, and *Good Will* was in town to provide support for their fundraising. When they finally completed the building, they invited the other denominations in town to share the facilities.[12]

Good Will's visit to the railroad shops at Big Springs in January, 1898, proved not to be a good month for work, according to E. G., but he felt good about their meetings at Cleburne, where they preached in the chapel car during the day at the huge shops of the Gulf, Colorado, and Santa Fe and at Second Baptist Church at night. The presence of the shops had more than doubled the town's population.[13]

When the Stuckers had visited Marshall in November, 1895, their mission had been just to the railroad workers and their families in the large shops. The Townsends' visit resulted in an appeal for the Reverend Townsend to become pastor of the pastorless First Baptist Church. The building was new—practically free from debt—and the congregation united, but E. G.'s heart was with *Good Will*. "Through the kind words of commendation of several of my friends, they have given me a call; but on account of my obligations to the car, I felt that I could not turn it loose at once." It seems interesting that Townsend would turn down the prestigious Marshall offer with the baby coming. Such knowledge should have caused him to consider a stable position seriously, knowing how difficult life on the chapel car would be with a baby.[14]

At Longview Junction, crowds filled the car day and night. "It was a time of patient seed sowing, but a spell of temporary illness interrupted us before we got to the reaping," Townsend explained in his monthly report to the Publications Society. Hollie was not feeling well.[15]

Just days after *Good Will* arrived at Longview, E. G.'s and Hollie's good friend and mentor George Truett of the First Baptist of Dallas had a tragic encounter while quail hunting with Capt. J. C. Arnold and the Reverend George W. Baines. Captain Arnold, a Texas Ranger who had recently become chief of police in Dallas, was a member of Truett's Church, and Baines, pastor of Cleburne's First Baptist Church, was a close friend of Truett. It was on the second day of hunting that Truett accidentally shot Captain Arnold in the leg, causing a serious wound that was not considered life threatening, but three days later Arnold died. Truett took to his bed in an agony of guilt and swore to never preach again, but in a dream he saw Jesus telling him "be not afraid. You are my man from now on," and it was said that Truett returned to the pulpit a changed man.[16]

With prayers for the healing of their pastor, the Townsends went to fulfill their engagement at Palestine, one of the many Texas towns with Biblical names. The general offices of the International & Great Northern Railroad were situated at Palestine in 1872, along with the Division's Employee Hospital. By accounts, this was one town that did not appreciate the coming of the railroad. Carl Avera wrote in his town history that when the railroad came to Palestine "a plague of locusts would have been more welcome." To ensure safety from flying cinders the railroad was placed one-half mile from the court-house in the center of "Old Town." Palestine's old guard hated

Good Will was placed on a siding at the Palestine International & Great Northern Railway station, a Victorian depot constructed in 1892. *Courtesy the Palestine Public Library*

the noisy, puffing engines, "the flying cinders that blackened their lace panels" in their Southern-style homes and brought danger of fire. The workers laying the tracks and manning the engines were dirty, unkempt, a noisy uncultured breed. They would have to have been a tough group to have endured the trials and hardships of railroad life.[17]

It was not that the citizens of Palestine were anti-progress. They were one of the first towns to have horse-drawn trolleys to carry travelers from the depot to nearby hotels and businesses, of which there were many. Many of those newcomers, including some blacks, had come to work for the railroad. By 1882 the whistle of the shops brought three hundred mechanics and laborers to work, their paychecks boosting the town's progress and causing some to moderate their early biases. But prejudices still ran high in the years since the Civil War, and tempers flared frequently between the black and white sides of town. Although there was friction between the black and white citizens, Palestine was a town that begged for immigrants, even erecting a special building to house them, and local citizens were happy to accommodate them because the more people who settled in town, the more money they pumped into the economy.

Good Will was sided near the massive late Victorian depot with its tower and gingerbread decorations. The Townsends' reason to come to Palestine was particularly to witness to the men in the shops who needed spiritual guidance, especially by reports of their attendance in the thirteen town saloons. Townsend would not have been the first to preach prohibition, for it had been debated heatedly on the streets of Palestine, and traveling evangelists had tried to rid the town if its nickname of "the toughest town in Texas" for many years without much success.[18]

By 1880, along with the usual collection of shops, Palestine had several churches, Methodist, Baptist, Presbyterian, Christian, and Catholic, plus two for the blacks in town. When *Good Will* came to town, the Baptist church had made a drastic move and abolished the church covenant. This was an extremely serious matter, for as the church history stated, "no Baptist church ever grew in spirituality without the covenant." Townsend had become increasingly disturbed, not only by the action of the Palestine church but by the number of churches they were finding along the routes that were in trouble. It was his profound conviction that unless the churches in East Texas received help, they were going to be lost to the convention to a large degree. "Taken as a whole, they are on the downgrade. There has been an awful apathy crept into them that paralyzed all their energies. It is also true of the other denominations to a very large extent. Many are split by petty internal dissentions; others are ignorant or indifferent towards denominational progress." Townsend was convinced that the answer was "prolonged and faithful prayer," and to obtain consecrated men for the pastorless churches.[19]

Townsend's more pragmatic concerns for the churches did not distract him from his passion to save souls. He reported, "One feature of chapel car work that impresses me very much is the readiness with which people come to the car for religious conversation. Almost every hour of the day some one comes to see the car, but concludes by sitting down to talk about his soul. I keep the front door open all the time, and the people come and go. We thus are some days literally preaching all day long." During such a conversation, a young cowboy from a nearby ranch left *Good Will*, as Townsend would say, "with peace in his soul."[20]

Galveston, the next stop on *Good Will*'s itinerary, had a celebrated Baptist past. Although the Presbyterians organized the first church of Galveston by not quite one month, the First Baptist Church of Galveston was one of the oldest in Texas, chartered in January, 1840, by Gail Borden, later of the Borden Milk Company fame. When Hollie and E. G. arrived in the principal port of the state, the city was in its glory. A new opera house had opened in 1894 featuring renowned performers like Oscar Wilde, Edwin Booth, Sarah Bernhardt, John Phillip Sousa, and Lily Langtry. The University of Texas Medical College started classes in 1891 and became the biggest employer on the island. The rich, fattened by the prosperity, were pouring money into new homes, churches, schools, and businesses.[21]

This trip the couple was not working with the beautiful, prosperous First Baptist Church but with two smaller churches in less affluent sections of town. Hollie had returned with her husband to the chapel car for the Galveston mission, for Harold L. Frickett, former pastor of the First Baptist Church of Galveston, mentions her presence in a letter written years later.

A tiny scripture card from the Townsends' visit to Galveston left a sweet memory for Frickett. He wrote to A. C. Gettys, president of Mary Hardin Baylor College (The University of Mary Hardin-Baylor), on June 7, 1954, and said that when his mother passed away May 16, 1954, among her effects he found a card that she had kept in her home for more than fifty years. In 1898, when the Townsends came to Galveston, she had lived close to where the car was sided and had attended the services. She told Frickett that she remembered being given the scripture card. On the card the handwriting of presentation is evidently that of Hollie Townsend. Frickett said to Gettys, "I am sending this to you and asking you to make disposition of it. If it has any historic value, I presume you will keep it, if not, you will dispose of it."[22]

As Frickett affirmed, E. G. and Hollie did minister to the congregation of Second Baptist in April, 1898, but they also worked with the Reverend and Mrs. Lane of Third Baptist Church. Both churches experienced growth during the Townsend tenure, but the couple grew to have special feelings for Lane and his little flock. Lane and his church were valiantly struggling to serve a difficult part of the city. W. M. Harris, a pastor in the Galveston area, spoke of the needs of the area around Third Baptist. "There the people are as thick as winter 'leaves upon the bosom of some forest stream,' and as dead, many of them, and right in the heart of this densely populated section is this church." Harris said that the building they occupied was a poor affair, and both it and the ground on which it stood belonged not to them, but to the cotton mills. Third Baptist was the lone building in the center of a depressed city block.[23]

The *Galveston Daily News* printed a long article on March 28 describing the work and the chapel car. The reporter observed, "At a distance the car would be taken for the private equipment for some railroad magnate, but upon the sign 'Chapel car,' under the eaves is seen, and this motto, 'Go ye unto the world and preach the gospel,' on either side."[24]

Many of the headlines in the *Galveston Daily News* the week the Townsends arrived had to do with Spain's decision to refuse to accede to the demands of the U.S. government in the matter of Cuban independence. Even with the knowledge that war could be declared on Monday, April 25, the news did not stop the citizens from enjoying the week of April 17–24. Many attended the services of *Good Will*, this week in connection with the historic First Baptist Church. Other citizens enjoyed a dance at Forest Park held by the light guard club. Miss Ollie Cranford entertained friends at a euchre party, and guests attended a reception in honor of Dr. and Mrs. Ashton, although not held in their beautiful showcase home, Ashton Villa. Some spent a delightful evening at the theatre watching "A Proposal Under Difficulties." The Ladies Reading Club heard two papers, "Edward the Confessor" and the "Old Walls of London," carefully written and delivered by members dressed in the style of the day— brocaded silk skirts and puffed lawn waists in checked or plaid taffeta.[25]

After leaving Galveston, E. G. and Hollie attended the Southern Baptist Convention at Norfolk, Virginia. During the convention, Diaz again came into the spotlight. President McKinley had pledged to send food, medicine, and clothing to Cuba to relieve the starving sickness of the people, with or without Spain's consent. A committee of the Southern Baptist Convention petitioned President McKinley to appoint Diaz to the staff of Gen. Nelson A. Miles, commander in chief of the American army, and the president made the appointment. When Diaz met the president in Washington, he fell on his knees and kissed the president's hand, and, with tears streaming from his eyes, thanked him. McKinley appointed Diaz as chief interpreter on Miles's staff, and when the army moved, he returned to Cuba where he had fled months earlier to save himself from prison or death. The *Standard* reported, "It is not generally known, but it is a fact, that Gen. Miles is a Baptist, and with Diaz on his staff, we may feel that the Baptists are fairly well represented in the greatest army of the world."[26]

Hollie and E. G. returned to Dallas, where E. G. had pastored his first church and where Hollie had served as a Bible Woman for the First Baptist Church. Their services were in a poor section of town where there was a struggling mission. They were touched by the plight of the women, many of them frail, care-worn, with a baby in their arms and a scarcely clothed toddler tugging at their dresses.[27]

Townsend would say, "We have had a busy, happy year. We three together have labored for the Lord and by his help have carried good will and hope into many a heart."

HAPPINESS, GRIEF, AND SOLACE

When *Good Will* pulled into a town, Hollie could hardly wait to see the children and their parents lined up along the track and waiting at the station. "They are sure it must be something wonderful. Outside printed in gilt, they spell out, 'Chapel Car Good Will,' and then [the inscription on the side], 'Go ye into all the world and preach the gospel to every creature.' Then we hear a decision: 'It is the Salvation Army or some other Gospel business.'"

The couple would hang signs on the sides or ends of the car inviting all to come to the children's meeting in the afternoon, the preaching service at night, and the morning services. "The news that we are in town is freely circulated by the little folks and at the first service we have a car full. I play the organ and teach the children some bright songs and then have a prayer and ask them all to repeat some Scripture verse. . . . Some of them will say little snatches of a school speech and think that it is from the Bible. Often they sit and stare and say they have no Bible at home." Hollie was shocked by the behavior of the children in the towns. "Oh, the wickedness we find among the children in some of these towns. Little boys just out of the nursery swearing great wicked words, fighting, chewing foul tobacco, and sometimes drinking. What a privilege to carry the story of Jesus to these children!" [1]

Many of the men would come to *Good Will* just to see what the car was about. They had seen other unique rail cars sided at the depot, like the beautifully decorated car advertising the Texas State Fair. Men from stock ranches, lumber mills, mining camps, and railroad shops who would never think of dressing up and going to a regular church would attend the services. E. G.'s gentle manner and obvious compassion would encourage them to climb *Good Will*'s steps for individual prayer and counseling, as many had never had the opportunity to talk to a pastor about their problems. Hollie would tell how their private room, the living area, was often turned into an inquiry room for days and days. "We scarcely get time to sleep or eat for the troubled souls who come to us wanting to know the way of life." [2]

Newspaper reporters, denomination leaders, and her husband praised Hollie Harper Townsend's devotion to the advancement of Texas Baptist missions and her work with women and children. "She is modest, wise, consecrated and is a great soul winner and organizer, and is a power for good," her husband reported to the Publication Society in May, 1898. At Brenham, E. G. planned to attend meetings of the General Baptist Convention. When *Good Will* pulled into the depot at Brenham, Hollie was not standing on the vestibule eagerly watching for the children. She was approaching the birth of their child and was not well. [3]

At the convention, George Truett, president of the assembly, was dismayed at an impromptu tribute to the American flag by W. T. Tardy of Paris, a last-minute substitute for another speaker. One delegate described the young man's passionate delivery. "His voice took on the tones of the tempest in the forest. It would crash like the rumble of thunder, boom like the breakers, or roar like the cataract. Again it would ring out like an alarm bell at midnight, clamorous with threat and warning. Anon it would sob like the south wind through the magnolias, thrill like the strains of martial music or sink to the sweet cadences of a mother's lullaby sung over the cradle of her sleeping child."

It was discovered that his fervor sprang from the presence of two brothers, one in Manila with Dewey and one in Santiago with Sampson. The crowd rose to its feet and cheered his sentiment. Truett responded to the raucous response with disapproval. He pounded his gavel and called the excited crowd to order. He said that some present (no doubt some of the elder delegates) objected to such demonstrations at religious gatherings and in deference to their wishes, he requested that no further "outward and visible evidences of pleasure be made." [4]

The newspaper reporting the account of the conventions also reported on the progress of American troops in Cuba. "Dateline: Associated Press – June 23 [1898]. At 5 o'clock this morning 6000 trained American soldiers are encamped in the hills around Baiquiri and 10,000 more rest on board the transports off shore, ready to join those who have embarked as soon as available launches and small boats can carry them ashore."[5]

Just a month later, on August 27, 1898, little over a year after their marriage and their coming to *Good Will,* Hollie died a short time after giving birth to a boy. The death notice in the Dallas paper listed "Mrs. E. G. Townsend, 27 years, No. 306 Wood Street; cause of death not given."

J. M. Carroll, State Baptist leader, praised Hollie. He noted that it was through her marvelous Christian influence that Annie Jenkins, then a school girl, was so deeply impressed by Hollie that she would give her life as a missionary to China. Carroll said that in all the annals of Texas Baptists there has never been among our women workers a more "nobly useful" woman than Hollie Harper. "God called her to greater tasks on high. I never think of her untimely death without a feeling of inexpressive loss—a loss that all of our people sustained when she went Home."[6]

When Hollie left the chapel car to deliver their baby, left behind on *Good Will* was the quilt made for her by the Cottage Home girls and Elli, its colorful silk ribbons resting on a crimson background, emblematic of the devotion of the unique young woman.

One of the last things that Hollie did was to write a tract for the Publication Society describing life on the chapel car.

> My porches are rather small, but my yard is as big as—Texas! In this yard is always to be found the choicest flowers, for the children bring them to me every day, until I often have every vase full and in desperation bring in the dish pan to hold the love offerings. When we pull in at a little country station, we attract more attention than a circus. All the boys and girls and big folks too, come crowding around the car to see what it means, such a fine car—it cost seventy-five hundred dollars—and it does shine![7]

A grieving Townsend praised the "spiritual power and brotherly love" of his many friends at the convention, many of which rode with him on the MK&T to Temple, including Miss Elli Moore. From Temple, the group boarded the train to Belton and Baylor Female College's Cottage Home residences. After the fellowship at Belton, the young widower headed south to Taylor, where he reported, "and here we are lodged, and here we again begin our chapel car life. In much weakness, sorrow and loneliness of heart do we set our faces on the work? At every point we miss the touch of the vanished hand and the sound of the voice that is still. Yet hitherto God has supplied all our needs, and in his strength, do we now stand."

Townsend's references to "we" probably meant singer and organist Thomas Moffett who had joined the car soon after Hollie's death. Moffett had been working on chapel car *Emmanuel* with missionary B. B. Jacques and his wife for several years in California and Nevada towns. Publication Society Secretary Robert G. Seymour suggested that, after Hollie's death, he come to Texas and assist Townsend on *Good Will*.[8]

The Chapel Car Conference at St. Louis provided E. G. with a change of venue and the compassionate fellowship of his peers on the other Publication Society chapel cars. W. G. Brimson, Publication Society official and general manager of the Quincy, Omaha, & Kansas Route, entertained the chapel car missionaries on his luxurious private railcar "Marialys," which proved to be a memorable event. Brimson, with his many railroad connections as president and general manager of the Chicago & Eastern Illinois, Calumet & Blue Island, Chicago & South Eastern, Chicago & Kenosha, Joliet & Blue Island, and Milwaukee Bay View & Chicago railroads, had proven to be a valuable friend to the chapel car movement.

By 1898, five American Baptist Publication Society chapel cars were in service, and the missionaries would share stories of their disappointments and victories. *Evangel*, the first Baptist chapel car, had been working in cooperation with another Southern Baptist state, Louisiana. Like Texas, it was a strong Catholic region. At Donaldsonville, the Reverend Thomas and his assistant started a chapel, and at Woodworth, a mill town, they had good meetings. Even though the last week they were there both the saw and planing mills ran two hours overtime at night, greatly impeding attendance at the meetings, they completed the meeting house that had stood so long unfinished. *Evangel* had held one of its most profitable meetings at Olla, Louisiana, a sawmill town along the Natchez Trace, near the Castor Springs resort area. Thomas baptized several people in the Castor River in the presence of about a hundred onlookers.[9]

Emmanuel, the second car, had worked in Texas with the Wheelers in 1894 and had visited many of the "Hell-on-Wheels" towns in California and Nevada. B. B. Jacques was experiencing quite different weather than his fellow workers in Texas and Louisiana. At

Medford, Oregon, it had been ice-breaking time, so those who wanted to be baptized had to wait for warmer weather and warmer water. In one Oregon town, a Methodist minister came to the meetings in the car, and told Jacques, "This is the best thing I ever saw. I am going to petition the Methodist conference to build me a chapel car." No record has been found that the Methodists ever built such a car.[10]

Earlier in the year, *Emmanuel* had come into Grants Pass, along the rough and rocky Rogue River where gold had been found in 1851. The Reverend Jacques knew something about how Townsend was feeling at the loss of Hollie. Mrs. Jacques's health broke at Grants Pass, as it had on previous occasions, and Jacques called in a physician who told them that if she wanted to live, she must leave the work. "No one can tell the struggle it was for her to step out and say "good-bye" to the dear car for a time at least, but weakness compelled her to do it, and thus I was left alone," her disheartened husband wrote.[11]

On *Glad Tidings, #3,* Charles Herbert Rust had recently finished missions in Wisconsin, where he discovered, like the Stuckers in the Panhandle, the constant threat of fires. At Plainfield, Wisconsin, a center of country trade in the Potato Belt, many homesteads had been destroyed by fire, along with churches and whole town blocks, as dry haystacks burst into flames fanned by the wind. The Rusts had come to help revitalize the church. An ever-present danger to the towns in Wisconsin, just as was true in Texas, was not fire but the influence of the saloons. In one Wisconsin town, Rust had been giving a talk on "Danger Signals" to a carload of children. The town was "full of wickedness, and there were saloons and beer barrels all around us." He told the children that he wished they could write "danger" (in their minds) over every saloon in the city. Instead, the children took him literally. They went from the chapel car and, taking chalk, wrote "DANGER" on the doors of the saloons, on the sidewalk in front of the saloons, and also upon the beer storage houses.[12]

Messenger of Peace, #5, the most recent Baptist car, dedicated in 1898, had been working Kansas. At the World Exposition of 1904 held in St. Louis, the newly dedicated *Messenger of Peace* had been on display for much of the exhibition. One of the outstanding personalities to visit the exhibit was Dwight L. Moody, who preached from the platform of the chapel car. A year after the Chapel Car

Conference, a desperately ill Moody would be placed on *Messenger of Peace* in Kansas City, taken to St. Louis, and transferred to another train that took him home to New York to die.[13]

Finding solace from the other workers on the chapel cars and in his work, E. G. soldiered on. Even though he had arranged for the care of his motherless son, always the baby and Hollie were in his thoughts. There would not have been a moment on *Good Will* that would not have reminded him of Hollie—her rocking chair, the pattern on the teacup she so admired, the Estey organ she so loved to play while her sweet voice lifted up an old favorite hymn, like Fanny Crosby's "Safe in the Arms of Jesus." At Taylor, the children who waved to him from the tracks as the chapel car pulled into the stations would remind him of her delight at their bright faces.

In December, 1898, Townsend and Moffett visited Yoakum, a ten-year-old railroad town with a population of more than five thousand. The first train carrying passengers into Yoakum in the summer of 1887 found just a tiny settlement, but two years later, after the headquarters of the San Antonio & Aransas Pass (SA&AP) Railroad established large shops there, the town boomed with eight hundred men employed by the shops.[14]

Many families, like the Patrick May family, had traveled to Yoakum from Missouri in the 1830s in an oxen-pulled covered wagon that served as their home for several months until they reached the Red River. The Mays, one of the founding families of Yoakum, became part of the Green Dewitt Colony. The Congress of Coahuila and Texas had granted them land under the Colonization Law enacted on March 24, 1825. There were provisions, such as each immigrant had to be certified as a Christian of good moral character and had to take an oath to uphold the federal and state constitutions and observe the Catholic religion.

Struggling to build a livelihood in the Bushy Creek area, Patrick May learned of the planning of the SA&AP Railroad. He agreed to deed two hundred acres of pecans, cottonwoods, post oaks, and huge, sprawling live oaks to the railroad, but he would be too worn out and ill to be present when the first engine came puffing into the little village of Yoakum in March of 1887.[15]

Fourteen passenger trains a day came in and out of Yoakum. There were many tracks in the yards, and one of the tracks would be near the depot for the loading and unloading of freight cars. John W. Hedge and Geoffrey S. Dawson describe the conditions that would have faced the chapel car as it was uncoupled from the passenger train that brought it into town and placed where the station master wanted it. "Basically the yard portion of a railroad is where cars are shunted around to place them in their proper place, and this would be accompanied by the constant shattering noise of car impacts and the sharp bark of the exhaust, as the engineer quickly accelerated in order to perform some required maneuver." [16]

During a two-week mission, the *Good Will* team made quite an impression on the pastor and the growing church that had just built a new building. "We are all pleased, even very much delighted with Bro. Townsend and Bro. Moffett, the singer." The coming of the car had two good effects. One of which was to introduce to the people in a very strong way the workings of the American Baptist Publication Society, which the pastor considered to be "the strong power for good, we have today among us." The other benefit was Townsend's preaching of the "good old gospel of Christ . . . Moffett sings Christ and does it well," Pastor J. T. Jenkins added. [17]

After their success at Yoakum, Townsend and Moffett went to Karnes City, a town on the SA&AP Railroad near Kennedy Junction, then on to Skidmore Junction and Gregory, where there were no churches. At Rockport, three weeks of meetings resulted, which the pastor reported were, "perhaps greater than that of anything held here in past years." [18]

Townsend had the opportunity along this line to witness to a diverse audience. At Gregory, he had a special concern for the Mexicans who came to the car. Although many of the Mexicans could speak some English, most of the older men and women could not, so Townsend gave them Spanish New Testaments. Townsend reported that one day a dozen or more Mexicans were gathered at a home and a gentleman was reading to the group from one of the Spanish New Testaments. Townsend also counseled a black woman on *Good Will* during their stay at Gregory. That was unusual, because generally blacks would not come on the car if there were whites present; they would stand outside and listen through the windows, although Townsend and the other chapel car missionaries would assure them that they were welcome on the chapel car. Townsend reported, "After the audience was gone, one, a colored woman, a cook in one of the families here, came back weeping bitterly and asked us to pray for her. 'I wanted to hold up my hand, but was ashamed to, but I do want to be saved.' We assured her of our prayers and tried to point her to the Christ." [19]

At Bryan, one of the larger towns *Good Will* visited, Townsend and Moffett did "untold good" in the town of almost four thousand. Pastor R. D. Wilson praised the two missionaries, stressing that although the meetings held "no great excitement," Townsend was an effective but "safe" revivalist, and his work would "stand the test." This was not the first time that E. G. had been labeled as not a "hell fire and damnation," crowd-exhorting preacher, although his subdued delivery at Bryan could have reflected that his thoughts were not quite focused on his preaching but on his personal loss. [20]

CHAPTER
TWELVE

NEW LIFE, NEW WIFE,
NEW MISSION

During Hollie Harper Townsend's illness, she had conveyed to her husband her desire that in the advent of her death he marry her dear friend Elli Moore. It would be hard to imagine Townsend's reaction to this kind of deathbed request, although he probably was not surprised. All that is known is that E. G. did comply with his wife's wish and married Elli Moore on September 13, 1899, in the chapel of Baylor Female College, providing a suitable and willing wife and a substitute mother for little Gale.[1]

Raised in La Grange, Texas, Elli came from a distinguished and well-to-do family. Her grandfather, Colonel H. J. Moore, was in command of the Texas forces that made the fight for independence at Gonzales, October 2, 1835. Elli, seven years older than E. G. was educated at the Baylor Female College when it was located at Independence. Admired across the state for the contributions she had made to the education of needy young women, she had resigned her position as a teacher at Baylor College in Independence to promote the Cottage Home work. It was said that she had given her jewelry and other personal holdings to ensure its beginning. Because of poor health, Elli left her duties at Baylor Female College to travel to Europe. When she returned, she directed the Cottage Home program where girls could live rent-free while attending classes.[2]

After his wedding to Elli Moore and a quiet honeymoon, E. G. met singer Vallie Hart at Mineola Junction in October. Thomas Moffett had left the car for a brief period, and Hart, who had been singing in revivals all across the state and serving as a traveling agent for the *Baptist Standard,* was substituting for him. Hart, considered by many to be "one of the finest gospel singers in America," was also proficient on the organ. In an issue of the *Texas Baptist and Herald,*

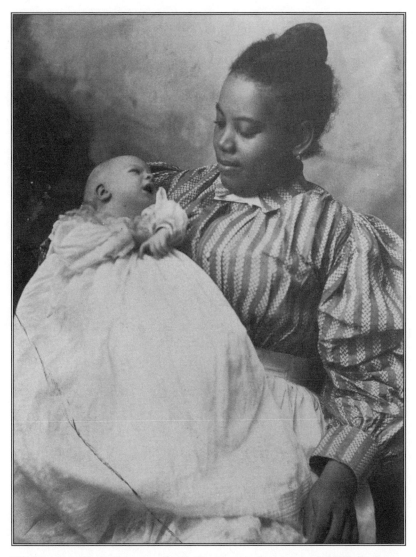

Elli Moore, who would marry E. G. Townsend after the death of Hollie, came from a wealthy Texas Baptist family. In this picture she is being held by a favorite family slave. *Courtesy Ernest Gale Townsend Papers, The Texas Collection, Baylor University, Waco, Texas*

a plea had been made to help Hart purchase a portable organ to use in his evangelistic work, so to be able to use the finely crafted Estey organ on *Good Will* would have been a delight.[3]

In 1873, shortly after the coming of the railroad to Mineola and the building of the first shacks that constituted the town,

T. L. Scruggs, said to have been of Baptist faith, came and set up a makeshift tabernacle for public worship. Itinerant preachers stopped there from time to time to conduct services. The Baptists erected the first denominational church of any kind in 1875, but the T&P and I&GN and Missouri, Kansas & Texas Irish workers wanted a Catholic church, and soon Mass was celebrated at a home in the community. A number of Mexican workers were employed by the railroad, as attested by their presence in the town's first cemetery, but it is dubious that they were welcome to attend Mass with the Irish. By the time *Good Will* arrived in Mineola, there were also Methodist and Church of Christ congregations. The services near the rail yards and shops would have drawn many to the chapel car, but many that did not enter the platform door would have stood outside or near enough to see the lights and hear the music.[4]

Just a month before Townsend and Hart came to Mineola, the mayor of the town had received a letter from the mayor of Greenville, Texas, warning him of a smallpox epidemic existing there. On the advice of the city health officer, the town was quarantined, and guards met every train arriving from Greenville, and no packages or passengers were allowed to embark. When word came that there were smallpox cases in Silver Lake and Grand Saline, both just a few miles west, an officer also met the T&P eastbound trains. A special officer guarded the road from the west to keep people out who might try to enter by other means of transportation. As Townsend and Hart were supposedly coming south from Belton and Townsend's recent marriage and honeymoon, the chapel car must have been permitted to stop and hold services.[5]

From Mineola, E. G. attended the Baptist General Convention at Dallas along with 2,390 messengers who voted on whether to seat Samuel Hayden. The vote stood "For seating Hayden," 557; "Against seating Hayden," 1,181. G. W. Truett, pastor of the First Baptist Church of Dallas, was relieved at the outcome of the vote and announced the convention's plan: to strengthen the frontier work, extending from the upper Panhandle around by El Paso, down the Rio Grande and across the southern coast from Laredo to Orange; in all, something like two thousand miles. And if that was not enough of a challenge, they vowed to supply the neglected places all over the state, supplement weak churches, revive failing churches, reunite discordant churches, and advance all churches toward a gospel standard of mission effort. The chapel car played an important role in this mission statement.[6]

In December, 1899, E. G. Townsend left his new wife Elli with his baby son. Then he and singer Thomas Moffett, who had rejoined the chapel car, traveled on *Good Will* to the border. On December 15, the *San Antonio Daily Light* announced that "the gospel car 'Goodwill' arrived in San Antonio over the Southern Pacific from the east yesterday afternoon," and that it would be sided on the Southern Pacific track at the passenger depot. After stopping in San Antonio for six days, Townsend arrived in Del Rio. Pastor Frank Marrs of Del Rio praised the Stuckers, who first came to the town in 1896 and accomplished much good. Now Townsend and Moffett's arrival was to encourage the new congregation in their drive to erect their own building. It would take more than two years before a church would finally be completed on lots donated by the Southern Pacific Railroad.[7]

With a full house with Pastor Marrs on board, Townsend and Moffett went west to Comstock. E. G. and Moffett probably occupied the berths in the living quarters, with Marrs sleeping on the deacon's bench that made into a bed behind the pulpit. There the trio worked with a new congregation located in that desolate area of the Devil's River. Marrs said, in spite of heavy rains, the chapel car was crowded.[8]

The Galveston, Harrisburg and San Antonio Railroad Company built a route westward through Val Verde County in the late 1880s, and along this line in thirty-mile intervals town sites were laid out, including the town of Comstock. The thirty-mile distance between towns was convenient in that it represented one day's travel by horse and buggy. In 1888 a post office was granted, and the same year George Washington Ames opened his general store. Increasing the opportunity for town growth, the Deaton Stage Line operated a six-horse stagecoach that changed teams four times between Comstock and Ozona. In 1889 the Philips Hotel began to serve travelers stopping overnight. A healthy sign for families who would come to the area, sometime around the turn of the century, a public school with one teacher and eighty-nine students opened.[9]

At the little station of Comstock, there were not a dozen houses in sight, yet from the ranches for twelve and twenty miles, the people came and filled the car. E. G. reported, "The reign of his Satanic

The Southern Pacific Railroad Pecos High Bridge was considered the eighth wonder of the world. Many men in the Comstock area worked on the bridge. *Courtesy the Center for American History, University of Texas, Austin*

Majesty has been so universal here in the past that they named one of their principal rivers after him, Devil's River." [10]

A gray-haired woman, the mother of twelve children, who had lived on a ranch all of her life, became interested in the meetings. She said, "I have never heard anything about the gospel, because I have never had any chance to go to preaching. But this you preach about is just what I have been longing for these many years." Townsend wrote that they organized a Baptist church there with fifteen members. The clerk of it, a young son of the mother mentioned, was sixteen years old before he ever heard a sermon.

Many of the men who lived in the Comstock area of the Devil's River worked for the Southern Pacific Railroad at the famous Pecos High Bridge. Because the previous rail route to cross the Pecos River was dangerous and difficult to maintain, construction started on the high bridge by the Southern Pacific Railroad in March, 1891. The construction left the original roadbed about three miles east of Comstock, proceeding northwest to the Pecos and rejoining the old roadbed at Shumla on the westside of the river. The bridge was 321 feet high and 2,180 feet long. At one time considered to be the eighth wonder of the world, the high bridge was open to railroad traffic in March, 1892.

Some passengers were afraid to ride across such a tall, spindly structure and would choose to walk, an almost inconceivable feat. At least one time, all passengers had to walk across the bridge because the wind was blowing so hard up the canyon that the trainmen feared the light wooden coaches might blow off the bridge. In 1910 the bridge was reinforced and shortened 665 feet, with rock fill placed at both ends. As it was valuable to the U.S. transportation system, the military guarded the bridge for many years, including during the Mexican Revolution and two world wars. It was finally replaced by a stronger concrete-and-steel structure in 1944.

When *Good Will* came to Comstock, some in the community still lived in caves in the bluffs, using willow limbs and river canes to construct crude homes. Tents were expensive, and few had money for things other than livestock. The most abundant construction materials available were railroad cross ties, which were used to build houses and barns and fence posts and to keep wood stoves burning. Life was hard, food was scarce—bread, potatoes, rice, coffee, chili, flour, beans, lard, sugar, some pork, and lots of goat meat were the staples, plus canned corn or tomatoes once in a while.[11]

After two weeks of services at Comstock, Townsend described his emotions about this part of Texas. "We are now on the southwestern border not only of Texas but also of the United States. Across the Rio Grande River in Mexico, the Santa Rosa Mountains lift their heads far above the clouds. This is the frontier of two republics. . . ."

After visiting Comstock, Townsend stopped at Langtry, the town made famous by Judge Roy Bean. Bean was still in office as the "law of the land" when *Good Will* conducted services in town. It was near Langtry, at Dead Man's Gulch, that a silver spike joined the transcontinental tracks of the Southern Pacific's Sunset Route January 12, 1883. The tracks stretched from New Orleans to San Francisco, tracing the steep canyon walls towering over the Pecos River. During the last decades of the 1800s, new towns and tent camps like Comstock and Langtry and Sanderson sprang up along the route— wild and lawless places crowded with railroad workers and the thieves, card sharks, and painted women who preyed upon them. It was Judge Roy Bean who would keep the peace, and in 1883 he moved his court and saloon to Langtry.[12]

Langtry was the first stop with Elli Moore Townsend on the car. It would have been quite an experience for the prim and proper Elli to view Bean's saloon and hear of how the judge so admired the actress Lily Langtry that he named his saloon and so-called Opera House after her, although it is more likely that the town was named for a Santa Fe Railroad construction foreman. No references have been found that indicate the judge came to any of *Good Will*'s services, although it was said that he had mellowed some in his later years. Even Bean would have had doubts about what would happen to his business if the churches and their anti-saloon attitude came to town.[13]

Brother Marrs would publicly tease Townsend about his lack of knowledge on the geography of the borderlands. On this, Elli's first trip on *Good Will*, Townsend tried to make her believe that the Rio Grande was a little creek of some canyon. Marrs later assured the congregation at Waco, where Townsend was planning to serve after leaving chapel car service, that even if E. G. did not know a creek from a river, his theology was well founded.[14]

At the I&GN rail center of Hearne, the car stood right at the round-house, and there would be as many men on the outside as on the inside. "When the windows are all up, they can hear equally as well outside," Townsend explained. Among the crowd of workers would be the Irish, Europeans, Mexicans, Chinese, and blacks. This mix was explosive in a town that prided itself on its concerted effort to restore white supremacy and where the Ku Klux Klan "grew by leaps and bounds." When the county election of 1896 came up, the Negro sheriff was quietly deposed before the election, and forty men with Winchesters were placed at the polling places to turn away all but Southern Democrats. A large crowd from the Brazos Bottom black community, on their way to the polls, accompanied by a brass band, was met at Little Brazos Bridge. The band's instruments were consigned to the river and the to-be voters were sent home.[15]

Townsend related, "One night, outside, there stood an engineer, cursing and abusing Christian people. He was reproved by one of the Christian yardmen. The man attracted a good deal of attention by his violence. Two nights after this he was shot and killed. It made a very profound impression on everyone. It is just this class of men that our work is among. Many times we are able to lead them to Christ."[16]

It is doubtful that the wealthy cotton planters and their families would have attended the meetings, but businessmen and others in the town would have come to the services held in the car, including some of the older citizens who could remember the legendary 1876 Methodist revival held by the evangelist W. E. Penn. The Methodist church had its beginnings in an upstairs room of Lambert's Saloon where the owner gave the minister permission to use the room but refused to discontinue his Sunday morning business during the services. So the clergyman preached "to the accompaniment of clinks, dice-rattles, and curses from below and the saloon band's secular blaring vied with the hymns." [17]

Somerville was the last stop for Townsend on *Good Will,* and it was a typical chapel car town not more than twelve months old. "More than a hundred houses have gone up in the last four months. There is not an organization of a church house in the place. There are plenty of saloons, and far into the night I can hear the shouts of their drunken carousals. Interest is growing every night. Last night and night before there were a number that promised to trust the Savior. It is my hope to organize a church here soon and build a house. I have the promise of a lot." [18]

Probably because of the desire to be with his little son, and because of Elli's desire to devote her time to the Cottage work, Townsend left chapel car work in early 1900 to pastor the East Waco Baptist Church. He and Elli Moore Townsend would become leaders of the University of Mary Hardin-Baylor at Belton. The Townsend Library on the Mary Hardin-Baylor campus is a memorial to E. G. and Elli Moore. Although university archives mark the leadership of E. G. and Elli, there is little relating to the illustrious chapel car ministry of E. G. and Hollie Harper Townsend. [19]

REVIVING EAST TEXAS TOWNS

Known not only for his years of ministry but also for his expansive size and good nature, the Reverend G. B. Rogers, who had pastored a number of Texas churches and had served as the financial agent for Baylor University during its most difficult time, came to *Good Will*.

In December, 1898, the *Standard* reported that Rogers had left his last pastorate at San Angelo and gone into evangelistic work. The new pastor at San Angelo described Rogers as, "one of the Lord's chosen vessels, pure gold," and questioned why Rogers, with his talents, had no offers of work. Then on March 21, 1899, while Townsend was still on *Good Will* and Rogers was still unemployed, Rogers's not quite twelve-year-old son, one of five children, died of meningitis. In addition to his grief over his son, Rogers was probably depressed over his inability to find a position that would fit his abilities and calling as well as support his family. In January, 1900, again the *Standard* pleaded for churches to use Rogers and "keep him busy," and by February his situation had improved as he was chosen to replace E. G. Townsend on chapel car *Good Will*.[1]

Rogers on February 3 went to pick up *Good Will* at Waco and confer with Townsend about the management of the chapel car. "I do not know what Bro. Townsend's general opinion of me is. I think it is good. I will vouch, however, for this statement, that he thinks I can ask more questions in detail than anybody he ever saw."

On his first trip on the chapel car, Rogers pulled out of the Waco station as *Good Will*'s new "conductor" on the MK&T, Train No. 4, then went on to Fort Worth, arriving there at 11:20 P.M. Green about chapel car operation and weary at the late hour, he reported with relief, "I found the yard master ready to serve me and put the car in the very best place. After finding out where I should like to be side-tracked, it seemed to be a pleasure to him to be exceedingly obliging. Soon the car was placed near the union station at the Main street crossing."[2]

Fort Worth was Rogers's home, and he was thrilled to have his first service on *Good Will* among friends. On Sunday, the chapel car was parked near the new T&P station ready to receive visitors. A large, fine-looking man came into the service one evening, took a seat about middle way of the chapel, and was much interested in the singing and preaching. At the close of the talk, he stood in response for prayer. When the benediction was pronounced, Rogers made his way back to him, and the man told Rogers how he came to be in the chapel car. He was bicycling by and he heard beautiful strains of music "the like of which I never heard in all my life." He circled around a time or two trying to locate the sound. Failing, he went up to a man and asked him where that music was coming from. The man pointed to the car and said, "Why they have a regular church over there on wheels," and he said, "Well, I'll just take that in," so he came in. He said that he was not in the habit of attending religious services, but he told Rogers, "I had my old wicked heart stirred tonight as I have never had it before. I never heard such sweet music. Of all the teaching I ever heard in my life you made it plainer to me than I ever heard it. I give you my hand and pledge you my word, sir. I am determined to live a better life."[3]

After the Fort Worth meetings, Rogers's former pastor expressed his excitement over the selection of Rogers to assume the duties of the chapel car. "No better man could have been selected for this responsible and great work. He is one of our best men."[4]

On February 4, Rogers traveled over the "magnificent route," the MK&T, to Houston where he found, like at Fort Worth, the railroad officials very considerate of the work. At his request, *Good Will* was sidetracked near the Grand Central Depot until arrangements for further travel could be made. Rogers traveled to several railroad districts of the city to evaluate the situation and reported, "The needs of the field simply beggar description. The destitution is appalling when we take into consideration how little is being done in the way of missions in this vast center of influence in Texas. I was besought almost with tears to side-track 'Good Will' in the fifth ward and hold meetings day and night for weeks in this territory." After praying for guidance in the matter, he determined to go on to East Texas, promising to return to Houston at a later date.

Houston East & West Texas (HE&WT) founder Paul Bremond was obsessed with the desire to open up the piney woods and bring progress and civilization to the East Texas region. The chapel car had visited many towns along his line from 1895 to after the turn of the century, although by the fall of 1899, the Southern Pacific had acquired control of the line. Wanting the railroad officers to know more about chapel car work, Rogers arranged with HE&WT General Manager N. S. Meldrum, "a most excellent gentleman," to come out on his line to work for a month.

G. B. noted, "I am now at the first station [Cleveland], forty three miles from Houston." Cleveland, the courthouse seat of Liberty County, was a small town of about three hundred inhabitants where the Townsends had held services earlier. General Manager Meldrum would have been well acquainted with the bustling, growing HE&WT rail community. In spite of the growth, there was no church building in town. Many railroad employees came to the services, no doubt remembering the chapel car from its earlier visit. People came from distances of ten miles or more away, despite the fact that the weather was bad, much rain had been falling, and the roads were almost impassable. According to the members of the Cleveland church, Rogers's ten-day revival was a "glorious" success, and the *Baptist Standard* reported, "The town is stirred as never before in its history." [5]

The person most responsible for the chapel car arrangements in a town would not be Meldrum but the station master, and the men in that position at Cleveland were W. P. Johnson and T. M. Peebles. It was the station master's job to be in constant communication with the other stations along the line and to report on the progress and positions of the trains. If the station agent was a religious man, he would be more likely to make pleasant arrangement for *Good Will*, but if the stationmaster was not a religious man, or was a member of a faith opposed to Baptist beliefs, he could make siding the chapel car very difficult. He could put it in an inaccessible place, surrounding it with busy freight and cattle cars, or providing no siding at all. At Cleveland, Johnson and Peebles must have been agreeable to the visit of the chapel car. Of course, if the general manager were on the car, Rogers would receive excellent service. [6]

The sawmill town home of the Bateman family. *Courtesy Temple archives, Diboll, Texas, University of Texas, Austin*

Although he was a big man, the children loved Rogers and would "go to him intuitively as to a friend." Rogers was so big that friends joked that his initials of G. B. stood for "great big." Along with the children's services, Thomas Moffett enhanced the chapel car ministry with his beautiful voice, and many in the small town would never have heard the hymns sung with such beauty.[7]

The church resolved to build a house of worship to cost about $1,000, and a few hours of house-to-house visitation resulted in a desirable lot and $300 toward the building fund. Rogers said, "Many outsiders, including the saloon-keeper, have donated liberally."[8]

Around the turn of the century, the East Texas timber companies drew tens of thousands into their sawmill towns. Between 1870 and 1907, the peak years for the sawmill industry, Texas production increased twenty times to a total of over two and a quarter billion board feet and placed the state third in rank among lumber-producing states. Sawmill work offered "long hours, low pay, little chance of advancement, an uncertain future, and, by the law of averages, a good chance of at least one serious injury." Despite the disadvantages, men needing work to feed their families would apply for employment.[9]

At Livingston, another mill town, results were not quite so encouraging. As was his custom, Rogers had sent ahead a message to the HE&WT agent announcing *Good Will*'s arrival. There was no answer! That should have been the first indication of problems. After the car arrived and was finally placed on a siding, people did not flock to the chapel car. Rogers and Hart would soon discover why there was not an enthusiastic response.[10]

Mill towns were known for fights, drinking, gambling, and prostitution, and during the time *Good Will* was in town, a longtime battle for prohibition was being fought. A town history relates that with the abundance of liquor available in the numerous saloons came problems. Women and children were being knocked off the wooden walkways by reeling men and were afraid to go to town on Saturdays. One woman told of hearing shots that killed eight men one afternoon. During that spring the fight for prohibition was won, but the laws that followed the election were not enforced. Taverns continued to sell alcohol, but their imbibing patrons were fearful of their criminal behavior being penalized, so a petition was presented to the Commissioners Court to request another election to reinstate the saloon business. The election was scheduled for August 30, 1902.[11]

During the night before the election, a fire started in the back of a store in town and spread quickly as there was no running water in town, and the bucket brigade could not control the blaze. By dawn on election day, the town was nothing but ashes and soot; all buildings lost except the brick courthouse. Not to be deterred, the alcohol option election proceeded as scheduled, and by the end of the day the "drys" had won the election to eliminate alcohol sales in Livingston. It was well known that the saloon keepers set the fire, and the good citizens of Livingston swore that not another saloon would be operated in town. As a precaution, the new buildings built in the business district were constructed of brick.[12]

Another problem in Livingston was the presence of the Union church, a conglomeration of several denominations like those frequently built by mill and coal companies. A Baptist church in town that would organize from the visit of the chapel car would draw from the membership and financial support of the Union church. If those two problems were not enough to keep people away from *Good Will*'s meetings, town folk would have to dodge mud and hogs on their way to the siding near the depot, as most piney wood lumber towns were free-range well into the twentieth century. As a necessity for keeping out the hogs and other animals, fences surrounded the one-room clapboard company houses.[13]

As improbable as it may seem, these possible distractions—the riotous life of the town, the presence of a Union church, or the nuisance of free-ranging hogs—were not the issue.[14] Rogers explained that the Livingston church, organized before the Civil War in 1860, did not cooperate in the Baptist General Convention of Texas and tended to be hostile to the chapel car's presence. "While the spirit of the people was cold and indifferent at first, it was wonderfully changed after we had preached and sung to them for a few days." According to Rogers, the services captured the whole town, and there was not a house large enough in the place to hold the people who came from far and near to hear the gospel. Rogers also preached at the black Baptist church, the first church erected in Livingston, on Sunday afternoon, and the members raised a significant donation for the chapel car of $3.35.[15]

T. S. Meese, a leader in the Baptist church, like many men in Livingston, had enlisted in the confederacy in 1861 and served with Capt. "Ike" Turner, a local farmer who, at twenty-two, was the youngest of his rank in Hood's Brigade. Fatally wounded at Fort Nansemond, near Norfolk, Virginia, Turner became a Polk County legend. Meese survived the battle at Fort Nansemond although severely wounded, then was captured at Gettysburg and later exchanged. After returning home, he engaged in farming and merchandising and was appointed sheriff and judge. Rogers would have had to win over tough veterans like Meese if the tenor of the meetings changed as drastically as Rogers reported.[16]

After waving farewell from the platform to members of the church and to an assortment of excited children, an exhausted Rogers would have settled on the leather-padded deacon's bench on the platform behind the organ and reflected on the success of the mission. As he watched out *Good Will*'s windows, it would have been difficult for him to ignore the beauty of the Polk County February landscape along the tracks—spring-fed streams, cedar thickets, great hardwood forests, violets, and climbing yellow jasmines, which blossom before the trees bud.[17]

Rogers did not seem to be a man of such idyllic inclination. He was not a student of philosophy. He did not possess the quiet charisma of an Edwin Stanton Stucker, who found the symbolism of bad and good seeds, or the dignified zeal of an E. G. Townsend, who used metaphors of pipe organs and men. Nor did he have the idealism of the younger men. His health was not good. His girth would have been a hindrance, especially in the cramped quarters of the chapel car where he would have had to turn sideways to walk the corridor between the chapel and the living quarters. The chapel car berth bed could not have provided much rest. He had few personal comforts on the chapel car, as his wife Katie, unlike Nettie or Hollie, generally stayed home with their children. His major strength was his long relationship with Texas General Baptist churches and politics. He was an old-fashioned preacher of the frontier style, not scholarly or restrained, with more of a hell-fire and damnation "Billy Sunday" approach. This delivery was what appealed to many in the small towns of East Texas.

In Groveton, like at Livingston, *Good Will* became part of an anti-saloon crusade. Rogers would again use his bombastic style to battle against the "devil alcohol." He reported on the situation when he arrived in March, 1900. "The curse of Groveton ever since it has been a town has been the liquor traffic. The saloon influence dominated. The churches, all but one, wax[ed] and waned and ultimately shut up their doors and went out of business; the saloon flourished like a 'green bay tree.' Satan and sin, riot and murder in the saloons all held high carnival over the fact that they were monarchs of all in sight."

The good citizens of the community became alarmed at their own lethargy and called for a local option election. *Good Will*, in response to earnest appeals for help, sidetracked right in the center of the town near the depot three days before the election. Rogers would relate, referring to himself, "The rum power had its hired man on hand to defend that side. With faith in God the chapel car missionary entered into the fight." The first night in the courthouse, Rogers thought he was speaking to almost everybody in town. Other speakers came from church and civil organizations to champion the cause. The election came on Saturday and the Prohibitionists won by a majority of thirty-four votes.

A pleased Rogers boasted, "The church much revived and determination to get a pastor and commence keeping house again for the

This church was originally built by the Baptists in Groveton, where G. B. Rogers held services in the chapel car and during his stay participated in an anti-saloon campaign. *Courtesy Groveton Public Library*

Lord. The town of Groveton has been practically redeemed. It is like a new place. Many say the change was brought about by the coming of 'Good Will.'"

Regardless of the influence of *Good Will*'s visit, the years between 1900 and 1902 were still filled with lawlessness. Fighting and killing were common and little was done to rectify the situation. Groveton town leaders tried to reform by passing a dry law, but that only encouraged the bootleggers to move in. In 1902, fires destroyed the wooden stores of the business district. Moody Stone, a staunch prohibitionist, operated a hat store and because he voted against the sale of whiskey, he lost his store in that fire. The outraged upstanding citizens organized the Groveton Law and Order League. Stills were destroyed, and many of the bootleggers were run out of town.[18]

Rogers had the condition of the railroad men at heart. He proclaimed that the "hunting up of the railroad man who has so long been deprived of Sunday and church privileges that the average church worker has ceased to think of him as a subject of gospel address," was the main purpose of the chapel cars.[19]

Thomas Moffett, bequeathed to Rogers by E. G. Townsend, was on board on this trip, but Rogers reported that the arrangement was only temporary. Moffett, Rogers said, was "a most estimable Chris-

tian man and a good, sweet singer of the gospel," but friction between Rogers and "the sweet singer" was beginning to be apparent.
The people at the meetings in Trinity saw in Rogers "a consecrated
man, a discreet and zealous worker for the upbuilding of the Re-
deemer's kingdom, and the tearing down of the strongholds of Satan." There was also praise for Moffett, and many formed strong at-
tachments for Brother Moffett. At Corsicana, next down the line,
great crowds again filled the car, and according to a report, men un-
used to attending church were attending and shedding tears. The
preaching of Rogers and the sweet songs of Moffett were touching
their hearts. The popularity and praise of Moffett could have been
part of the problem that would grow between the two men.[20]

Rogers, at odds with his singer, also had lessons to learn about
American Baptist Publication Society's policies regarding the chapel
cars. He requested that special books and Bibles in quantity be sent
to *Good Will,* but Robert G. Seymour, missionary and Bible secretary for the society, had to caution him to not sell the materials. The
railroads had made it clear that they would not provide free passage
if items were sold from the cars.

Seymour also warned Rogers not to let people other than the
chapel car missionaries travel on the chapel car. Rogers was going to
attend the Southern Baptist Convention at Hot Springs, Arkansas,
and thought it would be nice to take some friends along on *Good
Will.* Seymour wrote, "it is manifestly unjust to the railroads to carry
passengers unless they have a regular railroad ticket for which they
have paid full price. We have to be exceedingly cautious about such
matters. The railroads are very kind to us in carrying the cars and it
would be wrong for us to presume upon their kindness by accommodating those who would otherwise have to pay regular fares." At
times, it appears that Rogers forgot whose name was on the side of
the car and treated *Good Will* like it was "his" church-on-wheels, to
be used according to his rules.[21]

PRAISE, POUNDINGS,
AND PROBLEMS

On the way back from the Little Rock convention, the "golden singer" Moffett had been replaced by "golden singer" Vallie Hart, who had frequently served on the chapel car. Moffett would travel to California to work with the Reverend B. B. Jacques on chapel car *Emmanuel.* For the time being, Rogers seemed happy with his new singer.[1]

They stopped at Wills Point, on the summit between the Sabine and Trinity Rivers, the highest point east of Fort Worth. The *Wills Point Chronicle* reported, "Gospel Car Good Will was side-tracked here this morning and was placed on the Y where services will be held at 4 and 8 o'clock p.m. This car is the property of the American Baptist Publication society and its sole object is the preaching of the gospel. The car is in charge of Rev. G. B. Rogers, who is an excellent preacher. They have a special singer and good music." *Good Will* would have had one visitor who came to the car expressly to listen to the music. W. S. Wilder, a local agent for the Estey Organ Company, which claimed to "Lead the World," may have visited the chapel car to hear the organ that had been given to all the chapel cars by Colonel Estey of Vermont himself.[2]

During Rogers's stay at Wills Point, the scourge of small pox was mobilizing the town. "The city council passed an ordinance to fine every citizen who receives an out-of-town guest without first getting the permission of the mayor." Rogers in his reports did not mention whether he and Vallie Hart were required to be vaccinated in order to hold services but one group of citizens was. As in most towns in the South—regardless of the Thirteenth Amendment, the freeing of the slaves, and the years of reconstruction—the status of the blacks had not changed that much, in fact had worsened as to the hostile

attitudes of most whites. While the car was in Wills Point, the newspaper reported that the town blacks were "all vaccinated by force."
Town officials only requested that the white citizens be vaccinated,
but they forcefully vaccinated the entire black community.[3]

Not only was small pox a problem along the T&P line, but the
week *Good Will* came into town an attempt was made to hold up the
east-bound train at the water tank near Gladewater down the line.
The attempt was unsuccessful because when the fireman, who was
on the ground oiling the engine, was ordered to hold up his hands,
the engineer heard and immediately opened up the throttle and left
the would-be-robbers nursing their disappointment.[4]

There were reports of the Baptist chapel cars being attacked by
eggs and paint in Missouri, almost dynamited in a coal camp in West
Virginia, and struck by lightning in Colorado, and after the building
of three cars for the Catholic Church Extension Society, the Ku
Klux Klan frequently threatened the cars. But there had never been
a report of a chapel car being involved in a train robbery, although
several times it was a close call, and thieves did strike several of the
cars while they were sided in rail yards.[5]

Leaving the clamorous Wills Point yards full of cars being loaded
with oats and hay, Rogers was eager to take the car back to Houston
where he had promised the people in the desolate railroad areas that
he would return to help them. At meetings at Houston's Second
Baptist Church, Hart explained how the gramophone presented to
all the chapel cars by Thomas Edison, along with a choice of twelve
records, had added to the children's services. "We entertain them
with music and recitations from one of Edison's latest improved
gramophones, which is a great treat to both the young and old."[6]

The paper published a letter praising *Good Will*'s meetings.
"Everybody was completely carried off with Brethren Rogers and
Hart. We all rejoiced at their coming and lamented at their depar-
ture." While the paper was lauding the chapel car, Vallie Hart was
praising a special treat provided by the "good Baptist ladies and
ladies of other denominations." They had given a "sure-enough"
pounding—cakes, strawberry preserves, hams, pies, etc. for the
chapel car. For two men living on a chapel car without a woman to
cook for them, the fact that none of the "pounding" gifts needed to
be cooked, just eaten and enjoyed, was a special treat. Frequently at
towns, good-hearted ladies would donate foodstuffs for the missionaries. Rogers, who had to leave the meetings in Wills Point when his

wife in Waco became ill, especially appreciated the bountiful gifts and promised to return in late July for a revival meeting. Perhaps he figured that by that time, the chapel car larder would again be empty.[7]

Robert G. Seymour of the American Baptist Publication Society fired off another cautionary letter to Rogers. In Seymour's absence, the Publication Society had approved Rogers's request to take *Good Will* to Little Rock, Arkansas, to the Southern Baptist Convention. *Good Will* was not the only chapel car at Little Rock, as chapel car *Messenger of Peace* had arrived from Missouri with Dr. and Mrs. Sam Neil on board. This was not a good situation, Seymour explained. He thought they made a mistake in having two cars go to the convention because of the railroads. "Of course, you are not to blame but the railroad companies make a fuss if we go simply to exhibit; so we have to be very cautious when applications come to you to take the car to Associations and things like that, that we do not seem to be exhibitors." In spite of the subtle rebuke, Seymour praised Rogers, "We rejoice in your prosperity."[8]

Just as G. B. had promised, he and Hart returned to Wills Point where they remembered fondly the good meals provided by the Baptist ladies. Some of those same ladies, anticipating the services, would have purchased new finery. They had a wide variety to chose from, including the latest in footwear and fans and 26-inch, steel-framed parasols covered with good material for fifty cents at K. C. Mason Co. Their husbands could buy a new summer suit for $2.50, as the stock would change as the fall season approached. There were good crowds, but the *Wills Point Chronicle* reported that there was not as much interest as hoped, although folks from nearby towns helped fill the car. Since the chapel car had been to Wills Point several times, probably the curiosity had worn thin.[9]

Rogers was not feeling well when the car stopped at Ennis, a town made up of equal parts Mexicans, whose names were on early land surveys; blacks, who began as former slaves; Jews, who owned many of the original businesses; Czech Moravians, who settled in 1874; and French, who came in 1875. The town, booming after the coming of the railroad in 1891, was known for its fine schools rated among the very best in the state. The Baptist church was not in such stellar shape, and animosities toward the general convention caused a bitter split. Rogers probably would have preferred crawling into his cramped berth in *Good Will* or into a comfortable bed in the fine

Bardwell Hotel rather than dealing with another difficult situation. Instead he prepared to preach in a tabernacle made of lumber and canvas with a tin roof, built by the men of the new Baptist church, and the women worked buttonholes in canvas flaps for doors and windows. The meetings lasted for two weeks, and a member of the church praised Rogers as a "logical, tender, sweet-spirited preacher," who understood the Texas situation. Rogers, exhausted, although aided by Hart, looked to a few days rest.[10]

Elgin, the next town, created by the Houston & Texas Central Railroad in 1872, was a short stop of three days. At Victoria, on July 2, the *Daily Advocate* announced the arrival of the chapel car, stating it had come in on the 2:30 train and was sidetracked in the yards at the freight depot. Rogers preached at services on Smith's lot in the fourth ward. The local paper reported that they were drawing large congregations despite one of the heaviest and most continuous rains in past history. The rains caused the revival tent to blow down and people to scurry to the Presbyterian church.[11]

The chapel car came into Summerville at the courtesy of the Gulf, Colorado, and Santa Fe Railroad. Rogers described the town of seven hundred as "churchless, Sunday-schoolless, prayer-meetingless, utterly destitute of every religious influence and force. Think of seven hundred people utterly destitute of all religious privileges and services." When *Good Will* left, the state Board of Missions had made arrangements to send a half-time missionary to the town.[12]

Another matter of serious consequence for Seymour and Rogers was the "shopping" of the chapel car—the search for a repair shop that would do renovation work at a modest price. Rogers, not finding a Texas shop that would take the car, considered taking the car to Mexico, and Society Secretary Seymour told him to use his own judgment but cautioned him to keep the costs low. Rogers was fortunate, or so he and Hart thought at the time, that the Santa Fe shops at Galveston accepted *Good Will* for the needed work. They would revarnish the beautifully crafted Barney & Smith wood panels and seats, repair windows, repaint and revarnish the exterior, do light repair of air brakes and trucks, and freshen gilt lettering on the exterior sides of the car. The lovely stenciled rococo turquoise waves on the pale gold ceiling panels of the living quarters may also have needed retouching.[13]

In the heat of late August, *Good Will* crossed Galveston Bay on the barge for Bolivar Point. Rogers said the car "was taken in charge of that most excellent railroad, the Gulf and Inter-State" and pulled into the depot at Beaumont. According to the *Beaumont Enterprise,* the first service on Sunday, August 24, had a "small but appreciated" audience, and that the missionaries on *Good Will* invited church workers of all denominations to attend. Because of the growing crowds, services continued for two weeks in the town auditorium located in the city park and at the Methodist and Baptist churches. Rogers proclaimed that Beaumont, where he had served as pastor seven years ago, was "one of the best churches in the state." [14]

The Barney & Smith Car Company was not the only supporter of catalpa trees, for in the Beaumont paper, a John P. Brown, secretary of the Indiana Forestry Association, on a trip to the west declared the tree to be "the best all around trees I know of. They are the best for railroad purposes and equal to the pine for lumber." Brown's only complaint was that the tree was difficult to grow, but E. G. Barney was growing them all over Dayton, Ohio. [15]

On September 6, 1900, a Friday, Rogers and Hart returned to Galveston, Hart's home, where they had an appointment to place the car in the Santa Fe shops for the needed repairs. Because of the illness of his wife, Rogers left the renovation of the chapel car in Vallie Hart's care while he traveled home to Waco. He boarded what he later learned was to be "the last train out of Galveston" before the Great Storm. [16]

SHELTER IN THE TIME OF STORM

On September 8 and 9, 1900, Galveston—"a shining palace built upon the sand,"—was struck with what was to be known as the "Great Storm of Galveston," still recorded as the greatest natural disaster in American history.[1]

Good Will had been in Galveston two years earlier. Hollie and E. G. Townsend had worked with the First and Third Baptist churches in Galveston and had gotten to know the Third Baptist Church pastor, Elder G. W. Lane, and his family well. Just in July, a column in the *Standard* praised Lane's work at Third Baptist. "They now have one of the coziest little churches in the city, and though most of the members are poor in this world's goods, they are going right ahead paying for it and don't seem a bit discouraged. Brother Lane for a good many years worked six days in the week in one of the large factories here as foreman of a department, and then preached two sermons on Sunday, getting up Monday morning feeling greatly refreshed. He has just recently given up his position in the factory, and will give the Lord all his time."[2]

At first, no one took the storm seriously—not the Washington Weather Bureau who refused to predict that the storm was headed for Galveston, nor the newspapers which did not report it, nor the families who played among the waves, and not the hundreds who came and watched the "grand" and "beautiful" raging waters. Galveston weatherman Isaac Cline had doubted the accuracy of the Washington forecast. As he anxiously watched the waves and the skies, he began warning the people along the beach and telling them to go home. As the waves crashed and the winds whipped across the island, driving the waters down streets and into homes and businesses, most of the citizens were trapped. They had waited too late to flee to safer ground.[3]

Tennesseean Cline's first assignment for the National Weather Bureau after his training and obtaining his medical degree was at Little Rock, Arkansas. From Little Rock, the Weather Bureau transferred him to a little weather station at Fort Concho, Texas, but to get to Fort Concho, he was to travel by train to Abilene. A Little Rock ticket agent explained to Isaac that Abilene, a boomtown, was too new to be on the railroad map, but the railroad had now reached Sweetwater, some thirty-five miles west of Abilene. Sweetwater was the wild west. Just a few days earlier, a dozen Chinese railroad workers had been gunned down by a group of drunken cowboys. The sheriff arrested the killers and brought them before Sweetwater's brand new judge, who had just opened a saloon. The judge, the infamous Roy Bean, had let the killers go.

Transferred to Abilene in 1886, Isaac could not believe his eyes. "He had entered a territory as alien to him as anything he could have concocted in a daydream." Isaac saw a city where E. G. Townsend on chapel car *Good Will* in 1897 would preach to thousands in the largest tent meetings in West Texas. Around Isaac, joists and beams were going up for new buildings, and "cowboys strolled around in high boots and spurs the size of daffodils, and wore pistols shoved into their waistband." Awaiting his railroad coach to San Angelo and his station at Fort Concho, and unable to find accommodations in the one hotel in town, he obtained a room above a saloon. At the saloon's entrance, Isaac saw a porter mopping up the wooden sidewalk. "That looks like blood," he said. "Yes sir," the porter replied casually without breaking his rhythm, and he explained that four well-off ranchers had gotten into a gun battle, and all had been killed.

Isaac found a friendly group at the First Baptist Church of Abilene, and there he found his wife, the lovely church organist. In March, 1895, Isaac, his wife, and young daughter moved to Galveston; his assignment was to establish the first Texas statewide weather service.

What Isaac saw in Galveston when he first arrived was just the opposite of Abilene. In Galveston, the city boasted beautiful homes and prosperous businesses, but behind the facade—five hundred saloons lined the streets, opium was readily available, and Fat Alley was wide open with prostitution. On September 8, 1900, his view of the city was beyond belief. He did not want to accept the fact that the storm that he had been told by his bosses at Washington, D. C. was not coming to Galveston had come. The tragedies of the following days, September 8 and 9, would be impossible to describe, just branded into the hearts of those who survived.[4]

The storm lasted fifteen hours and the water receded quickly after the wind died down, but it left behind more than 3,660 homes destroyed and as many severely damaged. John Edward Weems, in his book *A Weekend in September,* relates the story of YMCA secretary Judson B. Palmer, who taught Sunday school with Isaac at the First Baptist Church. His family became trapped by water in their home. As the plaster fell in great chunks and rain poured in through the shattered roof, he took his son in his arms and with his wife's arms around his neck, waited until the water began to rise around his feet. He grabbed the shower pipe with his left hand and held his son with his right, as his wife hung on. "I felt the water rise around my body to my neck and to my mouth. Just then, the whole north end of the house fell in; the roof settled on us, and we went down into the water together. I thought, it takes so long to die. I was possible unconscious for a time. Then I had another thought: I wondered what heaven will be like?"[5]

Palmer lost his wife and son. He was caught by the current and thrown onto some driftwood, and for three hours, he lay on top of a floating shed, cast about at the mercy of the storm. "As I drifted," he said later, "these words came to me: 'When thou passeth through the waters I will be with thee.'"[6]

Pastor Lane of Third Baptist Church and his entire family were swept out to sea. The Third Baptist Church still stood, although badly damaged. The fury of the storm destroyed the houses of the Second Baptist Church and also the church at Alta Loma (now Santa Fe). Most of the churches in Galveston were destroyed. I. T. Creek, pastor of Second Baptist, wrote that the few members left had decided to rebuild, "Most of us sleep beneath the waves. Those left are destitute; our church is in splinters, scattered far and wide."[7]

Dr. Harris, pastor of the Galveston's First Baptist Church, described the events as the storm hit. He had secured his family in the parsonage and their cow, old Betsy, was tied to the back porch rail. When the water became so deep around the parsonage that old Betsy was treading water and about to drown, Mrs. Harris brought her into the kitchen. When the tornado traveling ahead of the hurricane came to the church building, the steeples "fell like ten pins with the largest one spinning down and knocking the back upstairs bedroom out of the parsonage." The steeples then fell on both the church's buildings destroying them and almost destroying the parsonage as well. When the steeples fell, it frightened the Harris family so badly they ran into the street but quickly returned due to the danger in being outside. Harris and his family then walked a plank to the safety of their neighbor's home.[8]

R. C. Buckner, the acclaimed head of the Baptist Buckner Home for Children in Dallas, wrote of his experience in the storm for the *Baptist Standard*. Buckner was in Indian Territory when the storm struck and immediately headed toward Galveston knowing that there would be children needing help.

Buckner would relate of his journey on the Galveston, Houston & Henderson (GH&H) train from Indian Territory that at Denison the train experienced great rains, and the cars rocked on the track in the face of the storm. At Dallas, where he checked on his orphanage, there was a terrible downpour. At Houston, he found the First Baptist Church in ruins. He also discovered that no one could travel on to Galveston without a pass. Although the mayor's deputy denied him one, Buckner sent a request to the city attorney and told him why he wanted to go to the storm-devastated city, and he was given permission. On the train with him were General Scurry, going to enforce martial law, and George Dailey, a reporter for the *Dallas News*.

Two trains came into Galveston in the early hours of the storm, and Buckner was on one of them—a GH&H train. It had left Houston earlier in the morning. When it became impossible for the GH&H train to continue because of the rising waters, a relief train was sent, and it slowly made its way through the waters that got so deep they flooded the firebox of the locomotive. The relief train reached "just shy" of the Santa Fe depot in Galveston, "its engine a hulk of cold iron."[9]

The second train, a Gulf & Interstate (G&I), was coming from Beaumont. *Good Will*, after services at Beaumont, had been transferred from the railroad line at Bolivar Point near the great lighthouse just a few days earlier to a barge that carried it to Galveston. Because of the storm, this G&I train could not make connection to the ferry, and the conductor had ordered it back to Beaumont. It never made it back. Some of the passengers left the train and waded through the waves to the Bolivar Point lighthouse, where they took refuge along with others who had crowded in. The train and the passengers who had refused to flee were lost at sea.

When Buckner's train had to stop because of damage to the rails, he and others took passage on a country wagon going to Texas City. After seeing much devastation and suffering through water and mud, he managed to get a skiff to row him the eight miles to shore, although it took thirty-two miles through the high waves, changing positions in the tiny craft to prevent capsizing. Finally arriving at Galveston and climbing over tangled timbers near Twenty-third Street, he saw ruined business houses and people burning bodies. Sidewalks were impassable and the stench was impossible. "The first acquaintance I met was Vallie C. Hart, who had just started on a search for the chapel car. He said: 'If Bro. G. B. Rogers has not left the city he is lost.' Have seen nothing more of Hart; have heard nothing more of Rogers. I hope he is safe." [10]

Buckner struggled through the horror of the city—standing in bread lines along with a poor, half-naked girl and an elegantly dressed lady, and loaning money to several of the destitute. He managed to reach the MK&T depot where he was to pick up a number of orphans who had survived the storm from a matron of the Galveston Orphans Home. Most of these orphans had lost their parents in the storm. All but three of the eighty-three children and the nuns at the St. Mary's Orphanage near the shore had been lost in the storm.

Buckner was able to gather the children and put them into a boat headed to the mainland.

> Before we reached the mainland our boat stranded, and as they began to lower life boats to take us to the shore; there was no little excitement among some of the children. There was one dear 8-year-old especially who had had a terrible experience. She had drifted from a raft from which her mother and several children had been washed and lost; but this child was rescued four hours later floating on a bit of drift alone. Now, as the boat in which our dear orphans were being rowed shoreward, they struck up the song:
>
> > Pull for the shore, sailor,
> > Pull for the shore;
> > Leave that poor old stranded wreck
> > And bend to the oar. [11]

Although *Good Will* escaped major damage in the Galveston storm, this picture shows the chapel car on its side in a flood-damaged area. *Courtesy the American Baptist Historical Society, American Baptist Archives Center*

As the storm raged, *Good Will*, parked in a repair shed at the Santa Fe shops near the depot, was beaten by the gales, although surrounded by a huge engine and sturdy supports.

At the time of the storm, singer Vallie C. Hart was at his home with his family. Hart explained how his home was wrecked and how he and his family only survived by clinging to the roof of a nearby building. The chapel car's household goods, which had been stored in his home for safe keeping, were destroyed, but the chapel car was providentially protected. *Good Will* suffered some damage from the storm, although there are differing accounts as to how much and what kind.[12]

> I have visited the car sheds of the Santa Fe shops, where the car is, and the management has placed the car in the best possible position. The fearful storm demonstrated this. To the east of the chapel car on the track is placed a great engine, which protected the car from the drift in that direction, and the drift from the bay side was caught and held by large posts supporting the shed, and while the debris is piled up all around and inside the

shed, not one plank was hurled against the car. While one portion of the sheds was torn away and wrecked, that portion over
the Chapel Car *Good Will* was not harmed.

Upon my arrival at the sheds I found an old German citizen
looking after the interests of the Santa Fe property, and in-
quired of him about the safety of his family. He told me, between his sobs of grief, how he had struggled all night with wind
and waves trying to save his family, and that he had saved them,
but lost his home and its contents. When I went inside of the
car and played on the organ and sang songs of praise to the
Lord for our deliverance, he came to the window and listened.

I found that the books under the platform [in a drawer] had
not been injured, and I gave this old gentleman a German
Bible as a present from Chapel Car *Good Will.* He was so grateful for it! He said this Bible was the first and only thing he had
to begin life over with except the clothes on the backs of his
loved ones, and he and all his family would appreciate the gift.

The blankets, pillows, and mattresses, and chapel car silver
were all taken to my home for safekeeping when the car was
turned over to the contractor. Brother Rogers, as well as the
contractor, advised this, and all was wrecked with my home.
Since the storm I have found the blankets, pillows, and mattresses, but they are so damaged by wind and water that I do
not think it advisable to try and use them in the car. Later on,
when the debris is cleared, I hope to get the silverware.[13]

Vallie Hart praised God that his family and *Good Will* were
spared, but Isaac Cline lost his wife and his home in the storm. He
was able to find and save his little girl. The hurricane changed Isaac.
He questioned whether he was to blame for the thousands who had
died, and he knew he was responsible for not being able to save his
wife. The winter that followed was a time of soul-searching for him.
On February 10, 1901, Isaac came forward to formally become a
member of the First Baptist Church. At the baptism held in the
YMCA pool, "Y" Secretary Palmer, who had lost all his family, and
a hundred members who also had lost loved ones and homes, were
present to welcome Isaac into the fellowship of the church.[14]

G. B. Rogers would later say of his absence from Galveston during the Great Storm, "I feel humble before the Lord for deliverance
from the terrific storm. Praise the Lord for His goodness and for His
wonderful works to the children of men."[15]

HELPING STORM-TORN TOWNS

Even though Vallie Hart had testified on first glance that an engine and posts of the Santa Fe Railroad shed protected *Good Will*, there was considerable damage and structural problems resulting from the gale's force. Before the storm, workers had already removed the car windows for repair and painting, exposing all the golden oak wood to the fury of the drenching rains. However, the windows near the speaker's platform must not have been broken, as the pulpit Bible was not water-soaked and the organ could still be played. The chapel car would require two months more work before the shops could finish and release the car. Some of this delay would have been because of an overflow of repair work on other damaged Santa Fe cars.

The Publication Society was already in arrears and did not have the money to pay for the shop work. Seymour, of the Publication Society, was very concerned about the situation in Texas, not only concerning the additional funds Rogers said were needed to repair the chapel car, but also about some of the collections Rogers was taking from local churches and Baptist organizations. Rogers and Hart had been at odds for several months, and that situation had worsened after the storm and the situation of the repair of the car.

Hart had written to Seymour about some of his concerns over what Rogers was doing. "You will also see that Valley [*sic*] Hart informs me that it is his duty to resign that car. I am afraid they are out gathering what funds they can instead of pushing car work. It surely needs your hand down there." Seymour sent chapel car superintendent Boston W. Smith to Texas in November, 1900, to investigate the situation and to speak to churches about the work of the chapel cars and the need for funds for *Good Will*'s repairs. Texas Baptists responded by a donation of $535 and a loan to the Publication Society funds to pay the repair bill, and women's groups replaced the items that had been stored and ruined in the destruction of Hart's home.[1] In late November, *Good Will* finally left the Santa Fe shops and continued its mission.[2]

Good Will spent nearly two months in storm-swept South Texas, bringing cheer to places like Richmond, Sealy, Alvin, Alta Loma (now called Santa Fe), Hitchcock, Hillsboro, Brenham, and Houston. On September 12, the wind and rain had devastated Houston; many homes were destroyed, as well as the Baptist and Methodist churches.[3]

Rogers and the newly refurbished chapel car arrived in Brenham on a southbound Santa Fe freight to hold revival services at the same time Texas Governor Sayers was announcing his intention of sending a message to the Legislature concerning the matter of relief for the districts swept by the storm.

Rogers was ill with "the grip," according to the *Brenham Banner,* and services in *Good Will,* sided between the Santa Fe freight and passenger depots, were cancelled for several days as many in the community were also afflicted. The chapel car was also suffering— from a problem in the obstinate Baker heating apparatus—and after leaving town, singer Vallie Hart was to return *Good Will* to a repair shop, this time at Houston. Brenham itself was suffering—not only the aftermath of the Great Storm but the inclement backlash of a Colorado storm that left streets impassable and work being done on damaged buildings impossible.[4]

B. F. Riley wrote of Brenham, "Houses are demolished and the streets are barricaded with beams, bricks and stones, trees, telegraph poles and wires. Among the wrecked buildings is the Baptist church. The steeple in falling carried away the whole south end of the building. The remainder is practically useless for service. Other churches, among them one of the Methodist, were practically destroyed."[5]

At Weimar after the storm, T. E. Muse pleaded the cause of small and poor churches. "As to the ability of the wealthier churches in the cities of Galveston and Houston to rebuild their church houses we cannot speak. It is no question however, that the feebler churches of the city, and especially of the storm-stricken country the people inhabiting the stricken country are largely new settlers, and were in limited circumstances before the storm; they are now in a most pitiful condition, not only property ruined, but their crops are a failure."[6]

Six months later, by newspaper accounts, it appeared that life in Weimar was returning to normal from the storm's effects. While *Good Will* was in town, the SA&AP pay wagon had come in and the railroad men were fixed for the next thirty days. A mask ball was given at the Grohsinn Hall, the farmers were bragging over giant eight- and nine-pound turnips, and local boys were getting into trouble jumping beneath moving rail cars, catching on to the rods and traveling some distance before swinging out.

Rogers and Hart received good newspaper coverage, with a reporter commenting, "The church on wheels is a novel one, and proved a strong magnet in attracting people to the services, which were ably conducted and enjoyed by all who attended same." After the car left, an item appeared in the newspaper inviting the children who had attended the chapel car services to call on T. E. Muse and pick up the Bibles Rogers had promised them.[7]

Because the first skirmish of the Texas Revolution was fought there, Gonzales was one of the most hallowed towns in Texas history. By the turn of the century, the town had become quite a business center. In spite of increasing prosperity, religious leaders were complaining about the "godless" Bohemians in the area. The 1900 census listed 318 foreign-born Czechs in Gonzales who listed Moravia or Austria as their place of origin, although a town history relates that "calling a Czech a Bohemian was like calling a Texan a Yankee."[8]

Bohemia, a central Europe country bounded on the south by Austria, on the west by Bavaria, on the north by Saxony and Lusatia, and on the east by Silesia and Moravia, was populated mainly by Czechs and Germans. For centuries Bohemia was a bloody battleground of Protestant reform. Under the leadership of such men as Jerome of Prague, John Huss, and Ziska, the Bohemians fought their good fight and lost, and Catholicism was forcibly imposed upon the country. Not only had the descendants of these earlier Bohemians become hostile to the Catholic faith, but also as a result of the bitter wars, many developed a non-religious tendency that resulted in active unbelief and hostility to all religious influence. Not only were the so-called Bohemians known for their "riotist" lifestyle in Texas towns, but, as a further insult to the traditional Protestant groups, they frequently established atheistic Sunday schools.[9]

The Galveston paper reported February 7 that *Good Will* had been at Gonzales "in charge of Rev. G. B. Rodgers [*sic*], assisted by Mr. Hart, who presides at the organ. Several religious services have

G. B. Rogers decided to extend *Good Will*'s stay at Gonzales because of "a cry of spiritual dearth among the people." Five thousand bottles of beer and eight hundred gallons of whiskey accumulated during four years was poured into the street in front of the Gonzales jail during a prohibition campaign. *Courtesy Gonzales Public Library*

been given in the car and the chapel is quite popular." According to Rogers, "There was such a universal cry of such spiritual dearth among the church members" that they decided to extend their visit, although bad weather threatened the services. The pastor reported, "A better feeling obtains among the brethren at Gonzales because of this [chapel car] visit." [10]

The relaxed, although wet, tone of Rogers's meetings was decidedly different from when the Reverend Z. N. Morrell, the famous Baptist circuit rider, organized the Gonzales church in 1834. During one of his early sermons, Indians stole his horse and scalped a man nearby. As a result, Morrell's meetings became armed gatherings. Another night, the assembly heard "a shrill Indian whistle" and some shots, and the next morning one of the citizens who had refused to come to the meetings was found scalped near the church. [11]

The good ladies of Gonzales treated Rogers and Hart to another first class donation party, or "pounding," leaving their stomachs saturated and satisfied. If the ladies had ventured into the living quarters of the chapel car, they may have been shocked. With just men living on the car, cleanliness would not have been the priority. The washroom and kitchen area, with the odor of dirty laundry and scraps of food, would not pass the good ladies' inspection. Frequently in other towns, women would band together to tidy the chapel cars and wash and replace the linens.[12]

On the next day after the chapel car left the yards, a Southern Pacific switchman was run over by a freight engine and a string of laden freight cars and was fatally injured. The newspaper reported that the single forty-three-year-old had no relatives in Texas, but his comrades spoke of him as a sober, industrious, and most companionable man. Many of the railroad men the chapel car served risked their lives daily, especially the switchmen.[13]

When Rogers and Hart, along with Hart's wife, came into Richmond, they saw a town rebuilding after the storm and a church that needed a friend. Mrs. Hart had joined the car after its visit to the shops of the GH&SA. The Hart home had been destroyed in the Galveston Storm along with the household goods of the chapel car, and she and her husband and son had barely escaped with their lives. It is not clear why she joined the *Good Will* team, as it had just been four months since her home was destroyed. Maybe their home was being repaired and she had no place else to go. Regardless of the reason, Mrs. Hart's presence would have added to the impact of *Good Will*'s visit. She had suffered as a result of the storm, and as a woman and mother, she could relate especially to the women and children of the town.

After the storm of September 8 and 9, the *Galveston Daily News* reported, "The Richmond which existed one week ago has been wiped very nearly out of existence. That the loss of life was small is a mystery." The miracle was that only three lives were lost, these in the black community—a man, wife, and child who were killed by their Baptist church falling on them. They had quit their home and had run to the church for safety. The white Baptist church, built in 1889, was entirely destroyed. The *Daily News* described, "It seems as if it had been picked up by the terrific tornado and then literally shaken to pieces." The Methodist church lost half its roof and most of its windows, while the Episcopal church, with the exception of its belfry, escaped serious damage.

Businesses like Myers & Co. dry goods, McFarlane's feed store, Beasley's drug store, and Coaster's bookstore were chipped away and battered, almost beyond repair. Even George Reading's saloon did not escape the devastation.[14]

James Ross, a black farmer at Crabb, just outside Richmond, recalled the storm with a ballad he learned from an evangelist called "Sin-Killer," present in Galveston during the storm.

> It was on a September evening
> That the storm struck our town.
> How the mighty buildings crumbled
> And fell upon the ground.
> It was on a September evening
> That the storm struck our town.
> It seemed that God in heaven
> Looked upon us with a frown.
>
> There was an engineer and fireman,
> Both was pluckin' brave.
> Who thought about his wife and child
> While lives he tried to save.
> They said, Jack, the tide is rising
> And we must go across
> So they brought the train to the Island side
> But the fireman, he got lost.
>
> On that September evening
> The wind was raging wild
> I saw a woman clinging
> To her husband and her child.
> The man he battled faithful
> Their lives he tried to save
> But they sank beneath the rolling wave
> And filled the watery grave.

It was said that Ross's rich tenor voice shouted and chanted the verses, and the Pilgrim Baptist Church choir followed with the chorus:

> Wasn't it a sad time
> When de storm struck our town.
> Wasn't it a sad time
> When the storm struck our town.[15]

The remnant band of the Baptist church was "completely discouraged," but Rogers, Vallie, and Vallie's wife came into town, held services, visited, and prayed with the congregation. The members began to rebuild, as they could not accept their town without their church. The pastor thought he would have to seek a ministry somewhere else to support his family but stayed on because, despite their own losses, the members collected $400 for his annual salary.[16]

Leaving Richmond, *Good Will* headed to Sealy, on the uppermost edge of the Gulf prairie, another storm-tossed town. Before the GC&SF and the Katy reached Sealy, only two farmers lived there, not including the prairie chickens. With the coming of the railroad, the town increased to around fourteen hundred at the turn of the century, and many businesses served the needs of the rail workers, ranchers, farmers, and others who had come as a result of the boom. The school had more than two hundred students, and a town history notes, "The Word of God is taught in six churches for Whites and in several others for Negroes."[17]

Then the boom turned when the railroad decided to move its shops to neighboring Bellville. Churches in town had already seen the effects of the shops' move, and many of the families of St. John's Episcopal Church had already followed the shops to Bellville. The Baptist church was pastorless and the congregation discouraged.[18]

The storm only intensified the town's dark mood. I. B. Sigler wrote of his recollection during this period. For a time despair gripped the people. As a result of the storm damage, "many of the railroaders left and many of their humble homes fell into decay. Many were sold for a song." Some left the little town with its pleasant memories, while others stayed on to hope for better days. The Presley Ward family, leaders of the Baptist church, stayed but decided not to repair the damaged look-out tower on their 1893 ten-room "show place," just thankful that the English-imported bay window shutters or the front door with its colored glass and hand carvings had escaped damage.[19]

Among the people who poured into the chapel car, there would have been many who wept at the horrific memories of the weeks past. The sight of the art glass motto "God Is Love" above the platform, the golden oak pews, the brass lectern with its pulpit Bible, the sound of the Estey organ, and Vallie Hart's beautiful voice would have been both calm yet bittersweet, leaving them wondering if they would ever get to worship in a church of their own again. Several citizens were baptized during the chapel car services, including young Brother Wilson, the telegraph operator of the MK&T Railway. Rogers reported, "The outlook seemed very gloomy, but the chapel car left the small band in a hopeful state." By the end of 1901, Sealy as it once was had ended.

Rosenberg, named after Henry Rosenberg, first president of the GH&SA Railroad, was just a few stations away on the MK&T from Sealy. In 1881 Italian Count Joseph Telfener made Rosenberg his headquarters to begin work on his New York, Texas, and Mexican Railway. The line became known as the "Macaroni Line" because of the food preferences of the Italians who laid the tracks. The Southern Pacific bought the "Macaroni Line" in 1885, and a large Union shop served freight and passenger needs and handled the shipping of thousands of cotton bales and cattle. The town grew as German, Czech, Polish, and Mexican families swelled the population to nearly one thousand.[20]

Methodists and Baptists boasted houses of worship before 1900. Then came the Great Storm. Rogers reported that the churches of Rosenberg were badly damaged, and the First Baptist Church's building under construction was destroyed. *Good Will,* sided near the depot, became the temporary house of worship for many of the town's discouraged citizens who had stayed in the aftermath of the storm. Rogers wrote, "At Rosenberg, so little was left of homes that they were "pressed to live at all."

While *Good Will* was at Rosenberg, according to Rogers, the Baptist church doubled in membership with some of the "best people in the town" joining. Night after night for two weeks, storm-worn townspeople came to the chapel car. Outside in the streets and saloons, people could see the oil lamps through the windows and hear the strains of the Estey organ and people singing the familiar hymns as they rose in the cool air of a Texas night.[21]

Seymour, of the American Baptist Publication Society, reported, "Nearly all of our Baptist churches were demolished in that afflicted area, and the people were discouraged, and perhaps would not have started up church work again soon if the [chapel] car had not rolled in town and begun meetings. As it is now, they have been stimulated to new life."[22]

On March 9 in a former chapel car town miles away from the storm-tossed coast, the pastor of the Baptist church at Wills Point, where *Good Will* had served just a few weeks before, lost two of his children and all of his household goods in another storm. Brother J. H. Clouse's two children—Maggie, a sweet six-year-old girl, and an infant nearly three months old—were killed in the storm.

The pastor was bruised, and one of his little boys had his arm and leg broken, but his wife was not hurt seriously. Four others were killed in the storm, one drowned near the town, and several were seriously hurt.[23]

In Alvin every church was destroyed by the Galveston Storm. The Baptist pastor pleaded, "Our church house is wrecked and our people too poor to even rebuild their own homes without help. I see no prospect of salary from my field, but I must stay. We must have help to rebuild our house of worship. . . . Who will help us?" Others at the Alvin church wrote, "We are in the midst of death and destruction caused by the hurricane of Saturday night, September 8. Many are homeless and destitute. Some will die from injuries received. Last Sunday night was spent in burying the death." Someone did help the Alvin Baptists, in their own town. A town history records that the congregation of the Jewish synagogue across the street opened up its doors to the homeless Baptists until repairs could be made on their church.[24]

While *Good Will* was at Alvin, Marion Weaver, an orphan who had been rescued from the Galveston storm by Rev. Buckner, wrote about her experiences. She told of being in a room with other orphans and storm survivors when the wind blew a door in and the water rushed in. "We did not know what to do. So the yardman took two or three children and threw them into the yard. He was going to throw all of them into the yard, but he was ordered to stop. One of the children returned wet from head to toe. The other three went into a house next door. One of the little boys went under the water twice, and would have drowned had not a man caught him and brought him next door. Just think! While we were being mercifully saved thousands were being drowned and killed by falling buildings."[25]

Alta Loma, now called Santa Fe, a town on the GC&SF Railway, was rich in pears, figs, and oranges. Established in 1883, it was not until 1894 that the first wave of settlers came and discovered artesian wells that would provide nearby Galveston with 6 million gallons of drinking water daily. The Baptist church in town claimed to be the second oldest church built on the Galveston mainland. One of the charter members of the church was the wife of William Skirvin, who had led the first party of settlers from their homes in the north hoping to profit in the growing of fruit in the rich soil. The townspeople welcomed *Good Will*, and the services provided a bright note in the community where all the churches were badly damaged or lost.[26]

Rogers reported that there was "great spiritual power" in the meetings at Yoakum, which seems to have been one of the towns not damaged greatly by the storm. He would be more aware of the number of Mexicans working at the shops, although few would attend the chapel car services. A picture of the shops in 1903 shows men working dressed in Mexican clothing as many Mexicans were arriving to do the distributing of supplies and other railroad work. The town and the shops had grown since E. G. Townsend visited in 1898.[27]

It was at Yoakum that Vallie Hart decided to leave the chapel car to go into business. For quite a while there had been tension between Rogers and Hart, especially after the period of the Galveston storm. Records do not indicate exactly what the problem was, but Hart's new position would pay more than the chapel car stipend and be less stressful, and he would also have more time to spend with his family.[28]

The little town of Sweet Home had moved from its original site five miles from the tracks of the SA&AP Railway to a new plat along the route. Rogers, who needed a positive experience, wrote of the new community, "It is more homelike here, I think, than anywhere I have ever been, except my own dear home with my loved ones." From Sweet Home, Rogers left for Waco to rest at home and prepare for his Mexican border trip.[29]

SOUTH TEXAS TO
THE PANHANDLE

The Laredo Baptists pleaded for *Good Will* to come back to "this wicked Border city," and Rogers returned in the summer of 1901. The congregation had been growing since the Stuckers' visit in 1896, and they desperately wanted a church building. "Our house is the tail-end of everything in the way of church buildings. The other churches have handsome brick edifices. Ours is a little frame house, notable in keeping with the general appearances of the city." If they could build a new church—one of brick, of modern design, which would cost nearly $6,000—they wanted to give the old building to the Mexican church, which had none.[1]

Although many would come to see the chapel car or visit with Rogers in the living quarters, the revival services were held in a brush arbor built by the town leaders that would seat several hundred. The *Laredo Daily Times* reported that "there was a large audience in attendance at the revival services last night. The meeting is growing in interest, and there is every token of a wide-spread revival." The next day, the reporter described the services under the tabernacle as "very delightful."[2]

One night the text was "What shall I do with Jesus who is called Christ?" Those present heard their positions in life paralleled to that of Pilate. "Many a man in office today who will not do what he knows to be right because he is afraid he will displease the lawless rabble and they might combine and vote him out of office. Many a man today will not become a Christian because he is afraid it might hurt his business, or he might have to give up an iniquitous business. Many a young woman will not become a Christian because she would have to give up a worldly, frivolous life. Many a young man can not give up his love for the cup, or the gaming table or some other sin."[3]

As Rogers was without a "golden singer," his daughter, who had helped him before with the music, and her friend May Foster took time out for a sightseeing visit to New Laredo across the border. The *Times* commented about their tour, "There is much that is novel and of interest in our sister city across the border, to the visitor from other states, and their day will doubtless prove profitable as well as enjoyable." Perhaps the reporter was not aware that Rogers and the girls were Texans.[4]

A "splendid congregation" attended the Saturday meeting, where at first a "delightful breeze swept through the place," the *Times* reported, "and all things considered, it was good to be there." Then the weather changed, and Rogers, who had preached his sermon to the end, noticed the evidences of an approaching storm. The service was dismissed, and when the congregation was not more than three blocks away, and Rogers and the two girls were headed to the safety of *Good Will*, they heard the tabernacle fall.

Early Sunday morning, men in working clothes with nails and hammers proceeded to build up the tabernacle again, and it was ready for the eleven o'clock service. In his remarks Sunday, Rogers praised, "We have surmounted an obstacle and intend to go right on, giving God the best service that we know how." The reporter— who had been captured by Rogers's sermon on Hosea 4:17, "Ephraim is joined to his idols; let him alone," and Rogers's text, "Let me alone,"—editorialized, "There are men and women distributed throughout our town who should have heard the sermon."[5]

Alongside the newspaper columns of Rogers's complete sermon texts ran ads from local brewers who would have been aware of the chapel car's presence in town. Charles Moser boasted that he sold more beer than any other saloon in Laredo because he was honest and did not sell straight from the kegs and scalded his pipes every day. Moser declared, "I haven't more whiskey than all of the saloons in Laredo put together, but what little I have is the best goods in Laredo." Billie's Saloon described "mint juleps, milk punches, and all mixed drinks served with special care," and Sulnon's Saloon advertised W. W. W. whiskey, the genuine, at $1.25 a quart. Not to be outdone, Billie countered that he sold the same brand at $1.00 a quart. For the discriminating who did not want to quibble over costs, there was always the Hamilton Hotel Bar, with its liquors, bottled beer, and cigars.[6]

Pastor Marshall said, "Great odds were against the meeting. The devil rallied his forces but God gave us success." When Rogers wrote of the Laredo experience, he said that the fine edifice going up was in the Romanesque Revival style, and the presence of the chapel car received the thanksgiving of the people.[7]

While Rogers preached on heavenly themes, a sidebar in the paper reported an earthly event—another gusher had come in at Beaumont down the border, and the reporter predicted that "the production of oil by the wells there would probably be greater than those of the balance of the world." Texas Baptists were not missing out on this bonanza as ads were run in the *Baptist Standard* offering stock at ten cents a share in their tract on Spindletop.[8]

On July 15, Rogers and his new singer W. C. Garrett left for Cotulla. In the center of the ranching country northwest of Laredo, Cotulla had, along with most Texas towns the chapel car had visited, the reputation of a rough place in its early days. According to local legend, railroad conductors announced the town by calling out, "Cotulla! Everybody get your guns ready." Three sheriffs and nineteen residents were said to have lost their lives in gunfights in the town, but the balance of power was changing. When *Good Will* was pulled into the station, the two churches in town outnumbered the one remaining saloon.

Members of the Baptist church built a brush arbor, similar to the one at Laredo, a mile from town on the Nueces River and sufficient to accommodate several hundred people. The pastor of the Cotulla church advertised, "All the adjoining churches are invited to cooperate in the meeting. Provisions can be procured on the ground. We ought to have 50 campers from Laredo, Cotulla, Pearsall, Carrizo Springs, and other towns and stock ranches." No doubt the folks from the Methodist church, the other church in town, helped fill the chapel car.[9]

People did attend—from Austin, San Antonio, Laredo, Eagle Pass, as well as many other smaller places on the I&GN Railroad. Ranch men were in attendance with their families, some coming from their ranches as far away as 50 miles. Rogers, pleased and surprised at their attendance, said, "I really believe I have discovered the secret of how to reach the stock men. Hold camp meetings, camp with them; they take hold and nobly help to support the meeting, bring their families and as a matter of course, stay with them and attend the services; in this way they hear the gospel and are as easily reached and saved when they hear as any one else." One group did not attend the brush arbor meetings. In the chapel car, Brother Hernandez preached in Spanish for the Mexicans of the area, while the brush tabernacle meeting was proceeding in English.[10]

At Hallettsville, Rogers helped the pastor with a protracted meeting in the predominately German/Czech town, and he does not mention the disruptions of the so-called "Bohemians." The *Hallettsville Herald* reported that Rogers and Garrett had been holding a most interesting meeting; interest was unabated, and the congregations very large. Special appreciation was shown for the singing of Garrett. The article described *Good Will* as "splendidly arranged for the use to which it is put."[11]

The *Hallettsville Herald* had taken a potshot at the rowdy reputation of the neighboring town of Yoakum during the time Rogers and Garrett were in town. An insulted Yoakum resident responded in a letter to the editor, "We are not such a God forsaken place as you be led to believe, if you read our local dailies. True we have a fortune teller, some bad boys, gambling houses and 'other resorts,' But we are not an exception to the rule. We will wager a years subscription to the *Hallettsville Herald* that we have as few of the aforesaid evils in our town as any town of our size in the state."[12]

The railroad chapel car program was still the main focus of the Publication Society although auto chapel cars, now more readily available and cheaper than railroad chapel cars, were being put into service in other states. In 1900 the American Baptist Publication Society built their sixth rail chapel car, *Herald of Hope,* serving in Lower Michigan. *Herald of Hope* would be the last wooden car built by the Barney & Smith Car Company. Most railroad manufacturers had gone to steel cars, as it was becoming more difficult to bring the wooden cars up to railroad safety regulations. With the additional chapel car came more financial burdens. Seymour wrote Rogers and, instead of pointing out some infraction of policy as was usually Rogers's due, agreed to raise his salary to $150 a month or $1,800 a year. Rogers was to pay his singers out of his own funds, and he was to have one on the car most of the time. One of the reasons for this decision could have been that Rogers had continuing problems getting along with the helpers who were assigned to the car. The chapel car missionaries received anywhere from $1,200 to $1,800 yearly for their services according to training, experience, and seniority. This increase would help Rogers support his large family.[13]

Six years after *Good Will* first entered XIT Ranch lands, the chapel car returned to the Panhandle. When Edwin and Nettie Stucker stopped in Dalhart in 1895, it was called Twist Junction—mainly a cattle loading station with just a few houses. By 1901 Dalhart had become a prominent station with a new depot and a growing community surpassing Channing to the south.

On August 25, 1901, *Good Will* stood on a sidetrack in the recently assembled railroad yards. Rogers reported that he and Garrett arrived in Dalhart to look after Baptist interests in this new town that "had sprung up as if by magic in this far away Panhandle country." He was told that there were about two hundred men at work there on the new Chicago, Rock Island, and Mexican railroad. The town was only two or three months old and he reported, "everything seems to bid fair to roll up several thousands in a year of two. There is no church here of any sort—no regular preaching at all."

A group of eleven people assembled in the car, and after much discussion and a sermon, the First Baptist Church of Dalhart was organized. At first, services were held in the Little Red School House at 700 Conley Avenue until a larger school building was completed, a one-room frame structure at the corner of Fifth and Rock Island streets, occupied on November 4, 1901.[14]

Rogers had been told that Dalhart was prohibition county and wrote, "for once let it be said that the Baptists have beat the saloon and the Methodists to a new town." He may have been misinformed, for according to Lillie Mae Hunter, in June, 1901, the Reverend W. B. McKeown came to Dalhart and spent the night. "There was quite a rough crowd in town, and many had gathered at the whiskey store. Quite a number got drunk and gave a rough time most of the night." The hotel where McKeown stopped was disturbed during the night when seven men were knocked down and robbed. Next day, Sunday, he organized the Methodist Church (South) with seven members. Like the fledgling Baptist group at Texline, perhaps the seven Methodists were not able to survive their union, as town records indicate that the newly formed Baptist church was the first church of any denomination to make its appearance in Dalhart.[15]

Relations between the Methodists and the Baptists were sometimes bitter, generally on the matter of baptism and whether the scriptures decreed immersion or sprinkling. Some Methodists accused the Baptists of producing a new version of the Bible in which the Greek word "baptidzo" was translated to mean immerse only. In many towns, though, there was cooperation between the two denominations. The missionary societies joined for bake sales for civil improvement, and in 1903 the Baptists would donate the greatest amount of money in town toward the building of the Methodist church.[16]

In just a few months, Dalhart's newly formed Baptist church had become an active participant in town life, with the Baptist ladies offering a "Sock Social" with admission based on the size of a person's sock multiplied by three—a novel idea to say the least. For those of a more genteel inclination, there was no dearth of cultural activities in Dalhart. Evening entertainment included an instrumental trio, a recitation, vocal solo, male quartette, and piano and mandolin duet, and cowboys from Stratford, Channing, Texline, and other nearby towns were excited about a ball to be given by the young men of Dalhart in the school auditorium.[17]

As the crowds at the depot waved goodbye to Rogers and Garrett standing on the chapel car platform, and as the train pulled away from the town site, the landscape began to change. The two men could see that some things did not change in this land of the Panhandle—the windmills still dominated the barren landscape dotted by cattle. The Russian Thistle still skipped before the wind, bounding across gullies, and shaking out families and belongings at little settlements along the lines. Only now the tumbleweed was stopped by the growing presence of barbed wire.

Rogers probably thought of the journey past. Almost one thousand miles from Laredo to Dalhart—a passing panorama of landscape, culture, and history. How many more miles would *Good Will* trail behind Texas engines, bearing its message of hope?

TROUBLED TOWNS,
A WEARY ROGERS

When the Reverend Buckner of the Buckner Orphans' Home rushed to help the orphans of Galveston during the Great Storm, he probably never considered that his own orphans in Dallas would be in a similar danger. On September 11, 1901, one year after the Great Storm, a cyclone hit the home and centered on the barn, three hundred yards from the main building. About twenty boys, who had gathered at the barn after the day's work, saw the storm approaching and ran to the main building, but two remained on duty in the barn. The iron-roofed, 60 x 100 feet building was lifted from its rock foundations twice some feet into the air and crushed into kindling wood. John Long, an eleven-year-old, was killed outright, while Walter Jones, about the same age, was caught by falling timbers as he made his escape and received severe injuries. Many of the horses were injured, crops needed for the use and profit of the orphanage were damaged, and timber that had been stored for building projects was rendered unusable.

Buckner told of the children's reaction to the storm. "At the main building the children excitedly gathered in groups in the halls and corridors. Especially alarmed were those who had been saved from the Galveston storm last September." [1]

Delayed repercussions from the Galveston storm, although not so severe, appeared in a memo to Rogers from the Publication Society. Much to the chagrin of Seymour, *Good Will* seemed to need more shop work to repair storm damages. His letter reflects his frustration. "What is the matter with car? I supposed it was all right, so much has been put on it, fixed on it, it must be in A-1 condition. I am surprised anything is wrong. I suppose you will have it fixed right." Seymour cautioned Rogers, "Kindly secure from the Cotton

Belt people and others if possible an estimate of the expense of putting the car in the best possible condition and let us know what the cost would be. It seems too bad that we have had to spend so much money for so little results, but we shall have to make the best of the situation." [2]

Another Seymour letter a week later was of a different kind of problem—the issue of Vallie Hart's leaving the chapel car. Seymour tried to explain to a disgruntled writer that Vallie C. Hart left *Good Will* through his own resignation. Seymour replied that Hart was on the car with Rogers, and "they did not seem to agree very well and as the Car was put in the charge of Mr. Rogers we could not very well remove him upon a disagreement." Seymour stressed that they were very much pleased with Hart and his work and should have been happy to have him continue on *Good Will* if it had been possible. "We know about his gifts, his power of song and everything of a high order. We hold him in high esteem. The Society is endeavoring to hold its own in the State of Texas with all its work and trying to do the best we can under all circumstances." [3]

While Seymour was fretting over the expense of keeping *Good Will* in service, in the Panhandle at Channing, down the line from bustling Dalhart, the little congregation still without a church since Stucker's visit in 1895 had received help from some affluent Baptist laymen. At their Fifth Sunday meeting, W. B. Slaughter, son of George Webb Slaughter of the notable Slaughter Ranch, along with Deacon Oakes, a successful Channing businessman, made possible the publication of a paper to serve the church members and to advertise the meetings of the struggling organization.

Returning to Marshall, a frequent chapel car town, Rogers welcomed the men in the huge T&P shops into the chapel car. Many of the men had done repair work earlier on *Good Will* and had listened to Stucker and Townsend, so they were eager to visit in "their railroad church car" and hear the new preacher "preach." Rogers took the car by the switch engine to the shops each day at noon for forty-minute meetings with the men after they finished eating their lunch. He reported, "They crowded the car and listened eagerly to the word of the gospel."

After the noon services, E. W. Campbell, the division superintendent of the railway, had the car drawn back to the station where Rogers and his new singer, Hugh Hiett, held children's meetings in the afternoon and a public meeting at night. Rogers praised the co-

Shop railroad workers attended services in the chapel car at noon and midnight and took pride in repairing the car. *Courtesy the American Baptist Historical Society, American Baptist Archives Center*

operation of the T&P officers. "I must also make mention of extraordinary help rendered by Superintendent E. W. Campbell. He is a fine Christian character, and has an abiding interest in the spiritual welfare of the 600 men in the shops in Marshall." [4]

From Marshall, the chapel car headed to Fort Worth for the annual meeting of the Texas Baptist General Convention. It had not been quite three years since Hollie Harper Townsend's death, but she had not been forgotten. J. B. Cranfill, president of the convention, paid tribute to her memory. After seeing Gale Harper Townsend, the little son of Hollie and E. G., at the sessions, Cranfill spoke to those assembled, "On the day these thoughts are written down I saw the little boy for whom Hollie Harper Townsend gave her life, come into the house of God. He is not yet three years old. How like his mother is that sweet baby face! As he sat to-day and was so still as the strong preacher told of God and things divine, I prayed that his devoted mother would live again in him." [5]

Although some of the damaged belongings on *Good Will* had been replaced after the Galveston Storm, with no women on board, the decor and furnishings were in need of help. During the convention, a group of Baptist ladies came to the rescue and asked to clean and refurnish the car, and they were praised for their efforts. Mabel Cranfill thanked the women in the *Baptist Standard,* "A year ago you pledged yourselves to refit the chapel car Good Will. Right nobly and promptly did you redeem your pledge, and so you cheered the heart of the noble, consecrated man who has carried the gospel in this church on wheels into many destitute places."[6]

Leaving Fort Worth, Rogers returned to Lufkin, a sizeable timber center south of Nacogdoches with also a legendary "rough and tumble" reputation. Conductors on the HE&WT Railroad were said to admonish passengers to remain on the train when it stopped at the depot, and one conductor called out the stop with a warming, "Next stop, Lufkin . . . prepare to meet thy God." Whether the warning was in jest or serious, in fact, when the trains arrived, citizens often drifted to the depot to pick fights with passengers who dared to comment on the town's rough exterior.[7] Things in town were probably not as wild as rumored, as the First Baptist Church had more than a hundred members who had been meeting two Sundays a month and had expanded to every Sunday preaching.

Rogers, just like Edwin Stucker and E. G. Townsend, had long been concerned about the churches in East Texas leaving the Baptist General Convention. So at Carthage, located on the Texas, Sabine Valley, and Northwestern Railway just a few miles from the Louisiana border, he was pleased when crowds overflowed the chapel car and, by invitation, they met in the Opera House, the largest hall in town.

For many years, there had been an active Baptist church in Carthage, but, as Rogers explained, "In the last two or three years the downgrade has been rapid and disastrous." From preaching four Sundays in the month, the church had gone down to one Sunday a month. Because of a disagreement between two factions of the fading church, the "missionary" group withdrew from the increasing "hardshell" old church to form a new church. The new church, called Central Baptist, wanted to channel their missionary funds into the recently organized Missionary Baptist Association, loyal to the Baptist General Convention of Texas. "We found a united band of 22 workers who welcomed us and declared the Lord had sent us." Rogers added that the singing was fine, the membership doubled, a building lot found, and $1,100 secured toward the $3,000 needed to put up a new church.[8]

Back down the line from Carthage on March 8, 1903, the chapel car returned to the little town of Tenaha on the HE&WT Railway. The station agent had learned a few hours in advance that the car was coming, but it was nearly night when the rail crew sidetracked *Good Will*. A weary Rogers wrote, "We scarcely had time to light the lamps and did not have time to eat supper when the people began to pour into the chapel, and soon it was comfortably filled." The car was no stranger in Tenaha, though the missionaries in charge were. Five years before, E. G. and Hollie Townsend had held a great revival there.

In spite of the good response to the Townsends, Rogers mentioned the growing discontent of some at Tenaha who opposed the Baptist General Convention work. "It is true that there were some who never overcame their prejudices and never attended the meetings, and necessarily got no blessing out of it. Some attended with a view to find fault, and of course found their bone and went away and gnawed it and growled, and got no good out of it for their poor, starving souls." Rogers baptized nineteen in a creek in Brother J. R. Moore's pasture in the presence of about five hundred people. He challenged the crowd to contribute funds toward the church's debt, and before the meeting was over, the debt was resolved.

Not only was the financial condition of the congregation improved, but in the midst of overflowing crowds, "good members who had been cool toward each other on account of state issues, had their hearts melted, their troubles settled, and became as brothers should be toward each other."[9]

South of Tenaha, Timpson awaited the return visit of *Good Will*, but on the first night of the scheduled mission, the rains came and caused them to cancel the services. Rogers commented on Hiett's talent and character. "He finds consecrated men and women everywhere we go to help him in the service of song. He is at home at the organ and when singing his delightful solos." The Timpson people, who were so receptive to Hollie and E. G., remembered Rogers and Hiett by presenting each of them with a gold watch and chain.[10]

Rogers, in what seemed to be a recurring pattern, chafed at American Baptist Publication Society policies. Seymour chastised him on two issues. Rogers sent the society a bill to have his personal laundry done, and his boss responded, "We never pay any laundry for anybody. That is a part of personal expense which . . . everybody has and which comes out of their own private funds." The second issue was that although Rogers had been given permission to take up donations on the chapel car, he was not permitted to sell materials— like tracts and Bibles. Railroad officials had written to protest Rogers's disregard for this rule. Seymour sternly said that he hoped the railroad matter would be speedily adjusted.[11]

The Cotton Belt Railroad was not able to work *Good Will* into their shops as Seymour had hoped, so Rogers made arrangements to take the car to the Mexican International Railroad at Ciudad Porfiro Diaz, Mexico, across the border from Eagle Pass. On the way to Eagle Pass, Rogers stopped at Brackettville, a town of fifteen hundred inhabitants plus a thousand soldiers who were stationed there. Although by now it would seem that little would shock him, Rogers was aghast at the moral decay of the town. "It has six or eight saloons that do a thriving business day and night. . . . Gambling tables are many—how many I do not know; they run in open daylight and without blinds or screens—also seven days in a week." In spite of all the wickedness and vileness, Rogers professed that the Lord was doing great things in the meetings, and several dozen "gave their hearts to Christ," including a number of soldiers. Rogers complained that the new chaplain at the army post was a Catholic priest, "so the soldiers will be without the gospel."[12]

Crossing the International Railroad Bridge at Eagle Pass after leaving Brackettville, Rogers wrote, "I have just left Ciudad Porfiro Diaz, Mexico, where I have been to enter Chapel Car, 'Good Will' into the Mexican International railway shops. I failed everywhere in Texas, on account of the companies being crowded with their own work. The car is to be thoroughly overhauled. This is going to cost nearly $1,000." Rogers, in the *Baptist Standard,* pleaded for contributions to pay the bill, as *Good Will* was not the only chapel car having difficulty in finding shops for repair purposes. Seymour shared the problem in a society newspaper. "Shall we not pray that in some way God will see that these meeting houses on wheels, dedicated to his service, may be kept in good repair."[13]

Before leaving Ciudad Porfiro Diaz, Rogers and Hiett spent several days with the young Baptist congregation organized in 1902. The church now had more than thirty members using a rented room in a private house and longing for a building. "Our Methodist brethren have just completed a nice brick chapel. For $800 in United States money, a good lot could be bought and a nice little chapel erected." [14]

After preaching at a number of churches without the car, Roger picked up *Good Will* at the Mexican shops in late July. Back in the repaired chapel car, Rogers headed for Elgin. The town, which welcomed the chapel car, was sorely afflicted—the corn crop was dead, the cotton needed rain badly, water was growing scarce, and much sickness prevailed.

In a rare incident, Rogers's wife joined him to journey to Kansas City to attend the Second Chapel Car Conference in September, 1902. Along with the missionaries on the other five existing chapel cars, Rev. and Mrs. Rogers attended sessions on "Selecting Towns for Work," "How Long to Stay in a Place," "Gospel Singing in Chapel Car work," "Cooking on Chapel Cars," "Care of the Car," and "Meeting Railroad Officials." For Mrs. Rogers, who seldom worked with her husband on *Good Will* because of family responsibilities, it was an opportunity to learn more about the work of the chapel cars and visit with the other missionary wives. Mrs. Rogers would find her life not unlike that of some of the wives, and yet with others, quite different. [15]

Like Mrs. Rogers, on *Evangel, #1,* Mrs. J. S. Thomas was not traveling with her husband in Indian Territory and Arkansas; instead she stayed home with their children. On *Emmanuel, #2,* B. B. Jacques's wife, suffering depression, was absent from the car frequently. In her place, Brother Moffett, who had served so faithfully in Texas, was assisting with the work in California and Nevada. On *Glad Tidings, #3,* Mrs. C. H. Rust had decided to leave the work, although she loved it, and stay home with the two little girls born while she was on the chapel car. Her husband carried on the work in Minnesota and Wisconsin with the help of the Reverend E. A. Spears. Mrs. J. B. Jacobs was serving with her husband on *Messenger of Peace, #5,* in Missouri, and The Reverend A. P. McDonald, a Michigan district missionary, traveled the state on *Herald of Hope, #6,* while his wife stayed at home. Chapel life was hard on wives, especially if they had families. They had to choose between staying with and supporting their husband's work on the chapel car or staying home to raise their families.

After returning his wife to their Waco home, Rogers, reinvigorated from the fellowship experienced at Kansas City, traveled to

Thorndale. This little town had suffered a double tragedy when two town churches burned. It was determined that an arsonist had destroyed both the Baptist and Christian churches. "They were both in flames at the same time that night," Rogers reported. "Our chapel is the largest auditorium in town, consequently, we will not get to accommodate larger audiences than the car will hold." Although bad weather prevented several of the meetings, Hiett wrote, "Christian people of all denomination seem eager to join hands and hearts in a strong 'pull' for the betterment of the town. Quite a number of influential business men, who do not belong to any church, are willing to do all they can to help in the good work. Pray for us in this saloon-stricken, ungodly town." [16]

It had been rumored that the town saloons were responsible for the church fires. As in other towns, saloon owners had undermined the building and maintaining of churches that would encourage prohibition. The *Baptist Standard* published a study as to the growth of dry counties because of the work of Texas prohibitionists. Most of the progress for prohibition was accomplished since 1893. Of the 235 counties of the state, 104, nearly half, were wholly dry. Of the remainder, seventy-four were largely dry, many of them wholly dry save the county seat, and only fifty-eight were wholly wet. [17]

Up in the Panhandle where Rogers, while preaching at Dalhart, had praised the town for being dry, the *Channing Courier* received a copy of an ad a liquor company wanted them to run. The editor reported that as pay the liquor company would send 20 quarts of 12-year-old, absolutely pure corn juice, "warranted to make a millionaire of a pauper in 30 minutes after the first drink, and land him in jail after the second bottle, and send him to hell on the home stretch, lest he know how to drink and behave himself, and there are so few that can do that: no, not one in a thousand." [18]

Now Dalhart and Channing had churches, but Texline, hanging on the line between New Mexico and Texas, still was churchless. A railroad missionary, John Carney, lectured at the Texline courthouse September 11, 1902, and reported, "This is a railroad town, no church, no schoolhouse. They are going to have an election on local option September 13 in this county. Pray for us that we may win out in this end of the state." [19]

Rogers and Hiett returned to Milano for the closing days of 1902. It had been a long time since the town had seen such a great revival. Children, who had lined the tracks at the depot to await the coming of *Good Will*, crowded into the car to hear the "big" man tell them Bible stories and teach them songs. In order to handle the crowds, Rogers had purchased twenty-five camp stools and placed them in the aisle, on the platform and in other available space, making the seating capacity of the car about 150.[20]

Although friction from dissenting groups was still present at Palestine, Rogers's next stop, he reported that the services were having good results. It was not long before the men from the I&GN Railroad's large shops came to request that the chapel car arrange meetings especially for them, and Rogers preached to them twice a day at the yards. It would be at such times that railroad employees would spruce up the car, wipe down the varnished wooden sides with oil waste, wash windows, check the air brakes and journal box, and do other things to show their appreciation for "their" church car.[21]

Moving north out of the piney woods in January of 1903, *Good Will* arrived in Tyler, and, if Rogers and Hiett were lucky, the balky, coal-fed Baker stove would be taking the chill off the almost impossible to heat car. Regardless of the temperature, the religious climate in Tyler was more diverse than many Texas towns. Many of the Irish who came to work on the railroad were Catholic, and the Diocese of Dallas had established the Benedictine Sisters St. Joseph Academy. To add to the diversification, even within the Catholic church, a colony of Lebanese who practiced the Maronite Rite instead of the Latin arrived in town. The Jewish community of more than fifty families formed a *chevra kadisha*, a burial society, purchased a plot at Oakwood Cemetery, and organized an orthodox faction.[22]

The officials of the Cotton Belt shops, although they had not been able to repair *Good Will* earlier, placed the car on the best possible siding. The weather—pouring down rain—made it too inclement for the ladies to attend. They would not have appeared at such a momentous social and religious event in dripping skirts or bedraggled, beribboned bonnets. So the chapel car was full of men and boys. Boys always had a special place in the hearts of the chapel car workers. Frequently, missionaries on the chapel cars would relate that mothers tearfully had pleaded with them to reach their sons with the gospel so they would not end up in the saloons. Rogers planned to spend at least three or four weeks with the men and the families of the Cotton Belt, and he reported that many attending the services professed never having any church connection.

When the chapel car first came into Texas, there were those who feared that the influence of the American Baptist Publication Society would infiltrate the churches and create problems for the Baptist General Convention. This did not happen. There was nothing but public praise from the leaders of the convention. When President J. H. Gambrell was asked what he thought of the chapel cars, he responded, "I think the wisdom of God broached the idea into the mind and heart of the man who conceived the scheme." He declared that the chapel car did not detract from but added to church life and work. "Of course there is great opportunity for a foolish manager to do harm, but the American Baptist Publication Society does not employ foolish managers." Gambrell said that the car "reaches classes of people who are not ordinarily reached by our churches. As is well known these classes abound in our cities, especially railroad centers. I think that Texas Baptists are tremendously indebted for the work of chapel car 'Good Will,' without cost to our organized work."[23]

At Denison, where E. S. and Nettie Stucker first witnessed to the railroad men at the T&P shops, the car received a warm welcome and the men who filled the car probably noticed that after all its repairs and renovation, it looked almost as good as when it first arrived in Texas. In the yards at Waco, the welcome was not as warm. Railroad officials placed the chapel car in a poor place making it impossible to reach the mill and railroad workers that Rogers wanted in the meetings, so arrangements were made to have a tent erected near the Woolen Mills but close enough for the railroad employees.[24]

Others in the Texas Baptist family were becoming more aware of the plight of railroad workers. As a result of the death of a twenty-three-year-old railroad worker in Wilson C. Rogers's church in Dallas, the second funeral of men killed on the railroad that he had conducted in the past year, it caused him to think very seriously about the church's attitude toward the railroad men. Rogers pointed out that the train crews, the bridge gang, and the wrecking crews, also the yardmen, had few opportunities to attend church.

With the exception of the "yard men," these men take their lives in their hands every time they go on duty, and virtually offer them as a sacrifice to the public and to the corporations which they serve; and the "yard men" are subjected to many dangers.

Every time an engineer pulls open the throttle of his engine and starts on "his run," he cannot tell how far down the line will end his last run. The trusty fireman at his post, beside his engineer, stands faithfully by his comrade, and if one goes down both go down together. They are men who brave the storm of winter and summer, called on duty at all unseasonable hours, day and night, and must not shrink from duty. Think of the great responsibilities placed up on them, the life and property entrusted to their watchfulness and care. It takes a brave man to be a good railroad man." [25]

A weary G. B. Rogers reported to the *Standard* that illness in his family prevented him from holding but one meeting in June, a good one at Mexia. He returned for just one week at Groesbeck, the town made famous for the Parker's Fort Massacre, where many of the settlers were killed or captured by the Comanches and Kiowas on May 19, 1836, including Cynthia Ann Parker, mother of the great Indian chief Quannah Parker. [26]

The Houston & Texas Central had created Groesbeck in the 1870s, along with Mexia. Fatigued, even discouraged by the personal and pastoral problems that beset him, Rogers, his large frame stooping, seemed to see Groesbeck through ever-darkening glasses. Rogers reported the situation as "deplorable."

Visiting Methodist evangelists also had a problem with the state of religion in Groesbeck. Evangelists Henson and Hays during revival services in 1898 touched upon the topic of lodges. There were about eight different lodges meeting in town once or twice monthly. The visiting preachers believed that the men in the community should not belong to the lodges, but *Journal* editor Morse countered that the only way people could obtain affordable insurance was through their lodge memberships. He concluded that if people followed Henson's advice not to attend meetings, the lodges would fail, and the insurance would be lost. Morse's Methodist readers let him know that they thought he was anti-religion in his stand, but he responded that he had always supported the events of the Methodists in his paper. In the years between 1898 and 1903, although valiant efforts were made by a new Methodist minister to "fire up" the flock, the result was dismal, if not as deplorable as Rogers had assessed. The new pastor said that Groesbeck Methodists had become distracted by "other pursuits, such as the many club meetings and a

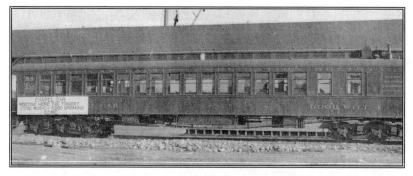

A sign would be hung on the side of *Good Will* to announce the services and invite townspeople to come. *Courtesy Norman T. Taylor Collection*

growing preoccupation with social refinement. Intellectual inquiry was beginning to temper religious zeal. Old-fashioned revivals were losing their appeal." [27]

Methodists were not the only ones who objected to the lodges, as Baptists frequently attacked the lodges using the argument that the scripture had specifically warned against secret societies.

Before the close of *Good Will*'s meetings, a new man was called to the struggling Baptist church at Groesbeck, amid a community that had been labeled as disenchanted with the good, old-fashioned gospel. Depleted and dejected, Rogers left the meetings in the new pastor's hands. Illness, both Rogers's and his wife's, gnawed away at his chapel car ministry.

CHAPTER NINETEEN

A TRIO OF TOWN PROBLEMS

Rogers was not ready to deal with more problems. He had enough of saloon-ruled towns and sick churches or towns with no churches at all. Yet waiting down the line were three towns with contrasting personalities and challenges.

Spring, a German town with a deceptively pure name on the I&G Railroad, where the Fort Worth division connected with the main line, was almost brand new, but it had not taken long for the town to establish a raucous reputation. Rogers decried while debarking from *Good Will* in the summer of 1903, that Spring had only a few businesses but "saloons galore" and "wickedness and ungodliness" were "without restraint."[1]

Rogers was not alone in his appraisal of the moral health of the little boomtown with its fourteen-track rail yard where several hundred were employed. "It was wild," Joe Monroe, an old railroader reminisced about the town's history. "There were five saloons and a gambling hall. Women would walk a block out of their way to get by Uncle Charlie's place because there were so many fights goin' on." Among the saloons was the Wunsche family's famed saloon (now the Spring Café, a popular tourist spot), finished just before *Good Will*'s visit.[2]

The Spring depot agent, R. L. Robinson, in addition to controlling the switches, selling the tickets, operating the telegraph, and managing the shipping of tons of potatoes in refrigerated boxcars developed by the Southern Pacific in 1886, would have made the arrangements for *Good Will*'s placement. Robinson had handled the siding of many unique cars that had come into the depot—circus cars, theater cars, photography cars, and even the decorated advertising car of the Texas State Fair. He probably had not arranged

Wunsche Bros. Saloon operated during the time chapel car *Good Will* was having services in the town. A tourist attraction, the tavern is still in business. *Courtesy Norman T. Taylor Collection*

for a car that so impressed the railroad employees—a railroad church car.[3]

Rogers proclaimed of the new town an old complaint, "no church, no preaching of any kind, no Sunday-school, no prayer-meeting, destitution was dense here at our door." He was able to drum up twenty prospective members for a church during the twelve-day mission and baptized several in Spring Creek. In spite of his efforts, there would not be a church building in Spring until the Sellers family donated land on which the Methodists built in 1909.[4]

Spring was not named after the creek, but instead because of a remark that a railroad construction worker who was laying tracks into the new town made about the balmy weather.[5]

Unlike young Spring, La Grange was one of the oldest of Texas towns, first settled by Austin's "The Original Three Hundred," who were then followed by German immigrants in the 1840s and Czechs and Moravians in the 1850s.[6]

La Grange, the home of R. E. B. Baylor, law professor and early supporter of the university that would bear his name, had fallen on hard times. In spite of the Baylor connection, the town of three thousand had no Baptist church in 1903 and few Baptist people. Although the town in the 1830s was a Baptist stronghold, the battle between the non-missionary and the missionary forces resulted in the church splitting. The breach between the two factions did not mean there was a clear-cut division of thought, as in most of the early Baptist churches; there was a blend of missionary and anti-missionary sentiments.[7]

The missionary debate, the 1867 yellow fever scourge, and the arrival of many immigrants resulted in hundreds of pioneer Baptists in and around La Grange fleeing. The membership of the once illustrious Baptist church dwindled down to three or four members who finally sold their building and closed.

Because of the influx of the large foreign element, La Grange had been targeted by many denominations as an area in great need of missionary work. A *Baptist Standard* letter stated that there were fifty-five thousand Bohemians in Texas and ten thousand in Fayette County alone. As before, Rogers complained, "These Bohemians are great Sabbath desecraters, drink beer and dance all day Sunday," and the Methodists agreed, adding to their list Mexicans, Scandinavians, Poles, and Italians flooding into the area. "They are not favorable to our ideas of law and order, and they are out of sympathy with our institutions."[8]

The pastor at neighboring Smithville, who had been doing mission work in the La Grange area, wrote of the situation there, "to tell the truth, there are very few Christians belonging to any denomination. The town is almost entirely controlled by a worldly element, which scarcely respect religion and have but little regard for morality . . . the liquor traffic is the basis of commerce. This business rules and dominates everything—politics, society, and religion. No church or preacher can succeed in this place only so far as they are permitted to do so by the combined saloon power." This opinion would cast aspersions on the Methodists and Presbyterians and three other churches that managed to minister to some degree in the town.[9]

Rogers and *Good Will,* like a battle-worn knight in his shining armor, came into town, but the tale did not turn out as Rogers had hoped. Adding to the saloon influence, the newspaper reported that the railroad stationmaster had placed the car in a bad spot, away out in the yards near the Katy freight depot, too far for the convenience of most of the town's people. Rogers, not to be denied his opportunity to restore a Baptist presence in La Grange, appealed to the county judge and the meetings were moved to the courthouse.[10]

Looking for a Baptist in La Grange was a "diligent search," but if there was one within a dozen miles, Rogers would find him. He had been told that only one Baptist was alive and living in La Grange, but before he left, he had found seven more.

"Looking for Baptists" was the avocation of all the missionaries on the chapel cars. One missionary told of visiting a little town where there was no Baptist church, and he had been told that there were Baptists in town, but no one knew who or where. First, he was referred to the barkeeper at the saloon, who then directed him to the storekeeper, who then guided him to another business establishment run by the mayor of the town. After the missionary stated his purpose of finding Baptists, the mayor said, "Ah yes, Baptists? What nationality are they?"[11]

In spite of eight possible candidates, Rogers decided not to attempt to establish a church. It would not be until 1920 that a Baptist church would again appear in La Grange.

One of those probably most distressed about the Baptist condition in La Grange would have been Elli Moore Townsend, wife of E. G. Townsend, former missionary on *Good Will.* Elli's grandfather, Col. John Henry Moore, built a blockhouse in what is now La Grange and named it Moore's Fort, and there settlers would take refuge from Indian attacks. He became a Texas War and Civil War legend in La Grange, and the most prominent of the Baptist leaders. One story told about Colonel Moore was that so great was his disappointment over the South's loss, he never laughed again and disapproved of those who were able to put aside their disappointment and once again enjoy life. Another story reflects his religious views.

Colonel Moore set aside the land for and built a church on his plantation. According to the story, Colonel Moore stood beside the preacher during the services in order to watch the congregation and prevent anyone from falling asleep.

Family legend also records that Moore was so stubborn that only his wife was ever able to influence his actions or opinions. He was so protective of his children that his disapproval of his daughters' chosen mates forced them to elope. Whether or not the colonel disapproved of Elli's mother, his son's wife, is unknown. Moore's controlling nature and influence may have been a factor in the demise of the Baptist influence in La Grange.[12]

Rogers deserved a break, and that came at Smithville, one of the towns visited by all the chapel car missionaries. Since the Stucker visit in 1896 and the Townsend visit in 1897, Smithville's reputation as a moral town had improved with the coming of more churches and a Railroad YMCA.[13]

The Railroad Ys brought the Christian witness to rail workers as well as provided a means of making railroad life and passage safer for all Americans. In the 1800s, particularly before rail unions, "life on the rails was cheap." Crews suffered impossibly long hours, unfit food, and infested beds. Many of the frequent train wrecks could be linked directly to excessive duty and unhealthy "rest" periods when "booze, gambling, wenching, and brawling" were favorite pastimes. As a result, thousands of railroaders were killed or maimed. The Railroad Ys provided a safe, wholesome home for thousands of railroad men across America, a place where they could find clean beds, good food, reading material, healthy physical activity, and spiritual guidance.[14]

Among the earliest religious activities of the Railroad Y associations were the gospel trains, usually composed of a Christian engineer, fireman, conductor, and brakeman, all men of outstanding character, gifted with simple and homely speech. Services were conducted in churches and railroad association buildings. The gospel trains visited railroad communities where no railroad association existed and promoted interest and sometimes organization of a Y branch. The service was simplicity itself—singing of old-time hymns, scripture and prayer, followed by thrilling recitals of personal experiences. Then would come an invitation to the audience "to entrain with the gospel crew as the train sped on toward the City of God."

Illustrations such as this one titled "The Last Call" were popular in YMCA publications. *From the author's collection*

YMCA officials explained that most railroad terminals were located in undesirable parts of the community and usually the district was "more or less thickly infested with saloons and other places of vice." When the men came in from their runs, they were in need of refreshment and rest, and they had great difficulty in securing good accommodations at any reasonable price, or any price. "Driven to the saloon," they would at least be sure to find companionship and a certain amount of recreation. The result was that they were often far from fit when the time came for them to take their trains out. The YMCA secretary emphasized that, with the complications of making up and getting the trains over the road, and the possibilities for preventing damage to goods, and accidents to life and limb, "if keen, bright men are in charge, it is not hard to see where railroads can make big savings by doing their part to keep the men in a fit condition." The chapel cars and the Railroad Ys worked together for the same goal, and in 1910, chapel car *Messenger of Peace, #5* would spend several years traveling on behalf of the Railroad YMCA.[15]

Great numbers came to *Good Will* during the ten-day mission at Smithville, and Rogers enjoyed a few days of respite from his earlier stops. Still he was tired. He wanted to go home to the comfort of his home, wife, and children. He had made his decision to leave the chapel car work. First though, he would hold his last mission on *Good Will* at the Dallas Lake Avenue Baptist Church, where the chapel car was packed for ten days of services. As he greeted the people climbing the steps onto *Good Will*'s platform, he had to have had bittersweet moments. His thoughts must have turned to the memories of all those towns and their troubles and victories. G. B., the great big man with the soft heart, must have had time for tears.

At the Dallas convention, the now much-beloved *Good Will* was on exhibit, this time visited by people who had come to know and respect the chapel car work. During the sessions, the Sunday School Board praised the presence of the American Baptist Publication Society chapel car, but few knew that its work in Texas would soon come to an end.[16]

On the Thursday afternoon of the women's meetings, a beautiful little boy was again put on the secretary's table in front of the gathering. The kiss he blew toward the audience brought tears to those who revered the memory of his mother, Hollie Harper Townsend.

THE END OF THE TEXAS LINE

The railroads continued to spread their network of tracks across the Lone Star State, and as the routes, rails, and shops were established, the face of Texas changed. At the beginning of 1900, more than halfway through *Good Will*'s journey, there was still less than ten thousand miles of railroad in Texas, only about five percent of the U.S. railroad mileage. At the turn of the century, the lower Rio Grande Valley still had virtually no railroad mileage. Vast areas of the South Plains, the Panhandle, and West Texas were without railroads. Still the flow of immigrants who followed those few lines made a tremendous impact on Texas life and growth as well as on Texas life and faith.[1]

Helen Mae Barnes in *Country Faith and Fate* recalls that times have changed since those days in the 1890s when a church steeple was still an uncommon sight on the Texas prairies and in the piney woods, for now, more than one hundred years later, Texas has never boasted so many churches. "Ragged choirs are long since replaced by electronic voices resounding from cathedral ceilings (and digital images projected on screens). Multi-hued robes now encase sophisticated choir members, securely hidden from sight in lofts of gold inlay, cleverly balconied" above the back of sanctuaries. She reflects, "Let's not forget it wasn't always so."[2]

Spanning those years, from 1895 to 1903, chapel car *Good Will* traversed Texas, seeking the lost among the thousands of settlers who had made their homes in churchless settlements along the tracks. During its eight-year journey, it helped to heal denominational rifts and encouraged discouraged churches while bringing the gospel to more than one hundred railroad towns.[3]

Edwin Stanton Stucker, the first missionary on *Good Will*, did not forsake his call to preach after leaving *Good Will*—if not just to railroad men. He served as a Publication Society mission secretary and evangelist, traveling all across the nation, while his wife Nettie cared for her family.

A. J. Diaz, after his brief but unique time on the chapel car, returned to Cuba, and would repeatedly try to regain favor with the Southern Baptist Convention but remained in disfavor.

Eugene Gale Townsend, pastor and teacher, along with his second wife Elli, became a force at Baylor Female College, which would become the University of Mary Hardin-Baylor. Texas General Baptists would long cherish Hollie Harper Townsend's memory.

G. B. Rogers served chapel car *Good Will* with dedication to the Baptist General Convention of Texas and a gifted call to preach the gospel. He was a mountain of a man with a heart of gold that touched many lives and churches, especially after the Great Storm of Galveston.

Each of them had left their message and mark in the railroad towns of Texas.

The first week in 1903, after the rousing gathering at Dallas, Rogers turned *Good Will* over to the Reverend and Mrs. T. S. Fretz. Fretz had received orders from the American Baptist Publication Society to transfer the car from Texas to Missouri and then Colorado to continue its ministry. Over the thirty-five years after leaving Texas, the car would serve in Missouri, Colorado, Utah, Nevada, Idaho, Oregon, and California.[4]

In January, 1938, the American Baptist Publication Society ordered the Reverend Morse Dryer to "park" a travel-worn *Good Will* "somewhere," as the railroads would no longer permit its passage. The ill Dryer wrote from California, where he had been serving on the chapel car for many months, about his disposition of the car. He wrote the Northern California Baptist headquarters that the "next week we [Dryer and his wife] go to Santa Rosa and Boys [Boyes] Springs in the 'Valley of the Moon' of Jack London fame to settle the chapel car on its permanent foundation. We think we have found a perfect place—no churches or religious meetings, many children and thousands of San Francisco folk vacationing all summer. We are in the midst of hotels, baths, hot springs and sports."[5]

A 1938 memo in the files of the American Baptist Historical Society notes that the chapel car was given to the Northern California Baptist Convention to be used as a stationary home and headquar-

Chapel car *Good Will* still exists, although in poor condition, on the same property where it was placed by the last missionary to serve on the car in 1938. *Courtesy Norman T. Taylor Collection*

ters for Morse Dryer. In 1940 the Northern California Baptist Convention sold *Good Will* for $275.00 to F. A. Maley of Boyes Springs. The Publication Society received its proportionate share of the money.[6]

The spot where Morse Dryer placed the chapel car in 1938 was where it stayed—behind the Boyes Hot Springs Hotel. For fifty-eight years the chapel car sat behind that hotel, waiting to be found—to be remembered—to be honored.

> In April 1998, my husband and I visited the last resting place of chapel car *Good Will,* a hundred years since E. G. Townsend lost his wife Hollie and set out on his mission to Del Rio and Comstock without her.
>
> There it was! Right where Morse Dryer left it. Within ninety feet of the fancy French doors opening into the luxurious lounge of the exclusive Sonoma Mission Inn & Spa, off hotel property, almost hidden by fence, pine trees, and landscaping.
>
> Greeted cordially the first week of April 1998 by the present owner and escorted to the location of the car, we felt shy, almost embarrassed—like two old friends seeing another old

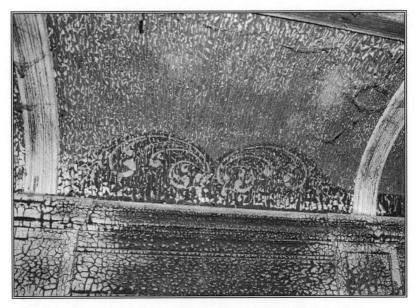

The graceful ceiling trim in the living quarters of chapel car *Good Will*, discovered when the car was found in 1998 by the author, had never been mentioned in chapel car reports. *Courtesy Norman T. Taylor Collection*

friend for the first time after many years. We knew *Good Will* would not be in great shape, maybe sad shape. After all, the car was 103 years old, and the present owners did not really know that their old railroad car had been a beautiful Baptist church on wheels once. It could be but a shadow of its former self.

Apprehensively, we looked the direction being led, trying to carry on polite conversation with our host, fearing yet longing for the first sight of the car which we had searched for with scant hope, [it] having been assumed destroyed, lost.

The faded, peeling exterior was what we had expected, but we did not expect the platforms to be gone, although the absent trucks did not surprise us. The parsonage-end door was open, and we peered into a darkness brightened by just shafts of light through the glassless windows. We stepped in, and my husband and the owner talked of the condition of the windows and walls while I looked up. What I saw surprised and amazed me.

The ceiling! It was painted in beautiful waves of turquoise on a golden background, along the sides and across the top,

waves and waves. Faded, cracking, peeling, but lovely still—
sumptuous, gracefully rococo, rolling, like the wind driven
waves of a storm-tossed, turquoise sea, caught and frozen in
tandem.[7]

As chapel car *Good Will* left Texas tracks behind in 1903, wind-
driven waves slapped against a new barrier protecting the once
"golden city" devastated by the Great Storm. A seawall, the most gi-
gantic structure of modern times—three miles long, sixteen feet
high, sixteen-foot base, five-foot top, with granite from Marble
Falls—provided the citizens of the city on the golden shore with re-
assurance and hope for a better future.[8]

G. B. Rogers, the last missionary on board *Good Will*, said of his
deliverance from Galveston during the Great Storm, "Praise the
Lord for His goodness and for His wonderful works to the children
of men." Those words could have been written in gilt letters across
the bright, varnished sides of chapel car *Good Will*, for they bespoke
the message and hope of all its missionaries.[9]

APPENDIX

American Baptist Publication Society
Chapel Car *Good Will, #4*

Missionary	Year	Mo.	Day	City	State	RR
	1894	10	01	Dayton	OH	Barney & Smith Shops
Rev. E. S. Stucker & wife	1895	05	01	Aurora	IL	—
	1895	05	17	Dayton	OH	C&SL
Rev. E. S. Stucker & wife	1895	05	28	Saratoga Springs	NY	D&H
Rev. E. S. Stucker	1895	06	05	Philadelphia	PA	—
Rev. E. S. Stucker & wife	1895	06	07	Buffalo	NY	NYC NYC&HR
Rev. E. S. Stucker, wife, & M. S. McMullen	1895	06	11	Aurora	IL	CB&Q
Rev. E. S. Stucker	1895	06	17	Chicago	IL	—
Rev. E. S. Stucker & wife	1895	06	22	Sedalia	MO	MK&T
Rev. E. S. Stucker, wife, & Mr. Gearch	1895	06	28	Fort Scott	KS	MK&T
Rev. E. S. Stucker, wife, & Mr. Gearch	1895	06	30	Fort Scott	KS	KCP&G
Rev. E. S. Stucker & wife	1895	07	06	North Topeka	KS	UP
Rev. E. S. Stucker & wife	1895	07	07	Dallas	TX	MK&T
Rev. E. S. Stucker & wife	1895	07	08	Denison	TX	MK&T
Rev. E. S. Stucker & wife	1895	07	17	Dallas	TX	MK&T
Rev. E. S. Stucker & wife	1895	07	20	Fort Worth	TX	MK&T
Rev. E. S. Stucker, wife, & Rev. M. D. Early	1895	07	26	Waco	TX	H&TC
Rev. E. S. Stucker, wife, & Rev. M. D. Early	1895	08	02	Texline	TX	FW&DC
Rev. E. S. Stucker, wife, & Rev. M. D. Early	1895	08	13	Canadian	TX	AT&SF
Rev. E. S. Stucker, wife, & Rev. M. D. Early	1895	08	17	Amarillo	TX	HE&WT
Rev. E. S. Stucker, wife, & Rev. M. D. Early	1895	08	21	Panhandle	TX	AT&SF
Rev. E. S. Stucker, wife, & Rev. M. D. Early	1895	08	25	Pampa	TX	AT&SF

Missionary	Year	Mo.	Day	City	State	RR
Rev. E. S. Stucker, wife, & Rev. M. D. Early	1895	08	29	Channing	TX	FW&DC
Rev. E. S. Stucker, wife, & Rev. M. D. Early	1895	08	31	Hartley	TX	FW&DC
Rev. E. S. Stucker, wife, & Rev. M. D. Early	1895	09	03	Twist Junction	TX	FW&DC
Rev. E. S. Stucker, wife, & Rev. M. D. Early	1895	09	08	Canyon	TX	AT&SF
Rev. E. S. Stucker, wife, & Rev. M. D. Early	1895	09	16	Hereford	TX	AT&SF
Rev. E. S. Stucker & wife	1895	09	26	Fort Worth	TX	T&P
Rev. E. S. Stucker & wife	1895	10	10	Belton	TX	MK&T
Rev. E. S. Stucker & wife	1895	10	15	Big Sandy	TX	T&P
Rev. E. S. Stucker & wife	1895	11	02	Marshall	TX	T&P
Rev. E. S. Stucker & wife	1895	11	20	Thurber	TX	T&P
Rev. E. S. Stucker & wife	1896	01	10	Temple	TX	GC&SF
Rev. E. S. Stucker & wife	1896	01	18	Waco	TX	H&TC
Rev. E. S. Stucker & wife	1896	02	01	Smithville	TX	MK&T
Rev. E. S. Stucker & wife	1896	02	09	San Antonio	TX	I&GN
Rev. E. S. Stucker & wife	1896	02	14	San Antonio	TX	I&GN
Rev. E. S. Stucker & wife	1896	02	20	San Antonio	TX	GH&SA
Rev. E. S. Stucker & wife	1896	02	23	San Antonio	TX	GH&SA
Rev. E. S. Stucker & wife	1896	03	14	Austin	TX	I&GN
Rev. E. S. Stucker & wife	1896	03	24	Waco	TX	H&TC
Rev. E. S. Stucker & wife	1896	03	27	Granite Mountain	TX	GM&MFC
Rev. E. S. Stucker & wife	1896	04	06	Eagle Pass	TX	GH&SA
Rev. E. S. Stucker & wife	1896	04	16	Ciudad Porfiro Diaz	MX	MI
Rev. E. S. Stucker & wife	1896	04	23	Laredo	TX	I&GN
Rev. E. S. Stucker & wife	1896	05	14	Del Rio	TX	SP
Rev. E. S. Stucker	1896	06	12	San Antonio	TX	MK&T
Rev. E. S. Stucker	1896	06	22	San Antonio	TX	—
Rev. E. S. Stucker	1896	07	21	Aurora	IL	—
Rev. E. S. Stucker	1896	08	30	San Antonio	TX	MK&T
Rev. E. S. Stucker	1896	09	01	Gainesville	TX	MK&T
Rev. E. S. Stucker	1896	09	04	St. Joe	TX	MK&T
Rev. E. S. Stucker	1896	09	08	Hennietta	TX	FW&D
Rev. E. S. Stucker	1896	09	12	Bowie	TX	FW&D
Rev. E. S. Stucker	1896	09	16	Decatur	TX	FW&D
Rev. E. S. Stucker	1896	09	20	San Antonio	TX	SP
Rev. E. S. Stucker	1896	10	01	Hillsboro	TX	MKT
Rev. E. S. Stucker	1896	10	10	Houston	TX	H&TC
Rev. E. S. Stucker	1896	10	11	Houston	TX	H&TC
Rev. E. S. Stucker	1896	10	13	Houston	TX	H&TC
Dr. A. J. Diaz	1896	11	01	Houston	TX	SP
Dr. A. J. Diaz	1896	11	03	San Antonio	TX	
Dr. A. J. Diaz	1896	11	05	El Paso	TX	
Dr. A. J. Diaz	1896	11	22	San Antonio	TX	IG&N
Dr. A. J. Diaz	1896	11	29	Laredo	TX	
Dr. A. J. Diaz & B. W. Smith	1896	12	04	San Antonio	TX	GH&SA
Dr. A. J. Diaz	1896	12	06	San Marcos	TX	I&GN
Dr. A. J. Diaz	1896	12	09	San Antonio	TX	

Dr. A. J. Diaz	1896	12	15	Houston	TX	
Rev. E. S. Stucker	1896	12	16	Houston	TX	
Rev. E. S. Stucker	1896	12	17	San Antonio	TX	IG&N
Rev. E. S. Stucker	1897	03	10	Dallas	TX	
Rev. E. G. Townsend & wife	1897	03	15	Dallas	TX	MK&T
Rev. E. G. Townsend & wife	1897	03	30	Smithville	TX	MK&T
Rev. E. G. Townsend & wife	1897	04	10	Cleveland	TX	HE&WT
Rev. E. G. Townsend & wife	1897	04	20	Shepherd	TX	HE&WT
Rev. E. G. Townsend & wife	1897	05	10	Shreveport	LA	T&P
Rev. E. G. Townsend & wife	1897	05	13	Wilmington	NC	—
Rev. E. G. Townsend & wife	1897	05	24	Tenaha	TX	HE&WT
Rev. E. G. Townsend & wife	1897	06	21	Sherman	TX	HE&WT
Rev. E. G. Townsend & wife	1897	06	29	Tenaha	TX	HE&WT
Rev. E. G. Townsend & wife	1897	07	17	Timpson	TX	HE&WT
Rev. E. G. Townsend & wife	1897	08	12	Thurber	TX	T&P
Rev. E. G. Townsend & wife	1897	08	22	Dallas	TX	—
Rev. E. G. Townsend & wife	1897	09	15	Thurber	TX	T&P
Rev. E. G. Townsend & wife	1897	10	10	Baird	TX	T&P
Rev. E. G. Townsend & wife	1897	10	14	Abilene	TX	T&P
Rev. E. G. Townsend & wife	1897	11	05	Abilene	TX	T&P
Rev. E. G. Townsend & wife	1897	11	07	San Antonio	TX	—
Rev. E. G. Townsend & wife	1897	11	11	San Antonio	TX	—
Rev. E. G. Townsend & wife	1897	11	19	Abilene	TX	T&P
Rev. E. G. Townsend & wife	1897	11	20	Baird	TX	T&P
Rev. E. G. Townsend & wife	1897	11	29	Sweetwater	TX	T&P
Rev. E. G. Townsend & wife	1897	12	10	Pecos	TX	T&P
Rev. E. G. Townsend & wife	1897	12	25	Big Springs	TX	T&P
Rev. E. G. Townsend & wife	1898	01	10	Cleburne	TX	GC&SF
Rev. E. G. Townsend & wife	1898	01	20	Marshall	TX	T&P
Rev. E. G. Townsend & wife	1898	02	04	Longview Jt.	TX	T&P
Rev. E. G. Townsend & wife	1898	02	20	Palestine	TX	I&GN
Rev. E. G. Townsend & wife	1898	04	05	Galveston	TX	GC&SF
Rev. E. G. Townsend & wife	1898	04	25	Galveston	TX	GC&SF
Rev. E. G. Townsend & wife	1898	05	01	Dallas	TX	GC&SF
Rev. E. G. Townsend & wife	1898	05	03	Norfolk	VA	—
Rev. E. G. Townsend & wife	1898	05	20	Rochester	NY	—
Rev. E. G. Townsend & wife	1898	06	05	Dallas	TX	MK&T
Rev. E. G. Townsend	1898	06	20	Brenham	TX	GC&SF
Rev. E. G. Townsend & wife	1898	06	26	Gainesville	TX	
Rev. E. G. Townsend & wife	1898	06	30	Border towns	TX	
Rev. E. G. Townsend	1898	08	05	Dallas	TX	MK&T
Rev. E. G. Townsend	1898	10	06	Waco	TX	—
Rev. E. G. Townsend	1898	10	13	Belton	TX	MK&T
Rev. E. G. Townsend & Mr. T. Moffett	1898	10	15	Taylor	TX	I&GN
Rev. E. G. Townsend & Mr. T. Moffett	1898	12	19	Yoakum	TX	SA&AP
Rev. E. G. Townsend & Mr. T. Moffett	1899	01	20	Dallas	TX	MK&T
Rev. E. G. Townsend & Mr. T. Moffett	1899	02	01	Karnes City	TX	SA&AP
Rev. E. G. Townsend & Mr. T. Moffett	1899	02	26	Skidmore Jt.	TX	SA&AP
Rev. E. G. Townsend & Mr. T. Moffett	1899	03	06	Gregory	TX	SA&AP

Missionary	Year	Mo.	Day	City	State	RR
Rev. E. G. Townsend & Mr. T. Moffett	1899	03	16	Rockport	TX	SA&AP
Rev. E. G. Townsend & Mr. T. Moffett	1899	04	08	Waco	TX	MK&T
Rev. E. G. Townsend & Mr. T. Moffett	1899	05	30	Gregory	TX	SA&AP
Rev. E. G. Townsend & Mr. T. Moffett	1899	08	04	Bryan	TX	H&TC
Rev. E. G. Townsend & Mr. T. Moffett	1899	09	05	Belton	TX	MK&T
Rev. E. G. Townsend & Mr. V. C. Hart	1899	10	22	Mineola Jt.	TX	MK&T
Rev. E. G. Townsend & Mr. T. Moffett	1899	11	09	Dallas	TX	MK&T
Rev. E. G. Townsend & Mr. T. Moffett	1899	12	07	Del Rio	TX	GH&SA
Rev. E. G. Townsend & Mr. T. Moffett	1899	12	27	Comstock	TX	GH&SA
Rev. E. G. Townsend, wife, & Moffett	1900	01	06	Langtry	TX	GH&SA
Rev. E. G. Townsend & Mr. T. Moffett	1900	01	10	Sanderson	TX	GH&SA
Rev. E. G. Townsend & Mr. T. Moffett	1900	01	14	Hearne	TX	H&TC
Rev. E. G. Townsend & Mr. V. C. Hart	1900	01	18	Somerville	TX	GC&SF
Rev. E. G. Townsend & Mr. T. Moffett	1900	01	31	Waco	TX	MK&T
Rev. G. B. Rogers & Mr. T. Moffett	1900	02	03	Waco	TX	MK&T
Rev. G. B. Rogers & Mr. T. Moffett	1900	02	04	Fort Worth	TX	T&P
Rev. G. B. Rogers & Mr. T. Moffett	1900	02	13	Houston	TX	MK&T
Rev. G. B. Rogers & Mr. T. Moffett	1900	02	17	Cleveland	TX	HE&WT
Rev. G. B. Rogers & Mr. T. Moffett	1900	02	26	Livingston	TX	HE&WT
Rev. G. B. Rogers & Mr. T. Moffett	1900	03	06	Fort Worth	TX	T&P
Rev. G. B. Rogers & Mr. T. Moffett	1900	03	10	Groveton	TX	MK&T
Rev. G. B. Rogers & Mr. T. Moffett	1900	03	22	Houston	TX	MK&T
Rev. G. B. Rogers & Mr. T. Moffett	1900	03	24	Trinity	TX	SLSW
Rev. G. B. Rogers & Mr. T. Moffett	1900	04	09	Corsicana	TX	SLSW
Rev. G. B. Rogers & Mr. T. Moffett	1900	04	19	Corsicana	TX	SLSW
Rev. G. B. Rogers & Mr. V. C. Hart	1900	05	17	Wills Point	TX	T&P

Rev. G. B. Rogers & Mr. V. C. Hart	1900	05	22	Fort Worth	TX	MK&T
Rev. G. B. Rogers & Mr. V. C. Hart	1900	05	27	Ennis	TX	H&TC
Rev. G. B. Rogers & Mr. V. C. Hart	1900	06	08	Elgin	TX	H&TC
Rev. G. B. Rogers & Mr. V. C. Hart	1900	06	15	Houston	TX	H&TC
Rev. G. B. Rogers & Mr. V. C. Hart	1900	07	08	Victoria	TX	T&P
Rev. G. B. Rogers & Mr. V. C. Hart	1900	07	21	Wills Point	TX	T&P
Rev. G. B. Rogers & Mr. V. C. Hart	1900	08	06	Waco	TX	—
Rev. S. G. Neil, wife, & Mr. V. C. Hart	1900	08	10	Somerville	TX	GC&SF
G. B. Rogers, S. G. Neil & wife, & V. C. Hart	1900	08	15	Galveston	TX	GC&SF
Rev. G. B. Rogers & Mr. V. C. Hart	1900	08	16	Galveston	TX	GC&SF
Rev. G. B. Rogers & Mr. V. C. Hart	1900	08	23	Beaumont	TX	G&I
Rev. G. B. Rogers & Mr. V. C. Hart	1900	09	06	Galveston	TX	GC&SF
Rev. G. B. Rogers	1900	09	12	Godley	TX	—
Rev. G. B. Rogers & Mr. V. C. Hart	1900	09	15	Weatherford	TX	—
Mr. V. C. Hart	1900	10	03	Sulphur Springs	TX	—
Rev. G. B. Rogers	1900	10	04	Blevins	TX	—
Rev. G. B. Rogers & Mr. V. C. Hart	1900	10	12	Tyler	TX	—
Rev. G. B. Rogers & Mr. V. C. Hart	1900	11	02	Galveston	TX	—
Rev. G. B. Rogers	1900	11	08	Waco	TX	—
Rev. G. B. Rogers	1900	11	15	Waco	TX	—
Rev. G. B. Rogers & Mr. V. C. Hart	1900	11	29	Galveston	TX	GC&SF
Rev. G. B. Rogers & Mr. V. C. Hart	1900	12	01	Dallas	TX	GC&SF
Rev. G. B. Rogers & Mr. V. C. Hart	1900	12	05	Denison	TX	MK&T
Rev. G. B. Rogers & Mr. V. C. Hart	1900	12	06	Plano	TX	SL&SW
Rev. G. B. Rogers & Mr. V. C. Hart	1900	12	07	Dallas	TX	GC&SF
Rev. G. B. Rogers & Mr. V. C. Hart	1900	12	08	Greenville	TX	SL&SW
Rev. G. B. Rogers & Mr. V. C. Hart	1900	12	09	Whitewright	TX	SL&SW
Rev. G. B. Rogers & Mr. V. C. Hart	1900	12	10	Gainesville	TX	MK&T
Rev. G. B. Rogers & Mr. V. C. Hart	1900	12	11	Denton	TX	MK&T

Missionary	Year	Mo.	Day	City	State	RR
Rev. G. B. Rogers & Mr. V. C. Hart	1900	12	12	Dublin	TX	TC
Rev. G. B. Rogers & Mr. V. C. Hart	1900	12	13	Brownwood	TX	GC&SF
Rev. G. B. Rogers & Mr. V. C. Hart	1900	12	14	Belton	TX	MK&T
Rev. G. B. Rogers & Mr. V. C. Hart	1900	12	15	Temple	TX	MK&T
Rev. G. B. Rogers & Mr. V. C. Hart	1900	12	16	Waco	TX	MK&T
Rev. G. B. Rogers & Mr. V. C. Hart	1900	12	22	Lancaster	TX	MK&T
Rev. G. B. Rogers & Mr. V. C. Hart	1901	01	05	Brenham	TX	GC&SF
Mr. V. C. Hart	1901	01	14	Houston	TX	GH&SA
Rev. G. B. Rogers, Mr. V. C. Hart & wife	1901	01	22	Weimar	TX	GH&SA
Rev. G. B. Rogers, Mr. V. C. Hart & wife	1901	01	24	Columbus	TX	GH&SA
Rev. G. B. Rogers, Mr. V. C. Hart & wife	1901	01	27	Waelder	TX	GH&SA
Rev. G. B. Rogers, Mr. V. C. Hart & wife	1901	01	29	Flatonia	TX	GH&SA
Rev. G. B. Rogers, Mr. V. C. Hart & wife	1901	02	02	Gonzales	TX	GH&SA
Rev. G. B. Rogers, Mr. V. C. Hart & wife	1901	02	16	Richmond	TX	GH&SA
Rev. G. B. Rogers, Mr. V. C. Hart & wife	1901	02	27	Sealy	TX	GC&SF
Rev. G. B. Rogers, Mr. V. C. Hart & wife	1901	03	06	Rosenberg	TX	GC&SF
Rev. G. B. Rogers, Mr. V. C. Hart & wife	1901	03	18	Alvin	TX	GC&SF
Rev. G. B. Rogers, Mr. V. C. Hart & wife	1901	03	22	Alto Loma	TX	
Rev. G. B. Rogers, Mr. V. C. Hart & wife	1901	03	27	Hitchcock	TX	GC&SF
Rev. G. B. Rogers, Mr. V. C. Hart & wife	1901	03	30	Hillsboro	TX	MK&T
Rev. G. B. Rogers, Mr. V. C. Hart & wife	1901	04	20	Temple	TX	MK&T
Rev. G. B. Rogers & Mr. V. C. Hart	1901	06	10	Yoakum	TX	SA&AP
Rev. G. B. Rogers	1901	06	22	Sweet Home	TX	SA&AP
Rev. G. B. Rogers	1901	06	26	Waco	TX	MK&T
Rev. G. B. Rogers & Mr. V. C. Hart	1901	06	28	Cotulla	TX	IG&N
Rev. G. B. Rogers, Aline & W. C. Garrett	1901	06	29	Laredo	TX	IG&N
Rev. G. B. Rogers, Aline & W. C. Garrett	1901	07	16	Cotulla	TX	I&GN
Rev. G. B. Rogers, Aline & W. C. Garrett	1901	07	31	Hallettsville	TX	SA&AP

Rev. G. B. Rogers & Mr. W. C. Garrett	1901	08	12	Fort Worth	TX	MK&T
Rev. G. B. Rogers & Mr. W. C. Garrett	1901	08	17	Dalhart	TX	CRI&M
Rev. G. B. Rogers & Mr. W. C. Garrett	1901	09	02	Waco	TX	MKT
Rev. G. B. Rogers & D. Pegues	1901	09	18	Marshall	TX	T&P
Rev. G. B. Rogers & Mr. H. L. Hiett	1901	10	07	Waco	TX	T&P
Rev. G. B. Rogers & Mr. H. L. Hiett	1901	10	11	Tyler	TX	
Rev. G. B. Rogers & Mr. H. L. Hiett	1901	10	14	Waco	TX	MK&T
Rev. G. B. Rogers & Mr. H. L. Hiett	1901	11	07	Fort Worth	TX	MK&T
Rev. G. B. Rogers & Mr. H. L. Hiett	1901	11	12	Waco	TX	MK&T
Rev. G. B. Rogers	1901	11	14	Alamogordo	NM	—
Rev. G. B. Rogers & Mr. H. L. Hiett	1902	01	18	Lufkin	TX	HE&WT
Rev. G. B. Rogers & Mr. H. L. Hiett	1902	02	07	Carthage	TX	GC&SF
Rev. G. B. Rogers & Mr. H. L. Hiett	1902	03	08	Tenaha	TX	HE&WT
Rev. G. B. Rogers & Mr. H. L. Hiett	1902	03	17	Timpson	TX	HE&WT
Rev. G. B. Rogers	1902	04	16	Waco	TX	MK&T
Rev. G. B. Rogers & Mr. H. L. Hiett	1902	04	22	Houston	TX	MK&T
Mr. H. L. Hiett	1902	05	06	Brackettville	TX	—
Rev. G. B. Rogers	1902	05	14	Ciudad Porfiro Diaz	MX	MI
Rev. G. B. Rogers & Aline Rogers	1902	05	26	Columbus	TX	—
Rev. G. B. Rogers & Aline Rogers	1902	06	07	Elgin	TX	—
Rev. G. B. Rogers & Aline Rogers	1902	06	12	Jewett	TX	—
Rev. G. B. Rogers	1902	07	16	Minden	LA	—
Rev. G. B. Rogers	1902	07	23	Ciudad Porfiro Diaz	MX	MI
Rev. G. B. Rogers	1902	07	25	Gause	TX	I&GN
Rev. G. B. Rogers & Mr. H. L. Hiett	1902	08	14	Houston	TX	I&GN
Mr. H. L. Hiett	1902	08	23	Bigfoot	TX	—
Rev. G. B. Rogers & Mr. H. L. Hiett	1902	09	20	Waco	TX	MK&T
Rev. G. B. Rogers & wife	1902	09	27	Kansas City	MO	—
Rev. G. B. Rogers & wife	1902	10	09	Kansas City	MO	—
Rev. G. B. Rogers & Mr. H. L. Hiett	1902	10	11	Waco	TX	MK&T
Rev. G. B. Rogers & Mr. H. L. Hiett	1902	10	21	Chilton	TX	

Missionary	Year	Mo.	Day	City	State	RR
Rev. G. B. Rogers & Mr. H. L. Hiett	1902	11	06	Waco	TX	I&GN
Rev. G. B. Rogers & Mr. H. L. Hiett	1902	11	09	Waco	TX	I&GN
Rev. G. B. Rogers & Mr. H. L. Hiett	1902	11	17	Thorndale	TX	GC&SF
Rev. G. B. Rogers & Mr. H. L. Hiett	1902	12	11	Somerville	TX	I&GN
Rev. G. B. Rogers & Mr. H. L. Hiett	1902	12	23	Milano	TX	I&GN
Rev. G. B. Rogers & Mr. H. L. Hiett	1903	01	10	Palestine	TX	I&GN
Rev. G. B. Rogers & Mr. H. L. Hiett	1903	01	11	Palestine	TX	I&GN
Rev. G. B. Rogers & Mr. H. L. Hiett	1903	01	14	Tyler	TX	I&GN
Rev. G. B. Rogers	1903	02	14	Terrell	TX	TM
Rev. G. B. Rogers & Mr. R. S. Coward	1903	02	21	Terrell	TX	TM
Rev. G. B. Rogers & Miss Lake Erie Parker	1903	03	23	Cooper	TX	TM
Rev. G. B. Rogers & Mr. R. S. Coward	1903	04	11	Denison	TX	MK&T
Rev. G. B. Rogers & Mr. R. S. Coward	1903	05	14	Waco	TX	MK&T
Rev. G. B. Rogers & Mr. & Mrs. Riley	1903	06	15	Mexia	TX	H&TC
Rev. G. B. Rogers & Aline Rogers	1903	07	03	Groesbeck	TX	H&TC
Rev. G. B. Rogers	1903	07	13	Waco	TX	H&TC
Rev. G. B. Rogers	1903	07	14	La Porte	TX	GH&N
Rev. G. B. Rogers & Rev. G. M. Daniel	1903	08	03	Spring	TX	I&GN
Rev. G. B. Rogers & Rev. J. D. Harling	1903	08	20	La Grange	TX	GH&SA
Rev. G. B. Rogers & Rev. J. D. Harling	1903	08	30	Smithville	TX	MK&T
Rev. G. B. Rogers	1903	09	12	Waco	TX	H&TC
Rev. G. B. Rogers & Rev. Thorn	1903	09	26	Bay City	TX	CANE
Rev. G. B. Rogers	1903	11	05	Dallas	TX	H&TC
Rev. G. B. Rogers	1903	12	14	Waco	TX	H&TC

NOTES

Chapter One. Stuckers Hear Chapel Car Call

1. Death certificate, State of Illinois, provided by Beverly Stucker Bennett; family records of Beverly Stucker Bennett and her son Davis Bennett, interview and visit, June 24, 2002, Ottawa, Kansas.

2. "A New Baptist Church," *Aurora Daily Beacon*, Wednesday, June 3, 1896, 1; Sterling/Rock Falls Daily Star, Aug. 12, 1914. According to his obituary, Packer invented a corn seeder, corn planter, windmill, and obtained several other patents.

3. *History of Ottawa, Kansas* (Ottawa: Ottawa Public Library, n.d.), 49.

4. *The History of Franklin County, Kansas* (Ottawa: Franklin County Historical Society and Friends of Ottawa Library, n.d.), 415. Harper would respond to the criticism that the University of Chicago did not stress biblical principles by saying, "We have more teachers in the Biblical work than any other institution in America," and he would say of the criticism about the approach of Higher Criticism at the University, "What is Higher Criticism? Simply a method of study. We take a book of the Bible, as the book of Job and we ask the questions: By whom written? For whom? When? And, what was the object of the writer? Because some who employ this method and ask these questions are infidels, shall you class all who ask them as such?" The full text of this speech may be found in the proceedings of the 1894 Baptist General Association of Illinois, 89–91.

5. Obituary of Nettie V. Stucker, *Ottawa* [Kansas] *Herald*, Dec. 27, 1941, 5; an inscription in the Bible given to Nettie by Edwin on their wedding day, provided by Beverly Stucker Bennett, their granddaughter.

6. The *Aurora Daily Beacon*, Wednesday, June 22, 1895, 8; *History of Ottawa, Kansas*.

7. In an interview with Beverly Stucker Bennett in Ottawa, Kansas, on June 25, 2002, Mrs. Bennett, Nettie's granddaughter, was shocked to discover that her grandmother played the organ and sang during chapel car services. She never knew that side of her grandmother, and only remembered that she was a sweet, quiet woman who loved to cook and care for her family.

8. Baptist General Association of Illinois, 1894, association statistics, 139.

9. *Brunell's City Directory [Aurora]* (Aurora: Aurora Public Library, 1893), 420; *Aurora Daily Banner*, June 9, 1894; Grant, *The NorthWestern*, 66.

Chapter Two. Chapel Car Unique Gospel Ministry

1. Taylor and Taylor, *This Train Is Bound for Glory*, 12.

2. Ibid.; Marks, *Road to Power*, 13–14.

3. Taylor and Taylor, *This Train is Bound for Glory*, 18–26; *Harper's Weekly*, Jan. 31, 1891, 90.

4. Taylor and Taylor, *This Train is Bound for Glory*, 20; The *Spirit of Missions*, December, 1890, 470.

5. Taylor and Taylor, *This Train is Bound for Glory*, 23; personal papers of the Reverend H. "Mac" Kennickell, Asheville, North Carolina. For more information on the cathedral car of North Dakota, see Taylor and Taylor, *This Train Is Bound for Glory*.

6. Information from Father Herman Page, Topeka, Kansas, whose father was a bishop in the Upper Peninsula of Northern Michigan, and articles by Lois Prusok, "The Church in Hiawathaland," and "The Episcopal Diocese of Northern Michigan," *Marquette Monthly*, January, 1996, and observations of the author when visiting the second Episcopal chapel car in Negaunee, Michigan.

7. For more information on the chapel cars of the Diocese of Upper Peninsula, see Taylor and Taylor, *This Train Is Bound for Glory*.

8. An observer, "The Mission of the Chapel Car," *Extension*, September, 1907, 11.

9. The information about the chapel cars was compiled from Taylor and Taylor, *This Train Is Bound for Glory*.

Chapter Three. Hearing the Tramp of Texas Millions

1. Baptist General Convention of Texas, Oct. 12–16, 1894 (Waco: *Baptist Standard* Printing House, 1894), 22.

2. Baptist General Convention of Texas, Oct. 11–14, 1895 (Waco: *Baptist Standard* Printing House, 1895), 27.

3. The *Colporter*, November, 1895, 5.

4. *Baptist Standard*, July 4, 1895, 5; Taylor and Taylor, *This Train Is Bound for Glory*, 77.

5. Taylor and Taylor, *This Train Is Bound for Glory*, 77; *The Pacific Baptist*, 3. Archive is located at the American Baptist Seminary of the West, Berkeley, California.

6. Taylor and Taylor, *This Train Is Bound for Glory*, 77; *Roswell* (New Mexico) *Register*, Apr. 3, 1895.

7. Taylor and Taylor, *This Train Is Bound for Glory*, 77; Proceedings, Southern Baptist Convention, May 11–15, 1894 (Atlanta: Franklin Printing and Publishing Co.), 42.

8. Executive Board of the Baptist General Convention of Texas, *Centennial Story of Texas Baptists*, 47.

9. Baptist General Convention of Texas, Forty-Sixth Annual Session, October 12–16, 1894, 58; Executive Board of the Baptist General Convention of Texas, *Centennial Story of Texas Baptists*, 47.

10. Proceedings, Southern Baptist Convention, May 11–15, 1894, 42.

11. Taylor and Taylor, *This Train Is Bound for Glory*, 32.

12. Trostel, *The Barney & Smith Car Company*, 180–225.

13. Ibid., introduction.

14. Minutes from the Seventy-First Anniversary of the 1895 American Baptist Publication Society, held at Saratoga, N.Y., June 1 and 3, 1895 (Philadelphia: American Baptist Publication Society), 15.

15. This description of *Good Will*, based on a variety of sources, including the Barney & Smith floor plans, is taken from the detailed studies of the chapel cars by Norman T. Taylor, who is restoring chapel car *Grace* at Green Lake, Wisconsin; "Chapel Car in Aurora," *Aurora Daily News*, Wednesday, June 12, 1895, 1.

16. Observation of Wilma Rugh Taylor and Norman Thomas Taylor on a visit to chapel car *Good Will* in October, 1994, located at Boyes Springs, Sonoma County, California.

17. *Aurora Daily News*, Wednesday, June 12, 1895, 1; *Fort Scott* (Kansas) *Daily Monitor*, June 29, 1895; *Fort Scott* (Kansas) *Daily Monitor*, June 28, 1895.

18. McBeth, *Texas Baptists*, 29.

19. Carroll et al., *A History of Texas Baptists*, 722; McBeth, *The Baptist Heritage*, 458; original source was Robert A. Baker, *The Blossoming Desert*, 159–60.

Chapter Four. Railroaders Love a Rail Church

1. Holden, *Alkali Trails*, 32–33; Jensen, *The American Heritage History of Railroads in America*, 122.

2. "Denison sold to highest bidder," *Sherman Democrat*, Centennial Edition, Aug. 12, 1979, 2; Troxell, *Texas Trains*, 224–25.

3. Maguire, *Katy's Baby: The Story of Denison, Texas*, 110.

4. Campbell, *Gone to Texas*, 320–21.

5. Spain, "Texas Baptists and Prohibition," 43–46; Vernon et al., *The Methodist Excitement in Texas*, 238.

6. Minutes of the Grayson Baptist Association, 1895, 16.

7. Hofsommer, *Southern Pacific, 1901–1985*, 31.

8. Moore, *The Story of the Railroad "Y,"* 53–54.

9. *Railway Age Gazette* 58, Feb. 26, 1915, 359.

10. Taylor and Taylor, *This Train Is Bound for Glory*, 39.

11. *Baptist Standard*, Thursday, July 4, 1895, 5.

12. Jensen, *American Heritage History of Railroads in America*, 192, has the target population of railroad employees across the United States during the

1890 "golden age" of railroading totaling more than 1,699,420, which is a different figure than the *Baptist Standard* reports; Seventy-First Anniversary of the American Baptist Publication Society, 1895, 49.

13. *Denison Sunday Gazette,* July 14, 1895; *Colporter,* July, 1895, 6; "Sunday Topics," *Sunday Gazette,* Denison, Texas, July 28, 1895, 3.

14. *Colporter,* October, 1895, 6.

15. Jensen, *American Heritage History of Railroads in America,* 194.

16. E. S. Stucker, "Noon Talks to Railroad Men," *Marshall News Messenger,* Nov. 7, 1895.

17. "Accident on the Texas and Pacific," *Sunday Gazetteer,* Denison, Texas, July 21, 1895, 2.

18. *Colporter,* October, 1895, 6; several photos show women attending chapel car meetings in other chapel cars, and that would be the common practice.

19. Proceedings of The Grayson County, Texas, Baptist Association, 1895, 15.

20. Taylor and Taylor, *This Train Is Bound for Glory,* 108; Seventy-Sixth Anniversary of the American Baptist Publication Society (Philadelphia: American Baptist Publication Society, 1900), 56.

21. *Colporter,* July, 1895, 6.

22. "Chapel Car Good Will," *Dallas Morning News,* July 18, 1895, 8.

23. "Children's Meeting at Chapel Car," *Dallas Morning News,* July 19, 1895, 8.

24. "Bound About Town," *Dallas Morning News,* July 20, 1895, 8.

Chapter Five. Scattering Canadian Gospel Seeds

1. Stanley, *Story of the Texas Panhandle Railroads,* 52.

2. Ibid., 46.

3. Ibid., 47, 52; Haley, *The XIT Ranch of Texas,* 210, 212.

4. "Chapel Car Work," *Baptist Standard,* Thursday, Aug. 1, 1895, 5.

5. Hamner, *Short Grass & Longhorns,* 230.

6. "Good Will," *Colporter,* October, 1895, 6.

7. In "Saints and Sinners: Waco Baptist Women's Work," *Texas Baptist History, the Journal of The Texas Baptist Historical Society,* vol. 18, 1998, Ellen Kuniyuke Brown presents an interesting study of the attitudes of Baptists of Waco and other Texas Baptists toward a witness to prostitutes. See Taylor and Taylor, *This Train Is Bound for Glory.* One particular incident involves the Reverend Hermiston on chapel car *Emmanuel* and a saloon girl called Carolyn who came to the chapel car, participated in the services, but felt that she was too bad for God to forgive her. She fled town and was killed in a buggy accident. The Reverend Hermiston preached her sermon.

8. Hunter, *The Book of Years,* 37.

9. Ferry, *Reminiscences of John V. Farwell,* vol. 1, 47, 65, and 79.

10. Stanley, *The Channing Story,* 11; Hunter, *The Book of Years,* 15.

11. "Chapel Car Good Will," *Colporter,* Oct., 1895, 6; Boston W. Smith, *The*

Story of Our Chapel Car Work, 31; Hunter, *The Book of Years,* 47; "History of the First Baptist Church of Texline, Texas," from church files at First Baptist Church, Texline, Texas; Hunter, *The Book of Years,* 38.

12. A history of the Texline Baptist Church notes that it was the second church to be organized in town, the first being a Methodist, but another town history states that the Methodist church was not organized until 1907.

13. Halberstadt and Halberstadt, *The American Train Depot & Round-house,* 30.

14. Stanley, *Story of the Texas Panhandle Railroads,* 55; Hamner, *Short Grass & Longhorns,* 245.

15. Stanley, *Story of the Texas Panhandle Railroads,* 55; Hamner, *Short Grass & Longhorns,* 245.

16. Haley, *The XIT Ranch of Texas,* 177; Laura V. Hamner, scrapbook.

17. Hunter, *The Book of Years,* 47.

18. Ibid., 28.

19. The 1893 Palo Duro Canyon Baptist Association.

20. Hunter, *The Book of Years,* 31.

21. Taylor and Taylor, *This Train Is Bound for Glory,* 79.

Chapter Six. Finding Surprises in East Texas

1. "State Board Meeting," *Waco Standard,* Oct. 31, 1895, 4; "An Understanding Reached," *Baptist Standard,* Feb. 6, 1896. 8.

2. Campbell, *Gone to Texas,* 308.

3. Plummer, *Historic Marshall Revisited,* 105; "A Pen Picture of the City of Marshall and Harrison County," a promotional booklet published by the Tri-Weekly Herald Book and Job Print, November, 1879, 11–12; Smith, *Story of Our Chapel Car Work,* 31; "Chapel Car Good Will," *Marshall News Messenger,* Nov. 4, 1895.

4. *Cultural Crossroads;* "A Pen Picture of the City of Marshall," 19; Plummer, *Historic Marshall Revisited,* 66.

5. Rebekah Baines Johnson, *A Family Album,* 93.

6. Plummer, *Historic Marshall Revisited,* 53.

7. *The Baptist Home Mission Monthly,* January 1898, 18.

8. Plummer, *Historic Marshall Revisited,* 53–70; "A Pen Picture of the City of Marshall and Harrison County," 9.

9. Plummer, *Historic Marshall Revisited,* 53–70, 30.

10. Ibid., 25; "Souvenir of the Allen House Dedication," The *Marshall Evening Messenger,* Feb. 13, 1895, a reprint of the *Marshall News Messenger* for the Harrison Historical Society.

11. Spratt, *Thurber, Texas,* introduction; Rhinehart, *A Way of Work and a Way of Life,* 45–46. (Marilyn D. Rhinehart, "Underground Patriots: Thurber Coal Miners and the Struggle for Industrial Freedom;" *Thurber Journal,* special ed., 1900, purchased by author at the Thurber Restaurant, located in the old store building, Oct. 19, 2001.)

12. Rhinehart, *A Way of Work and a Way of Life*, 60–61.

13. "Good Will," *Colporter*, January, 1896, 5; Rhinehart, *A Way of Work and a Way of Life*, 44–45.

14. Rhinehart, *A Way of Work and a Way of Life*, 100.

15. "Good Will," *Colporter*, January, 1896, 5; Rhinehart, *A Way of Work and a Way of Life*, 61.

16. R. W. Marshall, letter to the editor, *Baptist Standard*, Feb. 18, 1896, 9.

17. Johnson, *Smithville Then and Now*, 26; Pioneer Panola County, compiled by the Panola County Historical Survey Committee, 1976: From observations by the author during the writing of *This Train Is Bound for Glory*, including travel and research in hundreds of towns across America.

18. Johnson, *Smithville Then and Now*, 2; *Smithville Times*, July 16, 1992.

19. Mina F. Sayers, letter to the editor, *Baptist Standard*, Feb. 20, 1896, 8.

20. "Greatest Fire in Many Years," *Colporter*, March, 1896, 1.

21. "Storms Hit Central Texas," *San Antonio Daily Express*, Mar. 29, 1897, 1.

Chapter Seven. Border Towns, Big Decisions

1. Carroll, *A History of Texas Baptists*, 497.

2. "In the Shadow of His Hand: The First Century of the First Baptist Church of San Antonio, Texas, 1861–1961," in the archives of the Southwestern Seminary Library, 47; Carroll, *A History of Texas Baptists*, 497; *The Colporter*, Jan., 1896, 6; "Chapel Car Work," *Texas Baptist Standard*, Feb. 27, 1896, 9.

3. "The Gospel on Wheels," *San Antonio Daily Express*, Friday morning, Feb. 14, 1896, 8; Stucker log of travels, in Stucker file, American Baptist Publication Society, Valley Forge, Pa.

4. Frank W. Jennings, "San Antonio: The Story of an Enchanted City," *San Antonio Express–News*, 1998, 229.

5. "At the Sunset Baptist," *San Antonio Daily Express*, Wed. morning, Feb. 26, 1896, 8.

6. *Baptist Standard*, May 14, 1896, 8.

7. Dilmore, *The Story of the First Baptist Church of Marble Falls*, 32; Becker, *A Pictorial History of Marble Falls*, 17; "100 Pages of Marble Falls History, 1887–1987," Special Centennial Edition of the *Highlander*, Oct. 22, 1987, 6.

8. J. N. Marshall, letter to the editor, *Baptist Standard*, May 14, 1896, 8.

9. *Baptist Standard*, Apr. 26, 1900, 4.

10. Captain William Alexander Fitch, scrapbook, circa 1890s, Eagle Pass Public Library.

11. *Baptist Standard*, May 14, 1896, 8.

12. Ibid., "Del Rio Baptists: From Six Members to 1,450 in 70 years," May 24, 1966, newspaper clipping; notes on First Baptist Church history in vertical file, Val Verde Library, Del Rio, Texas; Taylor and Taylor, *This Train Is Bound for Glory*, 135.

13. Whitehead Memorial Museum et al., *La Hacienda,* 278; *Baptist Standard,* Feb. 18, 1896.

14. *Baptist Standard,* Aug. 6, 1896, 12.

15. Biographical Sketches of Val Verde County's Old Timers, Val Verde Historical Society, 1993, 2.

16. "Reverend Stucker Gone North," *Houston Daily Post,* Oct. 21, 1895, 5.

17. Campbell, *Gone to Texas,* 308.

18. Stan Green, *The Story of Laredo,* vol. 2, 19; The Executive Board of the Baptist General Convention of Texas, *Centennial Story of Texas Baptists,* 54.

19. E. S. Stucker, "Sermon Preached at Laredo, Texas, at the Close of a Series of Chapel Car Services," *Baptist Standard,* May 14, 1896. 6.

20. Taylor and Taylor, *This Train Is Bound for Glory,* 112.

21. *Baptist Standard,* Aug. 6, 1896, 12.

22. *Baptist Standard,* Feb. 27, 1896, 9.

23. V. V. Masterson, *The Katy Railroad and the Last Frontier,* 265–66.

24. The *Daily Hesperian,* Gainesville, Tex., Aug. 25, 1896.

25. Carroll, *A History of Texas Baptists,* 732–33.

26. "Good Will in the Shops," *Houston Daily Post,* Wednesday, Oct. 14, 1896, 3.

27. "Rev. Stucker Gone North," *Houston Daily Post,* Wednesday, Oct. 21, 1896, 5.

28. "Good Will in the Shops," *Houston Daily Post,* Wednesday, Oct. 14, 1896, 3.

Chapter Eight. Hero Diaz's Fall from Grace

1. Proceedings of the Thirty-Seventh Session–Forty-Seventh Year of the Southern Baptist Convention, May 6–10, 1892 (Atlanta: Franklin Publishing House, 1892), 43.

Note: A brief summary of the fascinating history of A. J. Diaz can be found in *The Missionary Work of the Southern Baptist Convention* by Mary Emily Wright, (Philadelphia: American Baptist Publication Society, 1892), 364–69, as well as in numerous accounts in the *Baptist Standard.*

2. *Encyclopaedia Britannica,* 1968 edition, s.v. "Cuba."

3. The Reverend I. T. Tichenor, *Conversion of Alberto J. Diaz and his Return to Cuba,* Maryland Baptist Mission Rooms, Baltimore, Archives, Southern Baptist Theological Seminary, Boyce Library, 4–13.

4. *Baptist Standard,* Apr. 23, 1896, 12.

5. Tupper, *Diaz, The Apostle of Cuba,* 28.

6. *Baptist Standard,* Apr. 23, 1896, 5.

7. Ibid., Apr. 28, 1896, 5.

8. Statement on the Situation in Cuba, by the Home Mission Board of the Southern Baptist Convention, Atlanta, 1903, Archives, Southern Baptist Theological Seminary, Louisville, 3.

9. Boston W. Smith, 1831–1908, scrapbook, "Merry Christmas," American Baptist Historical Society, Valley Forge, Pa.

10. Tichenor, *Conversion of Alberto J. Diaz and his Return to Cuba,* 11.

11. Statement on the Situation in Cuba, 4.

12. Smith, scrapbook.

13. *Baptist Standard,* Dec. 10, 1896, 9.

14. "San Antonio Notes," *The Texas Baptist and Herald,* Dec. 10, 1896, 6; "Dr. A. J. Diaz," *The Texas Baptist and Herald,* Dec. 17, 1896, 8.

15. *Baptist Standard,* Oct. 7, 1897, 16.

16. *Texas Almanac,* 1996–1997 edition, 42; Statement on the Situation in Cuba, 4.

17. Statement on the Situation in Cuba, 5.

18. Ibid., 30.

Chapter Nine. Honeymooning in Piney Arbors

1. Ramond, *Among Southern Baptists,* 502; "Dr. Townsend, Beloved Dean, Is Laid to Rest," Mary Hardin-Baylor newspaper, date unknown, found in the files, Mary Harden-Baylor University archives; Hollie Harper Townsend, letter to the editor, *Baptist Standard,* Sept. 21, 1897, 12.

2. Hollie Harper Townsend, letter to the editor, *Baptist Standard,* Sept. 29, 1897, 11; Hollie Harper-Townsend, "About Chapel Cars" pamphlet, Chapel Car Series No. 7 (Philadelphia: American Baptist Publication Society).

3. L. Katherine Cook, "Texas Baptist Women and Missions, 1830–1900," *Texas Baptist History, The Journal of The Texas Baptist Historical Society* 18 (1998): 41. J. B. Cranfill footnote in Carroll, *A History of Texas Baptists,* 862–63; see also Inez Boyle Hunt, *Century One: A Pilgrimage of Faith* (Birmingham, Ala.: Woman's Missionary Union of the Southern Baptist Convention, 1979), 23. There is mention of Hollie Harper in the letters from Annie Armstrong–Fannie Breedlove Davis; Patricia Martin, "Ordained Work—Unordained Workers: Texas 'Bible Women,' 1880–1920," *Texas Baptist History, The Journal of The Texas Baptist Historical Society* 18 (1988): 5; Hollie Harper, "Woman's Department," *Baptist Standard,* Aug. 18, 1896, 14.

4. Seventy-Fourth Anniversary of the American Baptist Publication Society (Philadelphia: The American Baptist Publication Society, 1898), 58–59.

5. "Sunday Morning Thoughts," *Baptist Standard,* Mar. 18, 1897, 4; Seventy-Fourth Anniversary of the American Baptist Publication Society, 1898, 59.

6. "Good Will," *Baptist Standard,* Apr. 22, 1897, 14.

7. "Revival," *The Dallas Morning News,* Mar. 6, 1897, 4.

8. T. C. Richardson, *East Texas: Its History and its Makers,* 706–707.

9. E. G. Townsend, "Chapel Car Good Will," *Baptist Standard,* Apr. 29, 1897, 13.

10. Hollie Harper Townsend, *Baptist Standard,* Apr. 22, 1897, 8.

11. Emma Haynes, *The History of Polk County,* 52.

12. "Over the River and Through the Woods, A Glimpse of Shepherd's

Past," the Shepherd High School Eleventh Grade English Honors Class, 1989–90, 16.

13. *Catch the Vision: First Baptist Church, 1896–1996, Shepherd, Texas,* published by the History Committee, 1996, 29.

14. *Baptist Standard,* May 27, 1897.

15. "A History of the First Baptist Church," *A History of Tenaha, Texas* (Tenaha: Tenaha Historical Society, n.d.), 172, 165; "Tenaha," *The New Handbook of Texas,* vol. 6 (Austin: The Texas State Historical Association, 1996), 252.

16. Recollections of Gloria Moore, Collection in Center, Texas, Public Library, 289 and 295.

17. "A History of the First Baptist Church," 172.

18. Anniversary Report of the American Baptist Publication Society, Rochester, N.Y., 1898, 59.

19. Ibid.; E. G. Townsend, "Chapel Car Good Will," *Baptist Standard,* July 22, 1897, 8.

20. Martin, "Ordained Work—Unordained Workers," 1.

21. Brown, "Saints and Sinners," 98. This article by Brown, who is archivist of the Texas Collection at Baylor University, is an excellent source concerning the role of women in Texas Baptist History.

22. Both Martin's and Cook's articles in *Texas Baptist History: The Journal of The Texas Baptist Historical Society* are excellent discussions of the status of women and preaching in Texas at the time of chapel car *Good Will*'s ministry; Mrs. Driver on chapel car *Good Will* and Mrs. Cutler on chapel car *Messenger of Peace* were both ordained. Mrs. Herminston, who served both on chapel car *Emmanuel* and chapel car *Grace,* was lauded for her preaching skills. Almost all the chapel car wives did some speaking other than to women and children, especially to the men at the railroad shops who seemed to be so touched by a godly woman, perhaps reminding them of their mothers and wives and sisters back home. All the chapel car wives, and some of their grown daughters, played the organ and helped with the singing; Seventy-Third Anniversary, American Baptist Publication Society, Pittsburgh, Pa., May 20–21, 1897, 98.

23. "Clergy Permits," *The Dallas Morning News,* June 6, 1898.

24. Herb Walker, *Good Old Camp Meeting Songs,* 10, 17.

25. Seventy-Fourth Anniversary of the American Baptist Publication Society, 59.

26. Baptist General Convention of Texas, Houston, Oct. 9–13, 1986, 66.

27. Seventy-Fourth Anniversary of the American Baptist Publication Society, 60.

28. Taylor and Taylor, *This Train is Bound for Glory,* 136–37.

29. Spratt, *Thurber, Texas,* introduction.

30. Hollie Harper Townsend, "Good Will," *Baptist Standard,* Oct. 21, 1897.

31. It would be in the spring of 1901 that a small church would be built for the Baptists. Pastor J. B. Vinson reported in the *Baptist Standard,* May 2, 1901, 16, "We are now worshipping in the new church house. We have bought a new bell and will soon have money to buy an organ."

Chapter Ten. Winning Souls in West Texas

1. *Baptist Standard,* Oct. 28, 1897, 6; "Sunday School Camp Meeting," *Abilene Reporter,* Oct. 29, 1897, 3.

2. "The Baptist Tent Meeting," *Abilene Reporter,* Nov. 5, 1897, 2.

3. Ibid.; *Abilene Reporter,* Oct. 22, 1897, 6.

4. "George M. Pullman Dead," *Abilene Reporter,* Oct. 29, 1897, 8.

5. "An Old Texan Talks," *Abilene Reporter,* Dec. 3, 1897, 5.

6. McBeth, *The Baptist Heritage,* 120; Carroll, *A History of Texas Baptists,* 722-23.

7. "Dr. Buckner Re-elected," *San Antonio Daily Light,* Nov. 6-7, 1897, 4 and 1.

8. "Greatest State Convention in History," *Baptist Standard,* Nov. 11, 1897, 2.

9. *Baptist Standard,* July 4, 1895, 5.

10. *Abilene Reporter,* Dec. 3, 1897, 5.

11. *Baptist Standard,* Aug. 18, 1898, 16.

12. "The History of the First Baptist Church of Pecos, Texas," www.mo.quik.com.grace.

13. *The New Handbook of Texas,* vol. 2, 155.

14. E. G. Townsend, *Baptist Standard,* Feb. 10, 1898, 8.

15. *Baptist Standard,* Feb. 24, 1898, 8.

16. McBeth, *The First Baptist Church of Dallas,* 135-37.

17. Avera, *Wind Swept Land,* 29.

18. Neyland, *Palestine (Texas), A History,* 42-43.

19. Dean, *History of the First Baptist Church, Palestine, Texas,* 21; *Baptist Standard,* Feb. 24, 1898, 8.

20. *The Baptist Teacher,* 250.

21. Ray Miller, *Galveston,* 131.

22. Correspondence from Harold L. Frickett to A. C. Gettys, Mary Hardin-Baylor College, June 16, 1954, Good Will folder, American Baptist Historical Society, Valley Forge, Pa.

23. *Baptist Standard,* Feb. 16, 1899, 8.

24. "Chapel Car Good Will," *Galveston Daily News,* Mar. 28, 1898, 8.

25. "Washington Is Excited," *Galveston Daily News,* Apr. 2, 1898, 1; *Galveston Daily News,* Apr. 24, 1898, 21.

26. "Resume of Southern Baptist Convention," *Baptist Standard,* May 19, 1898, 1; General Miles was the brother-in-law of Colgate Hoyt, railroad executive and a member of the Syndicate that built the first American Baptist chapel car, *Evangel.* Hoyt was a Baptist layman and a close friend of John D. Rockefeller and fellow trustee at the Fifth Avenue Baptist Church in New York. For more information on Miles, Hoyt, and Rockefeller and the chapel cars see Taylor and Taylor, *This Train Is Bound for Glory;* a loose page from a Baptist paper published in Dallas, name unknown, May 19, 1898, 1.

27. *The Baptist Teacher,* 694.

Chapter Eleven. Happiness, Grief, and Solace

1. "About Chapel Cars," *Baptist Standard,* Oct. 27, 1898, 12.

2. *Dallas Morning News,* Aug. 24, 1898, 7; "About Chapel Cars," *Baptist Standard,* Oct. 27, 1898, 12.

3. Anniversary Report of the American Baptist Publication Society, 59.

4. "Annual Meeting," *Brenham Daily Banner,* Brenham, Tex., June 22, 1898, 1.

5. "Annual Meeting," *Brenham Daily Banner,* June 23, 1898, 1.

6. Other babies born on chapel cars were the two daughters of the Reverend and Mrs. Charles H. Rush on *Glad Tidings,* and the son of the Reverend and Mrs. Allen on Chapel Car *Evangel;* Carroll, *A History of Texas Baptists,* 862.

7. Harper-Townsend, "About Chapel Cars." This same letter appeared in part in Mrs. W. J. J. Smith's *A Centennial History of the Baptist Women of Texas 1830–1930* (Dallas: Woman's Missionary Union, 1933), 161–63, and portions of it were used in McBeth, *Texas Baptists.*

8. *Baptist Standard,* Oct. 27, 1898, 9.

9. Smith, *Story of Our Chapel Car Work,* 17; Anniversary Report of The American Baptist Publication Society, 108–109.

10. *Pacific Baptist,* Nov. 16, 1898, 5–10.

11. Taylor and Taylor, *This Train Is Bound for Glory,* 83.

12. C. H. Rust, *A Church on Wheels,* 57.

13. Taylor and Taylor, *This Train Is Bound for Glory,* 164.

14. "Good Will," *Baptist Standard* June 20, 1895; Hedge and Dawson, *The San Antonio and Aransas Pass Railroad,* 28.

15. *Yoakum Community: The First Hundred Years, 1887–1987,* 285–86.

16. Hedge and Dawson, *The San Antonio and Aransas Pass Railroad,* 38.

17. *Yoakum Community,* 66; *Baptist Standard,* Jan. 13, 1899, 8.

18. *Baptist Standard,* Mar. 16, 1899, 9; *Baptist Standard,* Apr. 27, 1899, 8.

19. *Baptist Standard,* May 25, 1899, 8.

20. *The New Handbook of Texas,* vol. 1, 793; *Baptist Standard,* Sept. 7, 1899, 8.

Chapter Twelve. New Life, New Wife, New Mission

1. Eleanor James, *Forth From Her Portals: The First 100 Years in Belton.*

2. "The Townsend Papers," Baptist Collection, Baylor University Library, copied from *Baptist Standard,* July 30, 1958; Montgomery, *Ten Thousand Texas Daughters,* 142; *Baptist Standard,* Sept. 21, 1899, 12; Executive Board of the Baptist General Convention of Texas, *Centennial Story of Texas Baptists,* 238.

3. *The Texas Baptist and Herald,* Aug. 22, 1895, 4.

4. *Mineola: The First 100 Years,* 20–23.

5. Bruner, *Mineola and Its Mayors,* 61.

6. Carroll, *A History of Texas Baptists,* 785 and 783; "Third Day's Session," *Dallas Morning News,* Nov. 11, 1899, 4.

7. San Antonio *Daily Light,* Dec. 15 and 19, 1899; "Baptist Church, Val Verde County," *The History of Val Verde County,* 39.

8. "Chapel Car Work," *Baptist Standard,* Feb. 1, 1990, 9.

9. *The New Handbook of Texas,* vol. 2, 254.

10. "Good Will," *The Colporter,* March 1900, 7.

11. Jack Skiles, *Judge Roy Bean Country,* 121 and 129.

12. "Judge Roy Bean, the Law West of the Pecos," brochure, Texas Department of Transportation, March, 1998.

13. Ibid.

14. *Baptist Standard,* Feb. 2, 1900, 9.

15. "Good Will," *The Colporter,* April, 1900, 7; McCarver and McCarver, *Hearne of the Brazos,* 25 and 27.

16. Taylor and Taylor, *This Train Is Bound for Glory,* 139.

17. J. W. Baker, *A History of Robertson County, Texas,* 256; McCarver and Mc-Carver, *Hearne on the Brazos* 26.

18. "Good Will," *The Colporter,* March, 1900, 7.

19. Very little was found in Baylor University files of the chapel car ministry of the Reverend Townsend, a Baylor graduate, or of Hollie Harper-Townsend, a Texas Baptist Woman's Department editor and Baylor Female College and Cottage leader. At the campus of Mary Hardin-Baylor University, in Belton, Texas, in the Townsend Library, we found very little, almost nothing, about Townsend's years on the chapel car and his first marriage. The second Mrs. Townsend was a very influential graduate of Mary Hardin and a classmate of Hollie Harper-Townsend. Through her influence and his abilities, Rev. Townsend assumed high positions in the college.

Chapter Thirteen. Reviving East Texas Towns

1. "Good Will," *Baptist Standard,* Apr. 12, 1899, 16; *Baptist Standard,* Dec. 1, 1898.

2. "Good Will," *Baptist Standard,* Jan. 5, 1899, 8; "Good Will," *Baptist Standard,* Feb. 22, 1900, 13.

3. "Good Will," *Baptist Standard,* Feb. 22, 1900, 13.

4. *Baptist Standard,* Feb. 8, 1900, 9.

5. Seventy-Sixth Anniversary of the American Baptist Publication Society, 54. Rogers reported that there was a Catholic church in town, but he would not have considered it "a house of worship." *Baptist Standard,* Feb. 22, 1900, 13.

6. Maxwell, *Whistle in the Piney Woods,* 45.

7. *Baptist Standard,* Mar. 8, 1900, 9; *Baptist Standard,* Feb. 16, 1899, 8.

8. Ibid., Mar. 8, 1900, 9.

9. Sitton and Conrad, *Nameless Towns,* preface. Richardson, *East Texas,* 471; Robert S. Maxwell and Robert D. Baker, *Sawdust Empire: The Texas Lumber Industry, 1830–1940,* (College Station: Texas A&M University Press, 1983), 160, as quoted in Sitton and Conrad, *Nameless Towns.*

10. *Colporter,* April–May, 1900, 7.

11. Haynes, *The History of Polk County,* 131.

12. "Progress and Pyromania in Livingston," *Livingston Centennial Gazette,* Feb. 26, 1900, 1.

13. Sitton and Conrad, *Nameless Towns,* 39–41.

14. "Good Will," *Colporter,* April 1900, 7.

15. *Baptist Standard,* Mar. 15, 1900, 13; Haynes, *The History of Polk County,* 14–15; *A Pictorial History of Polk County, Texas: 1846–1910; Baptist Standard,* Mar. 15, 1900, 13.

16. *Historical Polk County, Texas: Companies and Soldiers Organized in and Enrolled From Said County in Confederate States Army and Navy—1861–1865,* Organization Ike Turner Camp, U. C. V. Unveiling, 1913, 19.

17. Haynes, *The History of Polk County,* 124, 13.

18. *Baptist Standard,* Mar. 29, 1900, 9; Ibid., Apr. 5, 1900, 9; Haynes, *The History of Polk County,* 121.

19. *Baptist Standard,* Apr. 5, 1900, 4.

20. Ibid., May 10, 1900, 9; Ibid., Mar. 29, 1900, 9; Ibid., June 7, 1900, 8.

21. Letter from Robert G. Seymour, Missionary and Bible secretary, American Baptist Publication Society to Rev. G. B. Rogers, Mar. 22, 1900 and Apr. 9, 1900, Archives American Baptist Publication Society, Valley Forge, Pa.

Chapter Fourteen. Praise, Poundings, and Problems

1. Correspondence from Robert G. Seymour to the Reverend B. B. Jacques, June 2, 1900, Seymour Collection, American Baptist Historical Society, Valley Forge, Pa.

2. "Gospel Car," *Wills Point Chronicle,* June 10 and 17, 1900, 5.

3. Ibid., June 24, 1900, 3.

4. Ibid., 5.

5. Taylor and Taylor, *This Train Is Bound for Glory,* see chapters on Catholic Extension Society chapel cars *St. Anthony, St. Peter,* and *St. Paul.*

6. *Wills Point Chronicle,* July 12, 1900, 5; *Baptist Standard,* June 28, 1900, 8.

7. *Baptist Standard,* June 14, 1900, 8; Ibid., May 31, 1900, 8; Ibid., Aug. 16, 1900, 9.

8. Letter from Robert G. Seymour to the Reverend G. B. Rogers, June 1, 1900, American Baptist Historical Society, Valley Forge, Pa.

9. "Protracted Meeting," *Wills Point Chronicle,* Aug. 2, 1900, 4; The Van Zandt County History Book Committee, *The History of Van Zandt County, Texas,* 57.

10. *Baptist Standard,* June 7, 1900, 4; Hawkins, *History of Ellis County Texas,* 121–23; "The History of Tabernacle Baptist Church," Ennis Public Library, Ennis, Tex.; Hawkins, *History of Ellis County Texas,* 124.

11. "Good Will," *Colporter,* September, 1900, 6.

12. Seventy-Sixth Anniversary of the American Baptist Publication Society, 1900, 53.

13. Letter from Thomas Seymour to Rev. G. B. Rogers, Aug. 1, 1900.

14. *Baptist Standard,* Sept. 20, 1900, 9; "The Chapel Car," *Beaumont Enterprise,* Aug. 24, 1900, 4.

15. "Must Protect the Forests," *Beaumont Enterprise,* Sept. 7, 1900, 3.

16. *Baptist Standard,* Sept. 20, 1900, 9.

Chapter Fifteen. Shelter in the Time of Storm

1. Elizabeth Hayes Turner lists five different sources for this phrase in her book *Women, Culture, and Community: Religion and Reform in Galveston, 1880–1920,* 29.

2. *Baptist Standard,* July 26, 1900, 9.

3. Larson, *Isaac's Storm,* 148.

4. Ibid., 58, 59, 67.

5. Miller, *Galveston.*

6. Weems, *A Weekend in September,* 100.

7. Carroll, *A History of Texas Baptists,* 794; *Baptist Standard,* Sept. 27, 1900, 8.

8. Bennett, "An Informal History of First Baptist Church of Galveston," 77.

9. Larson, *Isaac's Storm,* 162.

10. R. C. Buckner, "At Galveston after the Storm," *Baptist Standard,* Sept. 20, 1900, 13.

11. Ibid.

12. "The Great Galveston Storm," *Baptist Standard,* Nov. 8, 1900, 12.

13. "Good Will," *Colporter,* November, 1900, 6.

14. Larson, *Isaac's Storm,* 271.

15. "Good Will," *Baptist Standard,* Sept. 20, 1900, 9.

Chapter Sixteen. Helping Storm-Torn Towns

1. Correspondence from Robert Seymour to Boston W. Smith, Nov. 7, 1900, Seymour Collection American Baptist Historical Society, Valley Forge, Pa.

2. "Good Will," *Colporter,* November 1900, 6; *Baptist Standard,* Nov. 29, 1900, 1.

3. *Baptist Standard,* Apr. 4, 1901, 8; Ibid., Sept. 13, 1900, 12.

4. *Brenham Daily Banner,* Jan. 11, 1901, 4; Ibid., Jan. 15, 1901, 1; Ibid., Jan. 11, 1901, 4.

5. *Baptist Standard,* Sept. 13, 1900, 12.

6. "Storm-Swept Coast," *Baptist Standard,* Sept. 27, 1900, 13.

7. The *Weimar Mercury,* Weimar, Tex., Jan. 26, 1901; "Bibles for the Children," The *Weimar Mercury,* Feb. 2, 1901.

8. *The History of Gonzales County,* The Gonzales County Historical Commission, 1986, 47.

9. Grose, *Aliens or Americans,* 167–68; *The Home Mission Monthly,* November, 1896, 379; White, *A Century of Faith,* 154.

10. *Baptist Standard,* Feb. 28, 1901, 9.

11. Joe Tom Davis, *Historic Towns of Texas,* vol. 2, 42; *The History of Gonzales County,* 125.

12. Vallie C. Hart, *Baptist Standard,* Feb. 28, 1901, 9.

13. "Killed by the Cars," *The Galveston Daily News,* Feb. 8, 1901, 9.

14. *Around The Bend.*

15. Christensen, *Historic, Romantic Richmond,* 33.

16. *History of First Baptist Church of Richmond, Texas,* 10.

17. William A. Trenckmann, translated by his children William, Else, and Clara, History of Austin County, Texas, a supplement to the Bellville Wochenblatt, 1899, George Memorial Library, Richmond, Texas, 31–32.

18. "A Keepsake Edition of the Sealy News," Thursday, June 28, 1979, 49; Janie Brechin, "94 Year History of St. John's Episcopal Church of Sealy," in "A Keepsake Edition of the Sealy News," Thursday, June 28, 1979, 24.

19. *Sealy News,* Thursday, June 28, 1979, Sealy Public Library, Sealy, Tex., 49, 17.

20. *A Pictorial History of Rosenberg,* 4, 25–26, 76.

21. *Baptist Standard,* Apr. 4, 1901, 8.

22. Seventy-Seventh Anniversary of American Baptist Publication Society (Philadelphia: American Baptist Publication Society, 1901), 46.

23. *Baptist Standard,* Mar. 21, 1901, 8.

24. *The New Handbook of Texas,* vol. 1, 138; *Baptist Standard,* Sept. 20, 1900, 8.

25. Marion Weaver, *Baptist Standard,* Mar. 21, 1901, 15.

26. "The History of the First Baptist Church of Alta Loma," files of the Santa Fe Public Library; 1987 Orion English Students, "Our Town: The Communities of Alta Loma, Arcadia and Algca," collection in Santa Fe Area Public Library; *The New Handbook of Texas,* vol. 1, 132: Town history, Alvin.com.

27. Hedge and Dawson, *The San Antonio and Aransas Pass Railroad,* 59.

28. *Baptist Standard,* June 27, 1901, 9; Ibid., July 11, 1901, 16.

29. *The New Handbook of Texas,* vol. 2, 172.

Chapter Seventeen. South Texas to the Panhandle

1. *Baptist Standard,* July 4, 1901, 8; Ibid., Mar. 29, 1900, 9.

2. "The Revival Services," *Laredo Daily Times,* July 1, 1901; "The Revival Services," *Laredo Daily Times,* July 3, 1901, 1.

3. "The Revival Services," *Laredo Daily Times,* July 5, 1901, 3.

4. "The Revival Services," *Laredo Daily Times,* July 6, 1901, 1.

5. "The Revival Services," *Laredo Daily Times,* July 8, 1901, 4.

6. "The Revival Services," *Laredo Daily Times,* July 9, 1901, 3.

7. *Baptist Standard,* July 11, 1901, 9; Ibid., Apr. 11, 1901, 9.

8. *Baptist Standard,* July 11, 1901, 9.

9. *The New Handbook of Texas,* vol. 2, 364; *Baptist Standard,* July 11, 1901, 8; *Baptist Standard,* June 20, 1901, 8.

10. *Baptist Standard,* Aug. 15, 1901, 13.

11. *Hallettsville* (Texas) *Herald,* Aug. 1, 1901, 9.

12. Ibid., 1.

13. Letter from Robert G. Seymour to G. B. Rogers, Aug. 19, 1901.

14. "History of First Baptist Church," First Baptist Church, Dalhart, Texas.

15. *Baptist Standard,* Aug. 29, 1901, 12; Hunter, *The Book of Years,* 47; "A Centennial History of First Baptist Church, Dalhart, Texas, 2001."

16. Vernon et al., *The Methodist Excitement in Texas,* 103; Hunter, *The Book of Years,* 47; Hawkins, *History of Ellis County, Texas,* 67.

17. "Additional Locas and Miscellaneous," *Dalhart Texan,* Dec. 14, 1902.

Chapter Eighteen. Troubled Towns, a Weary Rogers

1. *Baptist Standard,* Sept. 19, 1901, 13.

2. Letter of Robert G. Seymour to Rev. G. B. Rogers, Oct. 17, 1901, American Baptist Historical Society, Valley Forge, Pa.

3. Letter from Robert G. Seymour to Rev. B. F. Riley, D. D., Oct. 4, 1901, American Baptist Historical Society, Valley Forge, Pa.

4. *Baptist Standard,* Oct. 24, 1901, 9.

5. Ibid., Nov. 7, 1901, 4.

6. Ibid., Nov. 21, 1901, 10.

7. Bob Bowman, ed., *The Lufkin That Was: A Centennial Album,* 12.

8. *Baptist Standard,* Oct. 10, 1901, 16; Bill O'Neal, *Central Baptist Church, Carthage, Texas, 75th Anniversary & Homecoming,* 1; Leila B. LaDrone, *A History of Panola County, Texas, 1819–1978.*

9. *Baptist Standard,* Mar. 27, 1902, 13.

10. Ibid.; Ibid., Apr. 17, 1902, 9.

11. Letter from Robert G. Seymour to Rev. G. B. Rogers, Mar. 28, 1902.

12. *Baptist Standard,* May 29, 1902, 9.

13. Ibid., Sept. 10, 1903, 7; "Conquest Missionary Course," June 7, 1902, American Baptist Publication Society, Valley Forge, Pa.

14. *Baptist Standard,* May 29, 1902, 4.

15. Ibid., Sept. 27, 1902, 10.

16. Ibid., Nov. 27, 1902, 16; Ibid., Jan. 1, 1903, 16.

17. Ibid., Oct. 30, 1902, 11.

18. Ibid.

19. Ibid., Sept. 11, 1902, 8.

20. Ibid., Jan. 23, 1903, 8; Ibid., Jan. 22, 1903, 16.

21. Ibid., Feb. 24, 1898, 9.

22. Smallwood, *Born In Dixie,* vol. 2, 476–77, 491.

23. *Baptist Standard,* Feb. 26, 1903, 16.

24. Ibid., June 11, 1903, 8.

25. Ibid., July 9, 1903, 13.

26. "The Fall of Parker's Fort," *Groesbeck Journal,* Friday, May 15, 1936, 1 and 8.

27. Cantrell, *Blest Communion,* 118.

Chapter Nineteen. A Trio of Town Problems

1. *Baptist Standard,* Sept. 24, 1903, 11.

2. *Spring: Lofts and Lore,* 9; "Ghosts of Spring's Roaring Past Called Back by Era's Survivors," Bill Porterfield, *Spring Chronicle,* Oct. 30, 1960, newspaper found in files of Harris County Public Library.

3. Don Hofsommer, "Not only a railroad, but an empire," *Trains,* March, 1998, 42.

4. *Baptist Standard,* Sept. 24, 1903, 11.

5. McGinley, *Just a Whistle Stop Away,* east vol. 4, 40, 21, and 38.

6. *Baptist Standard,* Sept. 24, 1903, 11.

7. McBeth, *Texas Baptists,* 19; Royce Measures, "Divided We Stand: The First Controversy Among Texas Baptists," *Texas Baptist History, The Journal of The Texas Baptist Historical Society* 19 (1999): 5 – 8.

8. Baptist Churches in Fayette County, a copy of a newspaper article, August, 1903, Church Box, La Grange, Texas Public Library; *Baptist Standard,* Thursday, Aug. 22, 1895, 5; Vernon et al., *The Methodist Excitement in Texas,* 237.

9. *Baptist Standard,* Sept. 24, 1903, 11; "La Grange, TX," The Handbook of Texas Online.

10. *Baptist Standard,* Sept. 10, 1903, 12; "Chapel Car Good Will," *La Grange Journal,* Aug. 27, 1903, 8.

11. *Baptist Home Mission Monthly,* October, 1897, 351.

12. Charles Wesley Corkran, "John Henry Moore, 1800 – 1880," (master's thesis, University of Texas, January, 1964), 301 – 302.

13. Crockett, *Early History of Smithville, Texas,* 29, 13; Johnson, *Smithville Then and Now,* 6.

14. Taylor and Taylor, *This Train Is Bound for Glory,* 168.

15. Ibid.

16. *Baptist Standard,* Nov. 12, 1903, 5.

Chapter Twenty. The End of the Texas Line

1. *The New Handbook of Texas,* vol. 5 (Austin: The Texas State Historical Association, 1996), 442.

2. Helen Mae Barnes, *Country Faith & Fate,* 129.

3. McBeth, *Texas Baptists,* 121 – 22.

4. For more on the story of *Good Will,* see Taylor and Taylor, *This Train Is Bound for Glory.*

5. A letter from Morse Dryer, missionary on *Good Will* to the executive sec-

retary of the Northern California Baptist Convention, in the files of the American Baptist Churches of the Northwest, Sacramento, Calif.

6. Taylor and Taylor, *This Train Is Bound for Glory*, 156.

7. The visit of the author to see chapel car *Good Will* in Boyes Springs, Calif., October, 1998.

8. *Baptist Standard*, July 23, 1903, 13.

9. Ibid., Sept. 20, 1900, 9.

BIBLIOGRAPHY

Manuscripts and Archival Collections

Alberto J. Diaz Collection. Boyce Library, Southern Baptist Theological Seminary, Louisville, Ky.

Channing Collection. Panhandle–Plains Museum, Canyon, Tex.

Channing Collection. XIT Museum, Dalhart, Tex.

Churches Files. Ennis Public Library, Ennis, Tex.

Churches Files. Val Verde Library, Del Rio, Tex.

Gloria Moore Collection. Public Library Center, Tex.

Good Will Files, Chapel Car Collection. American Baptist Historical Society, Valley Forge, Pa.

Hamner, Laura V., Scrapbook. Center for American History, The University of Texas at Austin.

I&GN File. Jewett Public Library, Jewett, Tex.

La Grange Photo Collection. La Grange Public Library, La Grange, Tex.

Robert Seymour Collection. American Baptist Publication Society, Valley Forge, Pa.

Stucker, E. G., File. American Baptist Publication Society, Valley Forge, Pa.

Stucker Family Records. In possession of Beverly Stucker Bennett, Ottawa, Kans.

Townsend Papers. Baptist Collection, Baylor University Library, Waco, Tex.

Townsend Papers. University of Mary Hardin-Baylor, Belton, Tex.

Trenckmann Collection. George Memorial Library, Richmond, Tex.

Turner, Ike Files. Texas State Library, Austin.

XIT Collection. Panhandle-Plains Museum, Canyon, Tex.

Interviews

Bennett, Beverly Stucker. Interview by author. Ottawa, Kans., June 24, 2002. Notes in possession of author.

Johnson, Jane C. Interview by author. Galveston County Historical Museum, Tex., Feb. 12, 2001. Notes in possession of author.

Jones, Keith G., rector of International Baptist Theological Seminary of the European Baptist Federation, Prague, Czech. Interview by author. Valley Forge, Pa., March 6, 2003. Notes in possession of author.

McBeth, Harry Leon, D.D. Interview by author. Southwestern Baptist Seminary, Ft. Worth, Tex., Oct. 17, 2002. Notes in possession of author.

Ray, Don. Interview by author. Channing, Tex., Oct. 17, 2001. Notes in possession of author.

Newspapers

Abilene Reporter. 1897.
Aurora (Illinois) *Daily News.* 1896.
Aurora (Illinois) *Daily Beacon.* 1895.
Aurora (Illinois) *Daily Banner.* 1894.
Baptist (Texas) *Standard.* 1895–1903, 1990.
Brenham Daily Banner. 1898, 1901.
Colporter. 1895–99.
Dalhart Texan. 1902.
Dallas Morning News. 1895, 1898.
Ft. Scott (Kansas) *Daily Mirror.* 1895.
Galveston *Daily News.* 1898, 1901.
Groesbeck Journal. 1936.
Hallettsville Herald. 1901.
Highlander (Marble Falls) Centennial Issue. 1999.
Houston Daily Post. 1895.
La Grange Journal. 1903.
Laredo *Daily Times.* 1901.
Marshall *News Messenger.* 1895.
Ottawa (Kansas) *Herald.* 1936, 1941.
Pacific Baptist. 1898.
Railway Age Gazette. 1915.
Roswell (New Mexico) *Register.* 1895.
San Antonio Daily Express. 1892, 1896, 1897, 1998.
San Antonio *Daily Light.* 1897, 1899.
Sealy News. 1979.
Sherman Democrat. 1979.
Spring Chronicle. 1960.
Sunday (Denison) *Gazette.* 1895.
Texas Baptist and Herald. 1896.
Thurber Journal. 2001.
Waco *Standard.* 1895.
Weimar Mercury. 1901.
Wills Point Chronicle. 1900.

Books and Articles

After Seventy-Five Years. Belton, Tex.: Student League and Alumnae Association of Baylor College, 1920.

Agnor, Margaret, ed. *Cultural Crossroads; Marshall-Harrison County, Texas,* Sam Houston Bicentennial Birthday Celebration, 1793–1993. Marshall: Cultural Potpourri Committee for Stagecoach Days, 1993.

Avera, Carl L. *Wind Swept Land.* San Antonio: The Naylor Company, 1964.

Baker, J. W. *A History of Robertson County, Texas.* Robertson County Historical Survey Committee. Waco: Texian Press, 1970.

Baker, Robert A. *The Blossoming Desert: A Concise History of Texas Baptists.* Waco: World Books, 1970.

The Baptist Teacher. American Baptist Home Mission Society, April 1898, 250.

Barnes, Helen Mae. *Country Faith & Fate.* Compiled by the Northeast Texas Writers' Organization. N.p.: Thompson and Sons, in cooperation with Northeast Texas Publishing, 129.

Battle, Charles S., ed., *Chicago Burlington and Quincy Railroad, for Eighty-six years, 1850–1937.* N.p.: n.p., 1937.

Becker, Billy. *A Pictorial History of Marble Falls: The Land Embracing the Falls on the Colorado.* Marble Falls, Tex.: The Highlander, 1999.

Bennett, Vernon E. *An Informal History of the First Baptist Church, Galveston, Texas.* Galveston: V. Bennett, 1970.

Bicentennial Commission. Polk County Historical Survey Committee, 1976.

Biographical Sketches of Val Verde County's Old Timers. Val Verde Historical Society, 1993.

Bowman, Bob, ed. *The Lufkin That Was: A Centennial Album.* Lufkin, Tex.: Lufkin Printing Co., 1981.

Bruner, Ora Pritchett. *Mineola and Its Mayors, 101 Years.* Marceline, Mo.: East Texas Genealogical Society, 1976.

Brown, Ellen Kuniyuki. "Saints and Sinners: Waco Baptist Women's Work." *Texas Baptist History, The Journal of The Texas Baptist Historical Society* 18 (1998): 98.

Campbell, Randolph B. *Gone To Texas: A History of the Lone Star State.* New York: Oxford University Press, 2003.

Cantrell, Myrna. *Blest Communion: A History of the Groesbeck Methodist Episcopal Church South, 1871–1939.* Groesbeck, Tex.: First United Methodist Church, 2002.

Carroll, J. M., A.M., D.D. *A History of Texas Baptists.* Dallas: Baptist Standard Publishing Co., 1923.

"Catch the Vision: First Baptist Church, 1896–1996, Shepherd, Texas." History Committee, 1996.

Christiansen, Roberta. *Historic, Romantic Richmond, 1822–1982.* Burnet, Tex.: Nortex Press, 1982.

Cook, L. Katherine. "Texas Baptist Women and Missions, 1830–1900." *Texas Baptist History, The Journal of The Texas Baptist Historical Society* 18 (1998): 41.

Corkran, Charles Wesley. "John Henry Moore, 1800–1880." Master's thesis, University of Texas, January, 1964.

Crockett, Silky Ragsdale. *Early History of Smithville, Texas.* Smithville: The Friends of the Smithville Library, 1990.

Davis, Joe Tom. *Historic Towns of Texas.* Vol. 2. Austin: Eakin Press, 1996.

Dean, Caddie Winston. *History of the First Baptist Church, Palestine, Texas.* Self-published, 1934.

Dilmore, Don. *The Story of the First Baptist Church of Marble Falls.* Marble Falls, Tex.: Marble Falls Historical Society, 1988.

Executive Board of the Baptist General Convention of Texas. *Centennial Story of Texas Baptists.* Dallas: Baptist General Convention of Texas, 1936.

Ferry, Abby (Farwell). *Reminiscences of John V. Farwell by His Elder Daughter.* Vol. 1. Chicago: Ralph Fletcher Seymour, 1923.

Grant, Roger H. *The NorthWestern: A History of the Chicago and North Western Railway System.* DeKalb: Northern Illinois University Press, 1996.

Green, Stan. *The Story of Laredo.* Vol. 2. Laredo: Border Studies, 1992.

Grose, Howard B. *Aliens or Americans.* New York: The American Baptist Home Mission Society, 1906.

Haley, Evetts. *The XIT Ranch of Texas and the Early Days of the Llano Estacado.* Norman: University of Oklahoma Press, 1929.

Hamner, Laura V. *Short Grass & Longhorns.* Norman: University of Oklahoma Press, 1965.

Halberstadt, Hans, and April Halberstadt. *The American Train Depot & Roundhouse.* Osceola, Wis.: Motorbooks International, 1995.

Hawkins, Edna Davis. *History of Ellis County Texas.* The Ellis County History Workshop. Waco: Texian Press, 1972.

Haynes, Emma. *The History of Polk County.* N.p.: Polk County Historical Society, 1996.

Hedge, John W., and Geoffrey S. Dawson. *The San Antonio and Aransas Pass Railroad, The Story of the Famous "SAP" Railway of Texas.* Waco: AMA Graphics, 1983.

Hefley, Kathryn. *Texline, the Front Door to Texas.* Texline, Tex.: Texline Centennial Committee, 1988.

"History of the First Baptist Church of Alta Loma." Files of the Santa Fe Public Library, Santa Fe, Tex.

"History of the First Baptist Church of Pecos, Texas." History Committee.

"History of First Baptist Church of Richmond, Texas." Centennial Committee.

"History of the First Baptist Church of Texline, Texas." First Baptist Church, Texline.

"History of Gonzales County." The Gonzales County Historical Commission, 1986.

"History of Gregg County." Longview Chamber of Commerce, 1957.

"In the Shadow of His Hand: The First Century of the First Baptist Church of San Antonio, Texas, 1861–1961." Archives of the Southwestern Seminary Library, 47.

Hofsommer, Don. *Southern Pacific, 1901–1985.* College Station: Texas A&M University Press, 1986.

———. "Not Only a Railroad, but an Empire," *Trains* (March 1998): 42.

Holden, William Curry. *Alkali Trails: Social and Economic Movements of the Texas Frontier, 1846–1900.* Lubbock: Texas Tech University, 1930.

Hunter, Lillie Mae. *The Book of Years: A History of Dallam and Hartley Counties.* Hereford, Tex.: Pioneer Book Publishers, Inc., 1969.

James, Eleanor. *Forth From Her Portals: The First 100 Years in Belton.* University of Mary Hardin Baylor; *After Seventy-Five Years.* Belton, Tex.: Student League and Alumnae Association of Baylor College, 1920.

Jensen, Oliver. *The American Heritage History of Railroads in America.* New York: American Heritage Wings Books, 1975.

Johnson, Rebekah Baines. *A Family Album.* New York: McGraw-Hill Book Company, 1965.

Johnson, Valerie Kite. *Smithville Then and Now.* N.p.: Self published, n.d.

Journal of The Texas Baptist Historical Society 3 (1983): 41.

LaDrone, Leila B. *A History of Panola County, Texas, 1819–1978.* Carthage, Tex.: Panola County Historical Commission, 1978.

Larson, Erik. *Isaac's Storm: A Man, A Time, and The Deadliest Hurricane in History.* New York: Crown Publishers, 1999.

McBeth, Harry Leon. *The Baptist Heritage.* Nashville: Broadman Press, 1987.

———. *Texas Baptists: A Sesquicentennial History.* Dallas: Baptistway Press, 1998.

———. *The First Baptist Church of Dallas: Centennial History, 1868–1968.* Grand Rapids, Tex.: Zondervan Publishing House, 1968.

McCarver, Norman L., and Norman L. McCarver Jr. *Hearne of the Brazos.* San Antonio: Century Press of Texas, 1958.

McGinley, Theresa Kurk. *Just a Whistle Stop Away, the History of Old Spring.* East vol. 4. Nacogdoches, Tex.: East Texas Historical Association, 2000.

Maguire, Jack. *Katy's Baby: The Story of Denison, Texas.* Austin: Nortex Press, 1991, 110.

Marks, Steven G. *Road to Power: The Trans-Siberian Railroad and the Colonization of Asian Russia, 1850–1917.* Ithaca, N.Y.: Cornell University Press, 1991.

Martin, Patricia. "Ordained Work—Unordained Workers: Texas 'Bible Women,' 1880–1920." *Texas Baptist History, The Journal of The Texas Baptist Historical Society* 18 (1988): 1.

Masterson, V. V. *The Katy Railroad and the Last Frontier.* Norman: University of Oklahoma Press, 1952.

Maxwell, Robert S. *Whistle in the Piney Woods: Paul Bremond and the Houston, East and West Railway.* Denton: East Texas Historical Association and the University of North Texas Press, 1998.

Measures, Royce. "Divided We Stand: The First Controversy Among Texas

Baptists." *Texas Baptist History, The Journal of The Texas Baptist Historical Society* 19 (1999): 5–8.

Miller, Ray. *Ray Miller's Galveston.* Galveston, Tex.: Cordovan Press, 1983.

Mineola: The First 100 Years. Mineola, Tex.: The Mineola Historical Society, 1973.

Montgomery, Marg-Riette. *Ten Thousand Texas Daughters: A Biographical Novel based on the Intimate Life Story of Mrs. Eli Moore Townsend.* San Antonio: The Naylor Company, 1950.

Moore, John D. *The Story of the Railroad "Y."* New York: Association Press, 1930s.

The New Handbook of Texas. Vols. 1, 2, and 5. Austin: The Texas State Historical Association, 1996.

Neyland, James. *Palestine (Texas), A History.* Palestine, Tex.: Empress Books, 1993, 1995.

Plummer, Edward W. *Historic Marshall Revisited.* Marshall, Tex.: E. W. Plummer, 1988, 105.

O'Neal, Bill. *Central Baptist Church, Carthage, Texas, 75th Anniversary & Homecoming.* N.p.: N.p., September 19, 1976.

"Over the River and Through the Woods, A Glimpse of Shepherd's Past." Shepherd High School Eleventh Grade English Honors Class, 1989–90, files of Shepherd Public Library, n.d.

"A Pen Picture of the City of Marshall and Harrison County." Promotional booklet published by the Tri-Weekly Herald Book and Job Print, 1879.

A Pictorial History of Polk County, Texas: 1846–1910. N.p.: The Heritage Committee of Polk County, 1978. *Around The Bend,* published by the Fort Bend Texas Historical Society, 1999.

A Pictorial History of Rosenberg. Dallas: Taylor Publishing Company, 1985.

Prusok, Lois. "The Episcopal Diocese of Northern Michigan." *Marquette Monthly* (January, 1996): 28.

Ramond, John Stanislaus. *Among Southern Baptists.* Shreveport, La.: Western Baptist Publishing Company, 1936.

Rhinehart, Marilyn D. *A Way of Work and a Way of Life: Coal Mining in Thurber, Texas, 1888–1926.* College Station: Texas A&M University Press, 1992.

Richardson, T. C. *East Texas: Its History and its Makers.* New York: Lewis Historical Publishing Co., 1940.

Rust, C. H. *A Church on Wheels.* Philadelphia: The American Baptist Publication Society, 1905.

Santa Fe High School English Students. "Our Town: The Communities of Alta Loma, Arcadia and Algca." Collection in Santa Fe Area Public Library, 1987.

Sitton, Thad, and James H. Conrad. *Nameless Towns: Texas Sawmill Communities, 1880–1942.* Austin: University of Texas Press, 1998.

Skiles, Jack. *Judge Roy Bean Country.* Lubbock: Texas Tech University Press, 1996.

Smallwood, James. *Born in Dixie; Smith County from 1875 To Its Centennial Year, The History of Smith County, Texas.* Vol. 2. Austin: Eakin Press, 1999.

Smith, Boston W. *The Story of Our Chapel Car Work.* Philadelphia: The American Baptist Publication Society, 1896.

Spain, Rufus B. "Texas Baptists and Prohibition: For or Against?" *Texas Baptist History, The Journal of The Texas Baptist Historical Society* 18 (1998): 43–46.

Spratt, John S., Sr. *Thurber, Texas: The Life and Death of a Company Coal Town.* Austin: University of Texas Press, 1986.

Spring High School South, American Cultures Class, comp. *Spring: Lofts and Lore.* Spring, Tex.: Spring Independent School District, 1977–78.

Stanley, F. [Stanley Francis Louis Crocchiota]. *Story of the Texas Panhandle Railroads.* Borger, Tex.: Hess Publishing, 1976.

———. *The Channing Story.* Austin: Center for American History, The University of Texas at Austin, n.d.

Taylor, Wilma Rugh, and Norman Thomas Taylor. *This Train Is Bound for Glory: The Story of America's Chapel Cars.* Valley Forge, Pa.: Judson Press, 1999.

Texas Almanac, 1996–1997 edition. Dallas: The Dallas Morning News, 1995.

The Texas Baptist Historical Society (1998): 43–46.

Trostel, Scott D. *The Barney and Smith Car Company: Car Builders, Dayton Ohio.* Fletcher, Ohio: Cam-Tech Publishing, 1993.

Troxell, Richard K. *Texas Trains.* Plano: Republic of Texas Press, 2002.

Tupper, Kerr Boyce. *Diaz, The Apostle of Cuba.* Philadelphia: American Baptist Publication Society, 1896.

Turner, Elizabeth Hayes. *Women, Culture, and Community: Religion and Reform in Galveston, 1880–1920.* New York: Oxford University Press, 1997.

Vernon, Walter N., Robert W. Sledge, Robert C. Monk, and Norman W. Spellmann. *The Methodist Excitement in Texas.* Dallas: The Texas United Methodist Historical Society, Southern Methodist University, 1984.

Walker, Herb. *Good Old Camp Meeting Songs.* Amarillo: Baxter Lane Co., 1977.

Weems, John Edward. *A Weekend in September.* College Station: Texas A&M University Press, 2000.

White, Charles L. *A Century of Faith.* Philadelphia: The American Baptist Publication Society by Judson Press, 1932.

Whitehead Memorial Museum and the Val Verde County Historical Commission. *La Hacienda: An Official Bicentennial Publication.* Norman: University of Oklahoma Press, 1976.

Wilkinson, J. B. *Laredo and the Rio Grande Frontier.* Austin: Jenkins Publishing Co., 1975.

Yoakum Community: The First Hundred Years, 1887–1987. Yoakum, Tex.: Yoakum Sesquicentennial/Centennial Book Committee, 1987.

INDEX

Page numbers in **bold** type refer to captions.

ISBN 1-58544-434-0

90000